SAM. FOOTE, COMEDIAN,

1720-1777

Frontispiece. Portrait of Samuel Foote by Cotes in 1765. Reproduced by Brookshaw in 1773. Courtesy of the Henry E. Huntington Library and Art Gallery.

SAM. FOOTE, COMEDIAN, 1720-1777

Simon Trefman

New York: New York University Press
1971

To Sunny

PREFACE

It is rare that a life as notorious, significant, and brilliant as Samuel Foote's should be so completely ignored in this century. Famed in his own day as wit, playwright, and actor, he was as much talked about as Garrick, Wilkes, Churchill, and Hogarth. Yet while all of these men had considerable attention paid to their works and lives, Foote continues to be known mainly to the specialist. Foote's own talents are partially to blame for this neglect. By writing plays mostly as a vehicle for himself and by using his wit and art to caricature the living, Foote became notoriously popular. But after his death, few of his plays were acted, except, perhaps, when Tate Wilkinson, "that mere, mere mimic's mimic," successfully aped Foote's acting, even to imitating the lurch of a cork leg. However, despite occasional obscurities, Foote's comedies are a surer and more lively guide to the temper of mid-eighteenth-century life than those of many other dramatists and actors who have received far more attention.

The stage at this time, although it lacked important dramatists, spent its energy and money on the arts of production. With Garrick as prime educator the audience was taught to appreciate naturalness in acting, realism in sets, authenticity in costumes, and, with Shakespeare at least, purity of text. The mid-century is traditionally seen by many as a golden time for actors who performed brilliantly and kept the stage a vibrant social medium despite the absence of great plays. Nor is this view wrong; but by its emphasis on positive qualities, one can lose sight of the continuous struggles waged under a surface calm imposed by the Licensing Act of 1737.

Although technically the monopoly enjoyed by Covent Garden and Drury Lane began when Charles II granted two patents, in practice the law was not always enforced, so that independent ventures kept the patentees from effectively imposing strictures on their writers and actors. When Fielding's satiric plays finally moved Walpole to push the Licensing Act through Parliament, there were some thirty-odd theatres and booths active in London.[1] By 1752 the Act took definite shape, and it became clear that only opera, ballet, pantomime, puppetry, and singing entertainments would be given license.[2] Legitimate dramatic theatre was limited to the existing patents, although it was possible for troupes to gain permission to act during the summer months when the regular companies took vacation.

This monopolistic control of the London stage gave an enormous power to the patentees that was not necessarily seen or intended by the originators of the Act. After 1737 any patentee, whether an actor-hating pantomimist like Rich, a profligate amateur like Fleetwood, or a theatrical genius like Garrick, had call on the law to stifle any dramatic venture that might threaten their investment.[3] As a consequence of that control, actors were unable to negotiate terms on an equitable basis; if they refused the terms of their articles, they would be forced to perform out of London. Playwrights were even more vulnerable than actors, who at least were necessary. Under these circumstances there was little pressure on the patentees to produce new plays. Indeed it was far more profitable to revive an old one and not pay for new sets, costumes, and third-night benefits for the author.

However, there were some pressures upon the patentees that could modify their power. Influential aristocrats could "persuade"

1. *The London Stage 1660-1800, Part 3,* ed. Arthur H. Scouten (Carbondale, Ill., 1961), I, xix-xl.
2. *Ibid.,* xlviii-lvii.
3. The Licensing Act increased the worth of a patent. By the time of Garrick's retirement the patent of Drury Lane was worth in excess of £65,000.

a manager to give a careful reading to a new play, or to allow a particular actor to star in a new role, or merely to replay a favorite piece. A playwright with no important friends found it almost impossible to have his play read—so few new plays were produced between 1740 and 1760. Opposing pressures could be applied also by those in the galleries, "the gods," as they were not so ironically termed. The incendiary quality of that group was such that the patentee risked the destruction of his theatre by going against their expressed wishes.

Much of the ferment in Foote's life—quarrels, law suits, and interminable feuds with theatrical personalities, especially Garrick—did not result merely from his aberrant and discordant wit, though he reveled in controversy and rarely lost with grace. As actor, playwright, manager, and, ultimately, parttime patentee, he reacted against the forces and interests generated by the Licensing Act; indeed, to a considerable extent his career was shaped by this opposition. Ironically, it was when he was granted a summer patent to the Haymarket and became a seeming fringe member of the dramatic establishment that his situation became most precarious. He had to invest considerable sums in leasing, buying, and improving his theatrical properties. He then had to depend upon the good graces of the Covent Garden and Drury Lane theatres not to extend their season too far into the summer months since he was dependent upon their actors, and their competition would thin his audiences. And if his personal relations with Garrick worsened after this time, it was not merely through envy.[4] Garrick could destroy him. Certainly he had reason for his fears, and when Drury Lane began to lengthen its season, Foote tried to retaliate by petitioning the king to extend the time limits of his patent. Though the request was refused, he continued to cope with the situation until he sold his patent to George Colman. The new owner, however, was eventually squeezed out as both houses extended their season to destroy the opposition, limited as it was.[5]

4. Thomas Davies, *Memoirs of the Life of David Garrick, Esq.* (London, 1808), II, 267.
5. Watson Nicolson, *The Struggle for a Free Stage in London* (Boston & New York, 1906), pp. 151-158.

Perhaps this control of the patentees can best be seen in its effect on the careers of some of the leading actors of the day. Barry, Macklin, Quinn, T. Sheridan, Woodward, Ross, Wilkinson, Mossop, T. Cibber, and even Garrick were forced to come to terms with the patentees or leave London and try the stages in Dublin, Edinburgh, or the provinces. Except for Wilkinson, who became head of a provincial troupe, and Quinn, who simply quit the stage, those who did leave London eventually returned. It was nearly impossible for even a first-rate actor to make a living outside the capitol, though for many life was intolerable in it. Rich of Covent Garden so loved his pantomime that he hated actors, especially successful ones. And, at Drury Lane, whenever Garrick took on an actor good enough to rival him in certain roles, a competition between the two inevitably developed; and just as inevitably the actor was driven off the boards by Garrick's brilliance or envy. Except for Barry who was hired under special circumstances, no major tragedian stayed long with Garrick.

It is more difficult to examine the effects of the monopoly on playwrights, for they did not work under contract. Certainly, the conditions made it impossible for them to depend upon their plays for financial support. A fairly successful play might make £500 to £700 during three benefit nights, but after the first nine productions the writer lost all rights to his play, no matter how many seasons it might continue to run. Furthermore, between 1740 and 1760 it was nearly impossible to have a new play accepted. During that period Rich at Covent Garden put on only six new tragedies and one new comedy, and from 1740 to 1750 Headly's *Suspicious Husband* was the only new play mounted (this does not include, of course, non-dramatic forms of entertainment, such as pantomimes, spectacles, and musical entertainments). Only after Rich's death in 1761 did Covent Garden begin showing a new play or two every year. The record at Drury Lane during the same period was more liberal mainly because of Garrick, who presented twenty-two new tragedies and four new comedies.[6] Yet even Garrick put on many of these plays only under pressure. In any case, the record for both houses is dismal. There

6. Information taken from *The London Stage, Part 3;* and *Part 4,* ed. George W. Stone (Carbondale, Ill., 1962).

was little encouragement for even the most talented writers to persist in producing for the stage. Though many important literary men of the time did write some plays, they were soon discouraged from continuing in that genre.

We can now see that despite the glamor of its practitioners, the theatre was almost reduced to a repertory depending heavily on revivals of Shakespeare's plays. Although Garrick and Macklin introduced a more naturalistic style of acting, to which were added more realistic scenery, improved lighting, and a greater degree of historical accuracy in costumes, the theatre was nearly impotent and ultimately self-destructive. It is even possible to say that had Garrick not been so brilliantly effective in managing Drury Lane, reformation of the Licensing Act would have come much sooner. His leadership forestalled the disintegration of the patent houses until the next century.[7]

As actor and dramatist, Foote could not adapt to the established needs of either house. His acting range was narrow, and despite his efforts, he failed in tragedy and could not succeed in comedy. He could not become the character he was to act, though he could caricature him. Yet his talents were theatrical; he was a monologuist, mimic, and master of the satiric revue. As a personality he was in great demand at the coffee houses and the mansions of the rich, but neither Garrick nor Rich wanted him, and only on occasion could they use him. Had he not had the contentiousness and drive to fight the patentees, he would have had a different career despite his talent.

7. Dewey Ganzel, "Patent Wrongs and Patent Theatres: Drama and the Law in the Early Nineteenth Century," *PMLA*, LXXVI (Sept., 1961), 384-396.

ACKNOWLEDGMENTS

The late Professor Edward L. McAdam, Jr., first suggested this topic as my dissertation advisor, and I shall remember him always as a kind and witty gentleman whose erudition and cheerful temperament made my task lighter. Dean George Winchester Stone, Jr., helped me to shape this book. He never failed to give me generously of his time, and I followed many of his suggestions. I am also grateful to Professor Arthur H. Scouten for reading the manuscript and for his detailed criticisms and corrections.

I wish to thank the following institutions for giving me permission to quote from manuscripts in their possession: The Folger Shakespeare Library, The Harvard Theatre Collection, The McGraw-Hill Book Company, The Henry E. Huntington Library and Art Gallery, and The Pierpont Morgan Library. Mrs. Mary C. Hyde also allowed me to quote an ALS from the Hyde Collection. The following English institutions were equally generous in giving me access to their collections: The Victoria and Albert Museum, The British Museum, and the Public Record Offices of Northumberland, Somerset House, and Guildhall. I would like to single out The New York Public Library, where I spent many intolerably frustrating days, as an indispensible source of books and newspapers. It would have been almost impossible for me to have written this book without its enormous collection so close at hand.

Finally, I take pleasure in thanking Helen C. Willard, Curator of The Harvard Theatre Collection, for her courtesies;

Professors Philip H. Highfill and George M. Kahrl for information promptly and generously sent; and my colleague, Arnold Asrelsky, for his help, encouragement, and for his endless patience in listening to Foote jokes. My wife, to whom this book is dedicated, suffered longest and helped the most.

CONTENTS

LIST OF ABBREVIATIONS

CBEL	*Cambridge Bibliography of English Literature*
DNB	*Dictionary of National Biography*
HLQ	*Huntington Library Quarterly*
MLN	*Modern Language Notes*
N & Q	*Notes and Queries*
PQ	*Philological Quarterly*
TN	*Theatre Notebook*

CHAPTER I

EARLY DAYS: DISSIPATION, DEBT, AND SMALL BEER, 1720-1743

If Samuel Foote's first biographer, William Cooke, is to be believed, the environmental and hereditary factors that shaped Foote into the most notorious wit and prodigal of his day were evident in anecdotes concerning his family background and his childhood. There were probably other equally interesting stories of Foote's childhood that would have shown Foote in another dimension besides that of mimic and prankster, but the anecdotes in the biography by Cooke were probably told to Cooke by Foote, who perhaps had begun by that time to see himself as the public saw him: an irrepressible comic who moved in a world of laughter.

A typical and revealing incident occurred when Samuel was about eleven. Overhearing the family discuss what was to be done with a man in the parish who had been charged with fathering a bastard, young Foote interrupted by saying he knew what the verdict would be and what the justices would say about it. Encouraged to go on, Foote screwed his face into a caricature of Justice D————:

> "Hem! hem! here's a fine job of work broke out indeed! a *feller* begetting bastards under our very noses, (. . . a common laboring rascal too,—) . . . we shall not have an

honest serving maid in the neighborhood, and the whole
parish will swarm with bastards; therefore, I say, let him
be fined for his pranks very severely; and if the rascal has
not money, (as indeed how should he have it?) . . . let him
be clapp'd up in prison till he pays it." Justice A———
will be milder, and say, "Well, well, brother, this is not a
new case, bastards have been begotten before now, and
bastards will be begotten to the end of the chapter; therefore though the man has committed a crime . . . —yet let
us not ruin the poor fellow for this one fault. . . ."

Samuel was very successful with his caricatures of the voices, like-
nesses, and attitudes of the justices, and he set the whole table
laughing. His father, however, demanded to know why he was
left out, for he was one of the quorum. Samuel obliged, imitating
Mr. Foote's matter-of-fact speech as he intoned the verdict,
twirling his thumbs the way his father did:

> "Why upon my word, in respect to this here business,
> to be sure it is rather an awkward affair; and to make sure
> it ought not to be; that is to say, the justices of the peace
> should not suffer such things to be done with impunity:—
> however on the whole, I am rather of my brother A———'s
> opinion; which is that the man should pay according to his
> circumstances, and be admonished—I say *admonished*—
> not to commit so flagrant an offense for the future." [1]

And his father laughed with the rest. This brief incident is particularly revealing because it dramatizes the talents that were to
catapult Foote into theatrical fame. His form of mimicry was
crude but he caught some outstanding feature in face, stance, and
voice of the person he was caricaturing, and, more important, his
mimicry was subservient to his wit. Foote was able to project what
the person *might* say in some particular situation, usually a ludicrous one, that made fun not only of the person's physical charac-
teristics, but satirized his mode of thinking as well. It was more

to his wit that Foote owed his success than to his ability as a
mimic.[2] The subject matter too revealed the direction of Foote's
interest. His wit and inclinations naturally turned to scandal. His
first recorded performance was about a bastard to be set on the
parish, his last piece of writing was to expose the hypocritical
attitudes of the Duchess of Kingston, a convicted bigamist of in-
ternational notoriety.

His father, after whom Foote was named, was educated as a
lawyer, and even though he is seen in some of the anecdotes of
Foote's childhood as an indulgent father and a lenient magistrate,[3]
he was obviously an ambitious and able man who achieved considerable success. Settling in the small town of Truro, Cornwall,
he was at various times mayor, Member of Parliament for Tiver-
ton, commissioner of the Prize Office, and receiver of fines for
the duchy.[4] His greatest achievement, however, was marrying
Eleanor Dinely Goodere, who came from an old aristocratic family
far above his in station and wealth.

Foote's mother was the daughter of a baronet, Sir Edward
Goodere of Hereford, who had married the granddaughter of the
Earl of Rutland thus allying himself with the Dinelys of Charlton
in Worcestershire. William Cooke, who met the lady when she
was celebrating her seventy-ninth birthday, describes her as being
very much like her son physically and temperamentally. Short
and fat, like Sam, she was still active and alert; but her talk, witty,
mirthful, and bawdy, revealed most clearly whom Sam resembled.[5]
Her family, ancient and aristocratic as it was, had many eccentrics,
mad, criminal, and harmless. The most notable explosion in the
Goodere family occurred in 1740 when her brother Captain
Samuel Goodere murdered his older brother, Sir John Goodere,
for his estate. According to Cooke, Mrs. Foote was to have profited
by inheriting some of Sir John's estates,[6] but, typically, she was to
write to her son not many years after her inheritance:

Dear Sam,
    I am in prison for debt: come and assist your loving
mother,
                                        E. Foote.

and Sam's response is a mirror image:

> Dear Mother,
>   So am I; which prevents his duty being paid to his
> loving mother by her affectionate son,
>   Sam Foote.
> P. S. I have sent my attorney to assist you; in the meantime,
> let us hope for better days.[7]

Even though she was probably left a considerable sum of money when her husband died, she must have mismanaged this sum too so that Foote was obliged to support her when he became successful.[8] In money matters too Foote was like his mother. He was frequently dogged by debt even during the peak of his earning powers. When Foote was in his twenties, Cooke has it that he ran through two fortunes and on coming into a third he dashed through town with his motto inscirbed on his new coach: *Iterum, iterum, iterumque.*[9]

Samuel was the youngest of three surviving boys born to the Foote family. Two children, Eleanor and Samuel, born April, 1712, and November, 1715, died in infancy.[10] The eldest brother, Edward Goodere, baptized November 5, 1716, [11] was educated as a clergyman, but despite his training he seemed to have been unable to make a living, for his brother Sam supported him with a pension of sixty pounds and occasional room and board.[12] An amusing anecdote by Cooke reveals Edward's dependence and his brother's chagrin at having such an unpromising member of the family so close at hand. During Foote's more prosperous years, one of Foote's friends, curious at seeing Edward lounging in the green-room at the Haymarket Theatre so frequently, asked Foote who he was. "My barber," was the laconic reply. On learning the true relationship, the friend chided Foote, who answered, "I could not disclaim *all* relationship with him, I was obliged to make him a brother-shaver." [13]

Almost nothing is known about the second brother, John, who was baptized on August 14, 1718.[14] It has been stated that when Foote left college in 1740, the prestige of having a rich older brother in Jamaica helped him socially.[15] A more popularly repeated story also had it that John changed his last name to Dinely in order to inherit his uncle's estate at Worcestershire, and that he died in 1758 leaving his estate to his son John.[16]

Samuel, the last child, was baptized January 27, 1720,[17] and early and late in life revealed those qualities usually associated with a youngest son. Undoubtedly spoiled by his parents, young Samuel must have been a terror to his schoolmaster in grammar school and a perpetual delight to his more repressed peers. Cooke reports him as being an instigator in most of the student rebellions against authority.[18] Richard Polwhele, a historiographer of Cornwall, was a student some years later at the same grammar school and under the same master, Mr. Connon, as Foote. Polwhele stated that Foote had shown great proficiency in acting Terence, but the old master sanctimoniously lamented the turn that this proficiency had taken—"That a school of morality should have been the nursery of buffoonery." [19] These must have been happy days for Foote, for according to this same source he frequently came back to Truro grammar school when he was a famed comedian to meet his old master, who dreaded his visits, and to delight the students. Polwhele remembers an incident in 1769 when he was still a student at the school, that Foote came to class and without approval dismissed all the students for the day.[20]

It is not known how well Foote did in grammar school, but it is likely that despite his abilities he lacked discipline and liked fun too much to excel in his studies. When he was seventeen, his family put in a claim to Worcester College, Oxford, to have Foote accepted because he was related to the founder, Sir Thomas Cookes. On June 29, 1737, Samuel Foote was officially accepted into the school, and part of the college record shows Foote's relation to Sir Thomas Cookes: "Pedigree submitted to Dr. Brookes, who reported upon it that Samuel Foote was Founder's kin—consanguineous and cognatus":

Sir Edward Dinely—Founder's mother

|

Sir Edward Goodere—daughter

|

Mr. Foote—daughter (Eleanor Goodere)

|

Samuel Foote

Samuel Foote was put under the care of the provost. Dr. Gower,[22] and again acted out the pattern that made him so memorable at grammar school. When Dr. Gower lectured him for his idleness, Foote would open the large folio dictionary he carried with him for these occasions and stop the doctor to look up each difficult word that was used in the scolding. But despite these stories, Cooke insists that Foote was not completely idle and that he became a competent Latin and Greek scholar.[23] In later life Foote was proud of his Oxford education, incomplete as it was,[24] and frequently took the liberty of laughing at those less educated than he. It is most probable, however, that Foote had a gentleman's education which included no more than a smattering of the classics, but with the help of his inventiveness and wit it took him farther than it would most people. In fact, it is surprising, given Foote's temperament, that he remained in college as long as he did. His first opportunity to leave college came in 1739, probably during the fall months, when he fell sick. He was advised by his doctors to go to Bath and take the cure. But the real cure for Foote was relief from boredom, and he befriended gamblers and "men of pleasure" at the resort. And when he finally returned to college, he returned in high style—in a rented carriage attended by two footmen in extravagant uniforms covered with lace.[25] A wild and exciting life continued to appeal to Foote, and his one taste of unhampered freedom clearly made college life far too restrictive. As the following extract from his college record will show, Foote continued to leave college without permission and finally stayed so long that he was dropped from the rolls:

January 28, 1740

Samuel Foote after a course of many irregularitys and lying out of the College, upon the 30th of December was imposed by the Provost, which he neglected to bring, but lay out of the College again on the 16th of January, and went the next day out of town without leave, for which reasons a citation was ordered to be put up as this day in the following form: Whereas Samuel Foote, Scholar of the College, has, in defiance of the Statutes and the authority of the college, presumptuously and insolently absented himself without leave asked of the Provost, this is to require the said Foote to return to the College within twenty days after the date of this present, and to answer to such things as shall be alledged against him, or to be deprived of his Scholarship and of all privileges and advantages belonging to it.

Feb. 25

The said Foote not appearing to the citation, his Scholarship was declared void this day.[26]

Despite his seeming haste to drop all chains, Foote repeatedly visited the college and kept up his friendships long after he had left. He never really reached a position in life where old friends would embarrass or bore him, for what he had been he continued to be; and those who liked him in his youth would see the same qualities to like in his middle age. Foote could always return because he seemed never to change or mature. This characteristic is reflected in his works as well, for there is no sign of development or deepening of concepts in his later works.

Upon leaving college, Foote decided to study law informally. He entered the Inner Temple and took chambers but did not put his name on the lists. [27] This form of independent study required far more discipline than Foote was ever to possess. In most of Foote's activities, the desire for money was usually the impetus— and when he had it, his main activity was to spend it. According to tradition, Foote came into some money at this time,[28] and he spent it building a reputation as a beau and a wit. A clubbable man, Foote began his days at the Grecian, a coffee house famed for Temple wit, and his evenings at the Bedford in Coven Garden where a more theatrical crowd gathered.[29] Appearing in sartorial spendor, Foote probably stunned the regulars by his uproarious stories and his gift for deadly repartee.[30] An interesting description of Foote at this time was given to Cooke by Dr. Barrowby, an eminent physician and critic of his day:

> He came into the room dressed out in a frock suit of green and silver lace, bag wig, sword, *bouquet,* and point ruffles, and immediately joined the critical circle at the upper end of the room. Nobody knew him. He, however, soon boldly entered into conversation; and by the brilliancy of his wit, the justness of his remarks, and the unembarrassed freedom of his manners, attracted the general notice. The buz of the room went round, 'who is he? whence comes he?' etc.; which nobody could answer; until a handsome carriage stopping at the door to take him to the assembly of a lady of fashion, they learned from the servants that his name was Foote, that he was a young gentleman of family and fortune, and a student of the Inner Temple.[31]

Unhappily, the fortune that the servant mentioned was rapidly dwindling, and Foote was moved to write his first piece:

> *The genuine Memoirs of the life of Sir John Dinely Goodere, Bart, who was murder'd by the contrivance of his own brother, on board the Ruby Man of War, in King Road near Bristol, Jan. 19, 1740 [OS]. Together with the Life, history, tryal and last dying words of his brother Capt. Samuel Goodere, who was executed at Bristol on Wednesday the 15th day of April 1741, for the horrid*

> *Murder of the said Sir John Dinely Goodere, Bart. Dedi-*
> *cated to the Right Worshipful Henry Combe, Esq. Mayor*
> *of Bristol. By S. Foote, of Worcester-College, Oxford, Esq;*
> *and Nephew to the late Sir John Dinely Goodere, Bart.*

He supposedly received 20 pounds for his account of the sensa-
tional murder and, according to Cooke, held out the condition
that his name be withheld as author.[32] But, though Foote later
may have claimed that he requested anonymity, the truth was
that he not only put his name to the pamphlet, he also identified
himself on the title page as nephew to the murdered man. He
added to *The genuine Memoirs . . .* a signed dedication to
Henry Combe, the mayor of Bristol, thanking him for bringing
the malefactors to justice. Though Foote, like many a character he
mocked in his plays, boasted of his aristocratic forebears, he
would not allow mere pride to deter him from exposing them to
public scandal for a fee.

Although it seems likely that portions of the Goodere estate
descended to the Foote family, Samuel seems to have received
little or none of it at this time. Driven by necessity, he undoubtedly tried many dodges, even work, to pay his debts and
return to the business of being a gentleman. On one occasion he
went into partnership with a Mr. Price.[33] to make and sell small
beer—Foote to advertise and sell the beer, Price to brew it. Johnson's anecdote about Foote and his small beer is well known,[34] and
one newspaper account substantiates Johnson's story of Foote's
superb salesmanship and the dismal quality of the beer he sold:
"Foote puffed off his small beer so well to the nobility that it
became as much in vogue as Mrs. Allen's claret. He soon, however,
quarrelled with his partner upon the small beer turning sour,
and lost his credit as the greatest puffer and small beer brewer
in Europe." [35]

Foote was reduced to a final expedient in attempting to recoup his lost fortune: marriage. On January 10, 1741, Foote
married Mary Hickes, a former neighbor of his from Truro. Proof
of this marriage was discovered in 1936 by John Wells Wilkinson,
whose photograph of the St. Clements Register reveals the neces-

sary information under the year 1740, but since this is an official document the date is Old Style and refers to 1741: "Mr. Sam¹. Foote of Truro & Mrs. Mary Hickes of this parrish were marry'd January 10th." [36] She was only seventeen when she married Foote,[37] and according to Richard Polwhele, "she was very pretty, and sensible enough to relish a witticism or a pun, and was educated as young ladies then generally were." Her parents were moderately comfortable for country folk, and she was given a "good estate" in St. Clements as a dowry.[38] Mary's father, who died at about the time of her marriage, also left two small estates worth about £140 a year to his daughter, but by "custom of the manor" the widow held the property during her lifetime.[39]

After a brief honeymoon in Truro, Foote mistreated his young wife cruelly. He soon squandered her dowry,[40] and was thrown in prison for non-payment of debt. Though his wife remained loyal to him, even living with him in jail according to Cooke, he treated her with public contempt and scorn. When his financial circumstances improved, he apparently deserted her, thus giving rise to the theory that he had never married. Fortunately, as Cooke asserts, "she died, however, in good time for both parties; before age came on to incite a further distaste in her husband; and before (as might perhaps have been the case) he had disgraced himself by adding ill treatment to neglect." [41] Even long after his wife's death, Foote's treatment of her was remembered by his enemies.

> Never drew drop of blood in all his life,
> Of Friend or Mistress,—save his virtuous Wife.
> What Kill his Wife?—He only lets her starve.
> No more.—He cannot death for that deserve.[43]

They had no children, and because of Foote's lack of commitment to the marriage,[43] almost no trace if its occurrence remained. Foote was certainly no family man, and Forster was correct in noting the lack of a settled relationship between Foote and any woman. He did have at least one mistress, for he mentions his natural sons, Francis and George, in his will. But even this relationship, if we can trust Cooke, was short-lived. She was his servant, and when Foote went to Paris she left him for a bass-viol player from the opera. Disappointed in her choice, she begged Foote to be taken in again. Foote laughed, "What Madam! Have you not been basely violated? and do you want to run your gamut on me?" [44] According to available anecdotes and memoirs, almost all of Foote's relationships with women, excluding his mother, were casual and filled with extremely flowery compliments, or brutal and resounding with devastating repartee. This detachment from women assumed great significance because it made Foote vulnerable to charges of homosexuality by his enemies. No proof exists to validate this charge, but anecdotes of this kind began to circulate as early as 1753 and eventually were used with such vicious authority in 1775 that Foote was forced to sell the Haymarket Theatre to George Colman the Elder in 1776.

At any rate Foote's marriage could not have helped him financially for any length of time. A "Statement of charges of debt against Samuel Foote" at Guildhall shows that Foote was sued for non-payment of debt by a small army of creditors including his mother and Lady Viscountess Castlecomer. He was taken before Sir William Chapple, Marshall of the Fleet Prison, and put into jail on November 13, 1742. He was released in a few months and almost immediately recommitted on similar charges. He was finally released on September 7, 1743, by the passage of a bill for the relief of insolvent debtors.[45] Undoubtedly worse would have happened to him had he not the help and protection of wealthy and titled people such as Francis Blake Delaval and his brother John. Theatre-struck themselves, they appreciated Foote's ability to entertain and encouraged him to seek his career on the stage.[46]

NOTES

1. William Cooke, *Memoirs of Samuel Foote* (London, 1805), Vol. I, pp. 18-22.
2. I think Samuel Johnson, who was fascinated by Foote, understood his real abilities when he disputed Boswell's notion that had Betterton

been alive to provide contrast, that great tragedian (superior to Foote in morals and acting) would have pointed up Foote's buffoonish ways and made him seem merely foolish. "If Betterton were to walk into this room with Foote, Foote would soon drive him out of it. Foote, Sir, quatenus Foote, has powers superior to them all." James Boswell, *Life of Johnson,* ed. George Birkbeck Hill, rev. and enl. L. F. Powell (Oxford, 1934-1950), Vol. III, p. 185. Hereafter referred to as *Life.*

3. Cooke, Vol. I, pp. 18-22.
4. Cooke, Vol. I, p. 4. He was elected mayor after the corporation manner, but the government disrupted the election. John Camden Hotten, *A Handbook to the Topography and Family History of England and Wales* (London, 1863), p. 30.
5. Cooke, Vol. I, pp. 12-13.
6. Cooke, Vol. I, p. 11.
7. Cooke, Vol. II, p. 4.
8. Cooke, Vol. II, p. 3. Foote also made a provision in this will for his mother. "Samuel Foote's Will Proved 22 October 1777 in Prerogative Court of Canterbury, Somerset House," manuscript written August 13, 1768, hereafter referred to as Foote's "Will," states: "And I give the Interest and produce of the then residue of my Estate unto my Mother Eleanor Foote Widow for & during the Term of her Natural Life."
9. Cooke, Vol. I, p. 61.
10. *The Register of Marriages, Baptisms and Burials of the Parish of St. Mary, Truro Co.* (Cornwall, Exeter: The Devon and Cornwall Record Society, 1940), Vol. II, pp. 381, 385; subsequently cited as *The Register.*
11. *The Register,* Vol. II, p. 386.
12. Cooke, Vol. II, p. 3 Foote;'s "Will" states: "After her Decease I give the Sum of Fifty Pounds a year to my Brother Edward Goodere Foote during the Term of his Natural Life."
13. Cooke, Vol. II, pp. 186-187.
14. *The Register,* Vol. II, p. 388.
15. Anon., *Memoir of the Life and Writings of Samuel Foote, Esq.; The English Aristophanes* (London [1788]), p. 7; and Cooke, Vol. I, p. 32, support this and give the brother's name as John.
16. Percy H. Fitzgerald, *Samuel Foote, A Biography* (London, 1910), p. 28.
17. *The Register,* Vol. II, p. 391.
18. Cooke, Vol. I, p. 17.
19. Richard Polwhele, *The History of Cornwall* (London, 1816), Vol. V, p. 204.
20. *Ibid.;* and see *Biographical Sketches in Cornwall* (London, 1831), Vol. II, p. 34, by the same author.
21. Fitzgerald, p. 13.
22. Cooke, Vol. I, p. 23.
23. Cooke, Vol. I, p. 29.
24. In his *Life,* Vol. II, p. 95, n. 2, Boswell relates that when Foote was at Edinburgh he made scurrilous game of Johnson. Boswell, to defend his idol, told Foote one of Johnson's denigrating remarks about him—that Foote was an infidel as a dog was an infidel; "that is to say he has never thought about the subject." Boswell says, "I never saw Foote so

disconcerted. He looked grave and angry, and entered into a serious refutation of the justice of the remark. 'What Sir, (said he,) talk thus of a man of liberal education:—a man who for years was at the University of Oxford.' "

25. Jesse Foot, *The Life of Arthur Murphy* (London, 1811), p. 429.
26. Cited by Fitzgerald, pp. 17-18.
27. Cooke, Vol. I, p. 30.
28. Cooke, Vol. I, p. 35. But I think it is more likely that he got the money just before he took his grand vacation at Bath in 1739. It is unlikely that his father provided him with enough money to live on this scale, and he was able to live extravagantly afterwards also as evidenced by his periodic escapes from college until his expulsion.
29. Cooke, Vol. I, p. 31-32.
30. On another occasion when someone wanted to reduce Foote's abilities to those of a mere buffoon, Johnson took exception: "But he has wit too, and is not deficient in ideas, or in fertility and variety of imagery, and not empty of reading; he has knowledge enough to fill up his part. One species of wit he has in an eminent degree, that of escape. You drive him into a corner with both hands; but he's gone, Sir, when you think you have got him—like an animal that jumps over your head. Then he has a great range for wit; he never lets truth stand between him and a jest, and he is sometimes mighty coarse." *Life,* Vol. III, p. 69.
31. Cooke, Vol. I, pp. 34-35.
32. Cooke, Vol. II, pp. 34-35.
33. Fitzgerald, p. 94, tentatively identifies Foote's partner as "Charles Price, better known as 'Old Patch,' a notorious swindler." When the brewing scheme failed, Price asked Foote to join him in a bakery. Foote supposedly replied, "No, as you have brewed, so may you bake; but I am cursed if ever you bake as you have brewed." This identification is supported by L. F. Powell, *Life,* 2nd ed., Vol. VI, pp. 448-449.
34. "Amongst the many and various modes which he [Foote] tried of getting money, he became a partner with a small-beer brewer, and he was to have a share of the profits for procuring customers amongst his numerous acquaintance. Fitzherbert was one who took his small-beer; but it was so bad that the servants resolved not to drink it. They were at some loss at how to notify their resolution, being afraid of offending their master, who they knew liked Foote much as a companion. At last they fixed upon a little black boy, who was rather a favourite, to be their deputy, and deliver their remonstrance; and having invested him with the whole authority of the kitchen, he was to inform Mr. Fitzherbert, in all their names, upon a certain day, that they would drink Foote's small-beer no longer. On that day Foote happened to dine at Fitzherbert's, and this boy served at table; he was so delighted with Foote's stories, and merriment, and grimace, that when he went down stairs, he told them 'This is the finest man I have ever seen. I will not deliver your message. I will drink his small-beer.' " *Life,* Vol. III, p. 70.
35. *Town and Country,* November, 1777, p. 597.

36. "The Life and Works of Samuel Foote," p. 180. Wilkinson had in
    tended to write a full life of Foote, but he stopped writing five volumes
    later with his hero still in his twenty-fourth year. A copy of his type-
    script is at the Huntington Library. Since scholars have only recently
    become aware of Wilkinson's typescript, and no one had thought to
    investigate the St. Clements Register, documentary proof of Foote's
    marriage is not widely known. Earlier biographers did not even be-
    lieve that Foote ever married. John Forster in *Biographical Essays*
    (London, 1860), pp. 347-348, stated that Foote's career shows no trace
    of any such "settled connexion." Later, a series of notes in *N & Q*,
    11th Series, XII (1915), 307, 347, 370, 466, supported this skeptical
    attitude. The articles concluded that searches had been made by
    Forster, Fitzgerald, and Joseph Knight, biographer of Foote in the
    DNB, and since no evidence had been found the question remains
    "shrouded in ambiguity."
37. *The Register*, Vol. II, p. 512.
38. Polwhele, *Biographical Sketches in Cornwall*, Vol. II, p. 36. See also
    Traditions and Recollections (London, 1826), p. 29, by the same
    author.
39 "A Perfect Schedule of all the estate real and personal of Sam¹ Foote
    Esqʳ," Guildhall Records, Debtor's Papers. Foote declared his posses-
    sions when imprisoned for debt in 1743. Cited by John Wells Wilkin-
    son in "The Life and Works of Samuel Foote," p. 970.
40. Polwhele, *Biographical Sketches in Cornwall*, Vol. II, p. 36.
41. Cooke, Vol. II, pp. 1-3, 66; Vol. III pp. 63-64.
42. Anon., *Asmodeus* (London, 1776), p. 13.
43. Cooke, Vol. III, pp. 63-64, notes that Murphy and some other friends
    of Foote persuaded him to take his wife back after he had left her
    She returned bruised because the carriage overturned, and Foote, cal-
    lous and mocking, punned on her bruises by comparing them to geo-
    graphical locations: the lumps on her head were the "Islands of
    Scilly," etc.
44. Cooke, Vol. II, p. 104. Another anecdote by Cooke, Vol. II, p. 103,
    supports Foote's jaundiced view of his mistress. A French visitor seeing
    Foote with his two young boys admired them and asked "Sont-ils par
    la même mere?" Foote replied, "Oui—by the same mare, but I have
    strong doubts whether by the same horse."
45. This information was originally found by J. W. Wilkinson, "The Life
    and Works of Samuel Foote," pp. 969-982.
46. Forster, p. 351.

CHAPTER II

FUT *VS* FOLDING:
WAR WITH FIELDING'S PUPPETS, 1744-1748

Opportunity coincided with Foote's wish to become an actor.
An actor's strike at the Drury Lane Theatre, probably captained
by its leading actors Garrick and Macklin,[1] was raised against
Charles Fleetwood, the owner of Drury Lane, and this strike
indirectly helped Foote to the stage. Fleetwood in gambling away
his own fortune also put his theatre on a precarious financial basis
by borrowing from unscrupulous money lenders against his assets.
The results of such mismanagement were the appointment of a
money lender as treasurer of the theatre; frequent failure to pay
the actors; disregard of legitimate complaints; and frequent retaining of costumes and other theatre property by bailiffs. The actors
were slighted also by the many presentations of spectacle and dance
to draw the mass audiences necessary to pay the mounting debts
and to fill Fleetwood's depleted pockets. In the 1742-1743 season,
eleven players decided they had endured enough abuse, and at
the end of the summer of 1743 they voted that acting would not
resume in September unless Fleetwood acceded to their demands
and that no one was to come to terms with the owner without the
consent of the rest of the group. Fleetwood was not beaten, even
though he was deserted by most of his company. A few key
performers, Mrs. Woffington, Delane, and Yates, remained and
were joined by strolling players recruited by Fleetwood. Later,
Theophilus Cibber and a few other players returned from Ireland

and further strengthened the forces of Drury Lane. Garrick expected opposition, and his trump card was to petition the Lord
Chamberlain, the Duke of Grafton, to grant the striking players
license to set up a rival company in the Haymarket Opera House.
Despite the players' long list of grievances, the petition was
refused; the Duke did not believe that the high salaries paid to
performers such as Garrick, Macklin, and Clive could warrant a
strike. This hope of a rival company was crushed in early October,
and without support of the theatre-going public, who took much
the same view as the Lord Chamberlain, the poorer players were
willing to give into Fleetwood if he would have them back. Urged
by them, Garrick negotiated terms with the owner. He received a
handsome raise for himself; some actors were forced to take cuts;
but Fleetwood insisted that Macklin's contract was not negotiable
—he would not under any conditions rehire the man he once
regarded as friend and protégé. Garrick tried to make amends to
Macklin by offering him six pounds a week until he could find
work if he would release the company from their agreement
requiring unanimous consent to terms contracted. Macklin refused, feeling he had been betrayed. Garrick, after clearing himself of the matter in a series of letters to the public, resumed
work, as did the other actors, at Drury Lane on December 8. The
rebellion had been quelled, and Macklin was out of work.[2]

Macklin's friends tried to keep Garrick from acting by raising
riots in the theatre, but the public, who came to see Garrick act,
did not take up Macklin's cause. After two days the riots were
controlled, and Macklin was forced to realize that his immediate
future lay outside the Drury Lane Theatre. He consequently
formed an acting school with a group of aspiring actors. He probably hoped, as T. Cibber [3] and William Gifford [4] had done before
him, to use an unlicensed theatre to present his plays and to make
money as well as to discomfit the managers of Covent Garden and
Drury Lane. It is not known how he raised his troupe, but it is
likely that Francis Delaval, a mutual friend of Foote and Macklin,
recommended Foote as a promising pupil. Interestingly enough,
despite later provocation of Macklin by Foote and Macklin's
angry retaliations, Foote continued to remain good friends with
the veteran actor. A hot-headed, inflexible man who had killed

a fellow actor in a burst of temper over a trifle, Macklin had an inflated opinion of himself as orator, actor, teacher, and dramatist. Foote could not resist pricking his bubble on a number of occasions, and Macklin, who had no humor in him, responded with little wit and great invective. Under these conditions, it was unusual that Foote would submit to Macklin's teachings at all. However, the rehearsals seem to have gone smoothly, and the first public announcement of Macklin's plans appeared in the *Daily Advertiser*, January 21, 1744:

> In a short time will be perform'd at the Theatre in the Haymarket, a Concert of Music, and the Tragedy of Othello, Moor of Venice. The character of Othello will be new dress'd agreeable to the Manner and Custom of his own Country. As both these entertainments will be perform'd by a set of Gentlemen for their own Diversion, no Money will be taken, nor any person admitted but by printed Tickets; which (by order of the Gentlemen) will be deliver'd gratis by Mr. Machlin, at his House in Bow-Street, Covent Garden; where Ladies, by sending their Servants, may take Places for the Boxes.[5]

The fiction that the play would be free was merely a device used to circumvent the Licensing Act of 1737.[6] The supposed authentic dress used in *Othello* was a touch provided by Macklin, who was extremely careful about such things ever since his great success as Shylock. Then, in 1741, he acted the Jew as villain, not buffoon, and he dressed "historically" with red hat, piqued beard, and loose black gown. Even Alexander Pope nodded and said, "It is very laudable." [7]

Finally, on February 6, 1744 at the Haymarket Theatre, Foote played Othello to Macklin's Iago. The famous quack Dr. Hill played Lodovico, and Yorke played Montano.[8] It is not completely surprising that Foote chose *Othello* to begin his acting career. It seems probable that this was a traditional role for the novice at this time and was played by such diverse talents as

Arthur Murphy, Tate Wilkinson, Spranger Barry, and Henry Mossop.[9] Of course Foote had not the figure, range, voice, or disposition ever to succeed in tragedy, but despite stories of the ludicrous burlesque that this *Othello* became,[10] it was, in fact, politely received.[11] It was stated that "the performance for chasteness and spirit, exceeded the most sanguine expectations of Mr. Macklin's friends." [12] This is mild praise, perhaps, in the exaggerated rhetoric of theatrical panegyric, but it was sufficient to encourage Foote to give several more performances. He continued to act *Othello* at the Haymarket on February 13, 20, 23, and March 2. On March 10, he played the role at Drury Lane as a benefit for a gentleman in distress. For his next role, he tried out comedy in the person of Lord Foppington in Vanbrugh's *Relapse* and repeated the role at Drury Lane on April 13, again as a benefit for a distressed gentleman. Foote closed his personal season at the Haymarket on April 26 with *Othello,* given as a benefit for a soldier.[13]

It is clear that Foote made little or no money from these appearances. Any profit made at the Haymarket must have been taken by Macklin, for it was his school; and the performances at Drury Lane, gratifying as it must have been to Foote to have a completely professional cast support him, were benefits, and the actors traditionally donated their salaries to the cause. Foote may have hoped for the instant recognition that came to Garrick, but if he received little adverse criticism, the praise was lukewarm— the words carefully chosen not to discourage a not untalented novice. He probably felt more at ease and had greater success with the comic roles, for after these maiden efforts at Othello, he rarely attempted tragedy again.[14]

His first success as an actor probably came to him in Dublin, where he next went to help Spranger Barry, who had made his first appearance at the Smock Alley Theatre on February 15, 1744. The dates have been disputed and no records have been kept of these early appearances, but it seems unlikely that Foote had the time to come to Ireland in the 1743-1744 season.[15] He probably acted at Smock Alley for part of the 1744-1745 season and played the comic roles that he later acted at Drury Lane when he returned to the London stage for the next season, in 1745-1746.[16]

Foote returned to Drury Lane on November 1, 1745, and continued acting through April 14. For the first time in London he played a variety of comic roles: Sir Harry Wildair in Farquar's *Constant Couple;* Lord Foppington in Vanbrugh's *Relapse;* Tinsel in Addison's *Drummer;* Sir Novelty Fashion in Cibber's *Love's Last Shift;* Bayes in Villier's *Rehearsal;* Dick in Vanbrugh's *Confederacy;* Young Loveless in Beaumont's *Scornful Lady;* and Sir Courtly Nice in Crowne's *Sir Courtly Nice.*[17]

These performances at Drury Lane established Foote as an actor in England. He met his former teacher, Macklin, there as well. Fleetwood's extravagances had finally caught up with him, and when he was forced to flee England to escape imprisonment for debt, Macklin was quickly rehired by the new owners.[18] For Foote, despite the prestige gained by acting at Drury Lane, the season could not have been satisfactory. Even though he played a number of lead roles, he was not a regular member of Drury Lane and undoubtedly received no weekly stipend, but was paid for each performance—perhaps on a percentage basis. He certainly did not play regularly, took on no supporting roles, and did not act in afterpieces as even more important actors did. For him to be taken on at these terms was extremely unusual, especially as an untried actor. Only well known players with large followings—Barry, Macklin, or Sheridan—could freelance and attract the audiences that would make it profitable for themselves and the owners. Perhaps Foote was encouraged by his success in Dublin and, no doubt, his friends were numerous and important. But, as can be seen by his roles, except for his modest success as Sir Harry Wildair, only one of his performances was worth repeating more than twice, and in six months' time Foote gave only nineteen performances at Drury Lane—not a profitable season in any sense. His friends may have encouraged him, but certainly the public did not. His inexperience and lack of subtlety must have impeded the great success he wished for, and Foote was not the man to begin with menial roles and work diligently at his craft until his labors were crowned with hard-earned stardom. He had to start at the top, and he would play second fiddle to no man. Fortunately for Foote, he had talent, wit, and inventiveness to equal his egotism; but until he found his métier as leading

actor in his own dramatic works, his career foundered in a series
of false starts and temporary successes.

At this point, Foote was so depressed that he wanted to resign
from the stage.[19] A letter from Garrick, who was taking the waters
at Cheltenham for his health, describes Foote as temporarily defeated in his ambitions but irrepressible:

> August 18, 1746
>
> I have come to this Place last Thursday, & a damn'd dull
> Place it is, notwithstanding We have Balls twice a Week,
> Assemblies every Night, & the facetious Mr. Foote to Crown
> the Whole: He is full of Spirits, abounds in Pleasantry,
> Plays at Whist for five pounds a Rubber, wears lac'd Frocks
> with dirty Shirts, & to the eternal Mortification of the
> Beaux Esprits he has renounced the Stage for Ever, & so
> (as Bayes says) farewell to Genius, humour & all that, *for
> damn him if he plays any more.*[20]

Perhaps Foote did not mean these words sincerely, for he was too
much of a showman to give up the stage so easily. But he was
subject to fits of despondency, and despite Garrick's picture of the
cheerful wit and reckless gambler, the reality was that Foote had
finished a dismal acting season with no prospects of being hired
for the fall, and that he was probably vacationing and gambling
on borrowed money. Under these pressures, Foote turned to a
subject entirely unsuited to him: theatrical criticism. Foote knew
the theatre, but he lacked the objectivity and discipline needed
to sustain a thorough analysis of the subject. The self-effacing
task of writing logically and unemotionally could not have been
endured by this mercurial monologuist, so that it is no surprise
that we have from his critical pen only two occasionally interesting essays, the first on tragedy and its successor on comedy.

*A Treatise on the Passions, So far as they regard the Stage;
With a critical Enquiry into the Theatrical Merit of Mr. G[arric]k,
Mr. Q[uin]n, and Mr. B[arr]y. The first considered in the Part of
Lear, and the two last opposed in Othello* was probably published

in February, 1747.[21] It contains little that is original or startling.
Foote describes the passions in their various categories of pain,
love, hatred, anger, etc., but he qualifies this by stating that all
passion really stems from the single passion of self-love or self-
preservation. He then analyzes, by interpreting the different parts
of the relevant Shakespearian play, the plausibility of Garrick's
acting in *Othello* and *Lear* and compares the acting of Quinn and
of Barry in *Othello*. The remarks Foote makes about Garrick are
typical and begin a long history of capricious and sometimes cruel
teasing of the highly sensitive actor. He begins his treatise by
describing a "little hero" whose reputation is based on fad. Foote
then piously bemoans the malice of the world that would think
he is referring to Garrick and swears that the man he has been
describing has been dead these thirty years. And to prove his
good will, he will protect Garrick's reputation by demonstrating
that he did not write such trash as *Miss in Her Teens*. His criticism
of Garrick's acting is also in this vein of teasing—for although
Foote pretends to be serious in his analysis of Garrick as Othello
and Lear, he is really maliciously damning Garrick with faint
praise. He ends his analysis of Garrick's Lear by stating that this
is one occasion when he is pleased with Tate's alteration of the
play (Lear lives happily ever after in this version) "because it has
prevented my commenting on Mr. Garrick's Manner of Dying,
about which, I am afraid, we should have some dispute." [22] Foote
was referring to Garrick's well known propensity for interminably
drawing out his dying scenes, which Foote later mimicked in his
production of *Tea*. His statements on Quinn and Barry merely
restate what had frequently been said about them: that Quinn
had nobility and grandeur, but that he tended to become monot-
onous and stilted; and that Barry could portray scenes of great
tenderness, but that his voice was too weak to represent the more
violent emotions. Foote still had loyalty to his old teacher and
had only unqualified praise for Macklin's portrayal of Iago.

On March 27, Foote's critical piece on comedy was published.[23] *The Roman and English Comedy Consider'd and Compar'd. With Remarks on the Suspicious Husband and An Examen
into the Merit of the present Comic Actors* is a more interesting
essay than the one on the passions. Foote writes of matter that

interests him personally, and because of this his objective mask
of critic occasionally drops. His style grows less pedantic and
more natural and witty as his own ideas break through his restate-
ment of current thought. He evaluates Plautus and Terence to
find that though their plots are more chaste than the English
ones (for he agrees with Collier about the immoralities of the
English stage), there is little variation in the Roman plays. One
can reduce all of Terence's plays to a formula:

> Two doating old Fools have a Brace of senseless Cubs
> for their Sons; the latter have a smart Servant allowed them,
> who has wit enough to gull the old Gentleman, and direct
> the young ones: A Girl, who sometimes exists in Name
> only, is the Object of young Master's Affections; but coming
> from the Lord knows where, and being the Lord knows
> who, why the Marriage is either impeded, or else a great
> Perplexity and Distraction results from it; but, however,
> it turns out at last, by the means of a Nurse, that Miss is
> a Citizen, a Friend's Daughter, perhaps; so the Casket and
> Trinkets are produc'd, and all Matters made easy.[24]

Foote then examines the English plays, especially those of Congreve, Ben Johnson, and Vanbrugh. He concludes that the English plays, perhaps because of the "complection of the inhabitants,"
have a greater variation in plot, characterization, and dialogue
than the plays of Plautus and Terence. Even though the Roman
plays have chasteness of plot, in terms of morality and unity,
the English plays seem to do very well without the unities of
time, place, and action because they observe the more important
unity of character. Vanbrugh comes in for especially high praise.
His comedies are claimed to be "unexceptionably the best in the
language" if one takes away their immoralities.

The most interesting part of Foote's essay is his comparison
of Garrick's portrayal of Abel Drugger with that of Colley Cibber.
Foote agrees that Garrick is by far the better actor, especially in
terms of correctness, for Garrick persuades you that he is the real

man while Cibber cavorts with squints and other facial distortions to draw laughs, and it is objected that this farcical conduct destroys the illusion of character. However, Foote's answer to these objections is most revealing: "Well, and what then? Don't Folks come to a Play to laugh? And if that End be obtained, what matters it how? Has not he the most Merit, who pleases the most? Suppose Garrick has the Approbation of Twenty or Thirty Judges in the Pit, shall I give up my Fun, which makes the inhabitants of both the Gallerys my Friends, for his Humour? No, hold a little, that will never do." [25] Here Foote suddenly drops his mask of objectivity and takes on the first person singular. He is not defending Cibber; he is defending his own farcical style of acting. All of Foote's fine theories of comedy are swept away in favor of the gallery's roar. One can also see more than just a touch of defensiveness as he reacts to Garrick's superiority as a comic actor. Foote remained truer to his pragmatic test of comedy than to any other theory, and it served him well. And perhaps Foote disliked Garrick because he knew that Garrick was a better actor than he, no matter which criteria he used. Unfortunately, Garrick was hypersensitive to criticism, and this failing made the little actor the perfect foil for Foote, who continued his satiric thrusts at him for another thirty years.

Despite Foote's protestations about leaving the stage and his brief foray into criticism, he did make another attempt at tragedy by playing *Othello* again at the Haymarket, on December 4, 1746.[26] Even though the performance probably reveals the desperate state of Foote's pockets rather than his willingness to try tragedy again, this single exhibition is interesting because it is the first time Foote rented a theatre and formed his own company. He apparently raised his own troupe of actors for this venture, and he used the same concert ploy in his advertising to evade the Licensing Act that Macklin did in 1744.

Thus financial desperation eventually forced Foote to defy the patent houses as, indeed, Macklin had tried to do with Foote's help in 1744. Macklin's school, of course, posed little threat to the patentees and was not even challenged by them. Foote's failure as an actor disarmed no one. Knowing that he could not compete with Drury Lane and Covent Garden with stock productions such as *Othello,* Foote proposed to strike back by mimicking the best known actors of the major houses. Foote gambled that the resultant controversy and publicity would net great profits—if he could keep his theatre open.

It is probable that he used the same actors he had recruited for *Othello* for his new entertainment, *The Diversions of the Morning; or, A Dish of Chocolate.*[27] This hash of mimicry and informal witty talk unveiled Foote's unique talents as no dramatic vehicle could. All testimony of that time reveals Foote's real failure as an actor. Short, stout, and broad of face, Foote would have to be a considerable performer to overcome these physical handicaps. But that was not an impossibility, and in comic roles these handicaps properly handled could become assets. The difficulty lay in Foote's total inability to accommodate himself to his roles. He could caricature the part by overplaying it, but he could not submerge his own personality to give the role its own validity. Johnson commented astutely on this trait as Foote revealed it even in his mimicry:

> No, Sir, his imitations are not like. He gives you something different from himself, but not the character which he means to assume. He goes out of himself, without going into other people. He cannot take off any person unless he is very strongly marked, such as George Faulkner. He is like a painter who can draw the portrait of a man who has a wen upon his face, and who, therefore, is easily known. If a man hops upon one leg, Foote can hop on one leg . . . Foote is, however, very entertaining, with a kind of conversation between wit and buffoonery.[28]

But in his new piece, Foote's acting was kept to a minimum, and he had wide range for both wit and buffoonery.[29]

A master puffer, and this time not restricted to the sale of small beer, Foote made sure that his *Diversions* would not die for lack of notice. The town became fully apprised of his efforts, for after spreading word, and probably giving interviews, to his wide circle of intimates and acquaintances at the coffee houses, Foote began publishing anonymous letters in the *Daily Advertiser* in which he threatened himself with a flogging if he dared to "take off" respectable people in his *Diversions*.[30] By stirring the waves of controversy, Foote caught one rather stupid fish in his net. Orator Henley, a flamboyant eccentric who gave speech lessons, heard he was to be one of Foote's victims and objected strenuously in the *General Advertiser* on April 21, 1747: "*Foote a Fool.* Whoever attacks my Reputation or Livlihood, is a mad Bull to me, and ought to be knocked down, prosecuted, etc. I hear I am to be hung up on Wednesday, at the Haymarket, by one Foote, a Fool." [31]

Foote's first notice for his eagerly awaited opening appeared on April 22, in the *General Advertiser:*

> At the Theatre in the Hay-Market, this Day will be perform'd a Concert of Music. With which will be given Gratis a New Entertainment, call'd 'The Diversions of the Morning.' The principal Parts to be perform'd by Mr. Foote, Mr. Shuter, Mr. Cushing, Mr. Costollo, Mrs. Hallam, Mr. Lee, Mr. Burton, Mr. Hallam, and Miss Moreau.
>
> To which will be added a Farce taken from 'The Old Batchelor,' call'd 'The Credulous Husband.'
>
> Fondlewife by Mr. Foote; Bellmour, Mr. Lee, Laetitia by Mrs. Hallam.
>
> With an Epilogue to be spoken by the B[e]d[for]d Coffee House.
>
> Tickets to be had at Mr. Waller's, Bookseller in Fleet-street. To begin at Seven o' Clock.[32]

It can be seen that Foote used the same concert device that he had used in December. But this time his publicity was too effective and his satiric intentions too feared for the patent houses to ignore his illegal opening. The actors especially were highly sensitive to Foote's threat of mimicking them.[33] James Lacy, the new part owner of the Drury Lane Theatre, alerted by the actors and alive

to his own interests, complained to the authorities about this
illegal competition from the Haymarket. The justice of the peace,
Thomas de Veil, responded to the charge by closing the doors of
the theatre and preventing the customers from entering on the
second day of performance, April 23.[34] Undaunted, Foote turned
to the aid of his powerful friends. With their help an agreement
was reached that Foote could present his play if the performance
did not compete directly with the patent houses. The result was
the first theatrical matinee. *The Daily Advertiser* of the twenty-
fourth carried this advertisement for the performance to be given
the following day—Foote had been delayed only two days:

> This Day at Noon, exactly at Twelve o'Clock at the
> New Theatre in the Hay-Market, Mr. Foote begs the favour
> of his Friends to come and drink a Dish of Chocolate with
> him; and 'tis hoped there will be a great deal of good
> Company, and some joyous Spirits; he will endeavor to
> make the Morning as Diverting as possible. (Tickets for
> the Entertainment to be had at George's Coffee House,
> Temple Bar, without which no Person will be admitted.)
> [Repeated April 27 with these additional comments:] Any
> Gentleman or Lady, with or without Tickets, will be
> admitted. Sir Dilberry Diddle will be there and Lady Betty
> Frisk has absolutely promised.[35]

Foote's cleverness regarding publicity may be seen in this
advertisement. Far from being obscure, it was clear to most people.
The device of a gathering for tea or chocolate or an auction of
paintings (Foote frequently varied the kind of event announced)
as a euphemism for a theatrical performance was clearly taken
from the advertisements of fights and auctions that were also cus-
tomarily given at noon. Professor Scouten in demonstrating this
idea cites a number of advertisements to prove this derivation.[36]

Foote's success was enormous; even de Veil helped by closing
the doors temporarily, which added to the notoriety of the performance. The crowds were so great that Foote had to drop all

pretense of "gratis" performances and take money at the door.[37] Except for slight changes and additions to vary his program, Foote and his rag-tag company continued to act through the sixth of June for a total of thirty-five performances. Garrick may have succeeded more phenomenally as an actor, but no one in the history of the English theatre had ever drawn such crowds by the sheer power of satiric invention.

It is impossible to reconstruct these early performances for they were never printed. Portions of his later performances, however, were printed, and through them it is possible to get an idea of what the more formal section was like. Two versions of the second act of the *Diversions of the Morning* appear in print. The version that was performed at Drury Lane in the season of 1758-59 is based on the *Rehearsal* form.[38] A pompous director teaches his inept pupils to act *Othello* in the presence of two disenchanted spectators. Most of this is a takeoff on Macklin and his school, and, of course, here Foote had inside information. The other version, acted at the Haymarket in 1763, is also called *Tragedy à la Mode; or Lindamira in Tears*.[39] The plot and some of the dialogue of the play was taken from William Whitehead's *Fatal Constancy or Love in Tears, a Sketch of a tragedy in the Heroic Style*. The *Rehearsal* form again is used, and in the original performance puppets took the parts in the tragedy rehearsal. Both of these versions are complete in themselves even though they are second acts. Badcock states that the first act was taken from Foote's comedy of *Taste*,[40] but I agree with Belden that since no contemporary accounts mention characters or the plot from *Taste*, Badcock's statement is improbable.[41] *Diversions of the Morning* probably consisted, then, of an act of burlesque in *Rehearsal* form and another more informal act in which incidents of the moment were satirized and individuals mimicked in Foote's uninhibited style. The epilogue by the Bedford Coffee House, for example, was a device used by Foote to mimic some of the eccentric personalities who frequented it. It is known that, besides Henley, he caricatured Christopher Cock, a fashionable auctioneer, and the Chevalier Taylor, a charlatan who professed to be an oculist.[42]

Since the actors from Covent Garden and Drury Lane said

that they would be ruined through Foote's mimicry, Foote graciously declared that he would provide them with proper situations, for they were completely unsuited to the aristocratic roles they played on stage:

> Quinn, from his deep, sonorous voice, and weighty manner of speaking, he apointed a watchman;—thus:
> "Past twelve o'clock, and a cloudy morning!"

> Delane was supposed to have lost one eye; therefore he fixed him as a begger man in St. Paul's churchyard, exclaiming:
> "Would you bestow your charity on a poor blind man?"

> Woodward puzzled him, he said, to find out any trade he was fit for: he therefore spoke the following speech in his voice and manner from *Sir Foppling Flutter* [Sir Courtly Nice]:—
> "Wherever I go, there goes a gentleman; upon my life a gentleman; and when you have said a gentleman (here dropping Woodward's voice and manner and assuming his own), why you have said *more than is true.*"

> Garrick he was also very severe upon, who was apt to hesitate in his dying scenes; particularly in the fall of Lothario, as thus:
> ". . . adorns my fall, and che-che-che-cheers my heart in dy-dy-dy-dying." [43]

The audiences came in unprecedented numbers to see these performances, and with his profits Foote disappeared, probably to France, to enjoy a long vacation.

He did not return to public view until November 4, 1747, when he gave his thirty-seventh performance of *Tea*, as he now called his piece, at the Haymarket.[44] He did not give many performances there, however, for Covent Garden was going through one of its poorest seasons. Rich lost Garrick, who had purchased a part of the Drury Lane patent, and Quinn to the Drury Lane company, whose members already included Mrs. Cibber, Mrs. Clive, Mrs. Woffington, Macklin, Mrs. Macklin, Delane, Mrs. Pritchard, and Yates. The thinned forces of Covent Garden could only make a meagre boast of T. Cibber, Ryan, and Mrs. Horton as their key performers.[45] Rich, therefore, needed an extra attraction badly and contracted Foote to give *Tea* as an afterpiece.

But the public did not respond well to the farce. *Tea* was given only thirteen times between November 11, 1747, and February 2, 1748, and there was little enthusiasm for Foote's performances as Bayes, Fondlewife and Sir Novelty Fashion.[46]

It is possible that the powerful attractions at Drury Lane eliminated almost all competition, but it is more likely that too many people had seen Foote give his performances the previous season and the novelty of the attraction was gone.[47] An additional reason for the lack of response was that the performances were tamer, for Foote did not give his imitations of actors at Covent Garden; that would be striking too close to home.[48] But he did continue with his other imitations, and on January 21 Foote delivered a new prologue to his *Tea*,[49] defending his mimicry by praising the personal satire of Aristophanes as an important contribution to Greek virtue:

> [In ancient Greece]
> Each reigning folly then was stamped
>   with shame
> Nor would the poet spare the culprit's
>   name:
> Th'offender with the offence was un-
>   derstood;
> And every satire was a public good . . . .
> And the state flourished with the growth
>   of wit.[50]

Statements like this soon earned Foote the nickname of the English Aristophanes, but his theory did not draw audiences. Foote had to find a place where he could give less inhibited performances to new audiences.

Foote left Covent Garden, went to Dublin, and on March 5 began to give morning performances of his *Dish of Chocolate* at the Capel Street Theatre.[51] Thomas Sheridan, manager of the Smock Alley Theatre and father of Richard Brinsley, had survived a number of costly theatrical battles with rival houses and desperately tried to avoid competition with Foote. Young Edmund Burke gives an amusing description of their encounter in *The Reformer* on March 17, 1748:

> . . . 'tis easy to perceive that Mr. F[oote]'s coming hither at such a Season was . . . in order to supplant Mr. S[herida]n in the favour of this City, by Exhibiting Entertainments still more monstrous and incoherent than the other could furnish them with. And this suspicion of Mr. F[oote]'s Design will seem better grounded, when we consider, that at his first coming hither (as I am well assured) our Manager paid him a visit, at which Time he very kindly offer'd him the Use of his House, and proposed to cooperate with him in any Piece of new-fangled Folly they might devise together: But the other obstinately refus'd, as thinking by the Elasticity of his Parts he had got the Wind of him; so taking a little House he set up for himself, where the other's best and most constant Auditors are continually flocking to him.[52]

Foote's competition with Sheridan also set off another rivalry that was to amuse the public. Harry Woodward, an actor from the Drury Lane Theatre who was famous for his portrayal of gentleman roles in comedy and of Harlequins in pantomime, resented Foote's mimicry of him. In retaliation he wrote a piece called *Coffee* to oppose Foote's *Tea*.[53] It is not known who won the battle, for each claimed victory.[54] But even though Foote's

Tea was successful at the box-office and Woodward's service was described as mere water on the leaves, Foote was thin-skinned enough to resent any spirited opposition to his satire. This encounter provoked much outward humor and considerable underlying anger on the part of the protagonists for the next few years.

Foote returned to the Haymarket Theatre on April 18, 1748, this time with new material called *Auction of Pictures,* wherein Foote "sold" portraits of various new characters. He advertised that his first performances would be for charity: "For the Relief of the Sufferers by a late Calamity . . . at his Auction-Room late the Little Theatre in the Haymarket Mr. Foote will exhibit for the satisfaction of the curious a choice collection of Pictures, all warranted Originals and entirely new. To begin at twelve noon." [55] Foote's new portraits were Thomas de Veil, the justice of the peace who had closed the doors of the Haymarket in 1746 and who had since died,[56] and Henry Fielding, who was satirized by Foote as Trottplaid, a pseudonym used by Fielding in his *Jacobite's Journal.*[57]

Fielding had shown public resentment of Foote in February when he sneered that Foote was so poor an actor that he was "fit only . . . to give Tea." He also blamed Rich for allowing Foote to appear at Covent Garden and "suffering private Characters to be ridiculed by Mimickry and Buffoonery upon his Stage." [58] In March, Fielding rented a house in Panton Street, and probably with the help of Thomas Yates, an expert puppeteer, he opened a puppet theatre which he advertised as Madam de la Nash's "Breakfasting Room." [59] Undoubtedly inspired by Foote's euphemism of *Tea,* Fielding advertised his establishment similarly:

At Ten in the morning, and at Seven in the Evening, Madam De La NASH Opens her large Breakfasting ROOM for the Nobility and Gentry in *Panton-street* near the *Haymarket,* where she will sell the very best of TEA, COFFEE, CHOCOLATE, and JELLIES. At the same Time she will entertain the Company Gratis with that Excellent old English Entertainment, call'd A PUPPET-SHEW . . .[60]

When Fielding heard of Foote's return to the Haymarket to continue his imitations, he advertised that his next puppet show
would include a satire on mimicry.[61] It was no coincidence that
the date of this performance was April 18, the same day that Foote
opened at the Haymarket.

Fielding's intentions were obviously clear to Foote, who retaliated by coming on stage chewing tobacco and "shabbily
dressed in complete black, except for two or three Chasms in his
Galligaskins, and the flap of his shirt hanging out," [62] in imitation
of the novelist. Obviously taken by surprise, Fielding took a
few days to prepare his rebuttal, and on April 21 he advertised
"The Comical Execution of Mr. PUPPET FUT, *Esq: Grocer and
Mimic*. With a New Scene *representing* TYBURN." The newspaper editor commented that this was only just for "as Mr. Foote
hath thought proper, instead of Tea to give Punch, Mr. Punch
will give Foote." [63]

Seeing the war broaden to the newspapers, Foote sent in a
protest to the *Daily Advertiser* complaining that the real Henry
Fielding had long since died and that an imposter was taking
his place:

> Whereas there is a dirty Fellow, in shabby black
> Cloathes, a flux'd Tye-Wig, and a Quid of Tobacco in his
> Jaws, that runs up and down calling himself Henry Folding,
> Esq; begging Money, and complaining of one Fut, a
> Grocer, from whom he says he received a severe Drubbing:
> Now this is to inform the Public, that the said dirty
> Fellow is an arrant Imposter, it being well known that the
> true Henry Folding died about four Years since, soon after
> the Publication of Joseph Andrews; and that he now lies
> interr'd in St. Paul's, Covent Garden, near the Remains of
> his old Friend and Patron, Edmund Curll, Bookseller, in
> whose service he lived and died.
>
> Note, The Said Imposter has gone by many Names;
> as Hercules Vinegar, Jonathan Wild, Punch, &c. and was
> Yesterday Morning seen by two or three People in Panton-
> Street, officiating as Jack Ketch to a Puppet-Show; and in

the Afternoon with his Wife and two Children hawking dying Speeches about the Streets.[64]

Angered, Fielding lost his temper and judgment. He brought Foote before his "Court of Criticism" in his *Jacobite's Journal* on the charge of character assassination:

> *Samuel Fut,* of the Parish of *St. Giles's,* Labourer, was indicted, for that he being a Person of an evil Mind and Conversation, and not having the Fear of either Law or Gospel before his Eyes, but being moved and seduced by the Devil, or some of his Imps, on the 18th of *April,* and at divers other Times, at a Place called and known by the Name of the *Scandal-Shop,* in the *Haymarket,* one Justice of the Peace, one Orator, one Poet, one Lord, one Auctioneer, and divers other Persons, did steal and take off, and with a certain Instrument, called a Hatchet-Face, value Three-halfpence, which he the said *Samuel Fut,* before a certain wooden Head, then and there did wear, and hold, them the said Justice of the Peace, &c in a certain Part called the Character, then and there wickedly, diabolically, and ridiculously, did maul and hack; and other Injuries to them did, against the Peace, &c.
>
> [The prisoner denied the charge but was pronounced guilty. His council then moved in Arrest of Judgment on the grounds that some of the persons mimicked were dead. The court ruled that this did not invalidate the charge:]
>
> That if any of the Persons mimicked were dead, the Offence was thereby heightened rather than extenuated; since to drag Persons out of their Graves, in order to ridicule them, could only be justifiable, in the case of notorious Criminals, whereas, on the contrary, one of these was a Nobleman of great Honour, and the other a Magistrate, to whose Care the Public were highly indebted, for having brought many notorious Rogues to Justice; many, perhaps, of the Prisoner's intimate Acquaintance; and had

he been now alive, the Prisoner, through his Means, would
certainly have shared the same Fate. . . .

I shall proceed therefore to pronounce the Judgment
of the Court; which is, that you *Samuel Fut* be p-ssed upon,
with Scorn and Contempt, as a low Buffoon; and I do, with
the utmost Scorn and Contempt, p-ss upon you accordingly.

The Prisoner was then removed from the Bar, mimicking and pulling a Chew of Tobacco from his Mouth, while
the P-ss ran plentifully down his Face.[65]

Though Professor Battestin defends Fielding's grossness by ele-
vating it to the level of Swiftian satire,[66] a different view of the
squabble would reveal little to Fielding's credit. A conviction of
moral superiority is not a license for abuse. In this newspaper
exchange, Foote is far wittier than Fielding, perhaps because he
had not been hampered by the need to justify his attack on moral
grounds. He only wanted to provoke a laugh—certainly a purer
motive than that of Fielding.

On May 4 Foote altered his usual advertisement for his
Auction by adding Joan's song to Punch from *The Pleasures of
the Town,* Fielding's puppet adaption of his *Author's Farce.* A
few words were changed:

> Punch, Punch, Punch,
> Take Care of your Hunch,
>   Take Care of your big strutting Belly;
> If once you should dare
> War with me to declare,
>   I'll beat your fat Head to a Jelly.
>   *Vide Fielding's Author's Farce.*[67]

Foote undoubtedly added to *Auction* new material on Fielding
with the printing of this new notice, and Fielding retaliated on
May 9 by presenting a puppet adaptation of the *Covent-Garden
Tragedy.* The lead role of Captain Bilkum was to be played by
"Mr. Puppet Fut." [68] This phase of the battle, however, lasted

only one week. *The Covent-Garden Tragedy* was replaced by *Bateman* on May 16, and Foote withdrew Joan's song from his advertisement on May 17.

The new caricatures and the quarrel with Fielding proved highly remunerative, and, as he had done the preceding year, Foote played his *Auction* into early June. He occasionally revised and added to his entertainment, and, as before, scheduled matinee performances until the end of May and then began his performances in the evening. He gave a total of thirty-six performances between April 18 and June 16.[69]

Certain patterns were emerging even at this early stage in Foote's career that were to persist throughout his life. Foote would continue to revise or replace material that grew outdated or began to pall, and he would continue to experiment with unusual and new theatrical pieces—though most of these would be satiric portraits bordering on libel, and in a number of cases they would be in part, or in whole, suppressed by the Lord Chamberlain. Travel also became an important part of Foote's life. He developed a love for France and continued to vacation there frequently throughout his life. In his work, too, travel became necessary, for whenever Foote had had a bad season or needed money, he would sail to Dublin, or, on occasion, ride to Edinburgh to recoup losses by playing his London attractions. For the most part these trips were successful and they saved him from financial disaster more than once. For Foote there was no pleasant cycle of work and vacation. His high living and heavy gambling forged a pattern of dissipation, consequent debt, and then the need for quick money to hold off the bailiffs. Foote's career as dramatist and actor seem to have been controlled by the forces of recklessness and necessity.

NOTES

1. James Thomas Kirkman, *Memoirs of the Life of Charles Macklin, Esq.* (London, 1799), Vol. I, pp. 277-287.
2. The information for this account of the actor's rebellion has been taken from a variety of sources. In addition to Kirkman the following books were also consulted: William Cooke, *Memoirs of Charles Mack-*

lin, Comedian (London, 1804), p. 134; John Genest, *Some Account of the English Stage from the Restoration in 1660 to 1830* (Bath, 1832), Vol. IV, pp. 51-55; Watson Nicholson, *The Struggle for a Free Stage* (London, 1906), p. 78; Alwin Thaler, *Shakespeare to Sheridan* (Cambridge, Mass., 1922), pp. 140-141; William Appleton, *Charles Macklin, An Actor's Life* (Cambridge, Mass., 1960), pp. 62-63; and *The London Stage 1660-1800, Part 3*, ed. Arthur H. Scouten (Carbondale, Ill., 1961), Vol. II, xciii-xciv, pp. 1061-1077.

3. In 1733, after Colley Cibber sold his share of Drury Lane to John Highmore, Theophilus Cibber, who had expected this share for himself, led a seceding group of actors to the Haymarket Theatre, and with the help of the Lord Chamberlain, who allowed them to act, forced Highmore to give in to their demands. It is thought that this unfair coercion prejudiced the Duke of Grafton against Garrick's petition even though Garrick had sufficient justification for his actions. See the account in Thaler, pp. 139-140.

4. Garrick achieved his fame by appearing at Goodman's Fields on October 19, 1741. The little theatre, managed at that time by William Gifford, proved so financially successful because of Garrick's phenomenal popularity that the patent houses felt threatened. Before the 1742-1743 season, Garrick was offered a highly profitable contract by Drury Lane, and the patentees of both houses put legal pressure on Gifford to force the closing of his Ayliffe Street theatre. Scouten, Vol. II, p. 999.

5. Cited by Scouten, Vol. II, p. 1085.

6. Thaler, plate opposite p. 140, reproduces a playbill advertising Garrick's debut in *Richard III:* "At the late Theatre in Goodman's-fields this day will be performed a Concert of Vocal and Instrumental Music divided into two parts.

Tickets at three, two, and one shilling. . . .

N.B. Between the two parts of the Concert will be presented an Historical Play called the Life and Death of

King RICHARD the THIRD. . . .

To which will be added a Ballad Opera of one act, called

The VIRGIN UNMASKED. . . .

Both of which will be performed gratis by persons for their diversion."

7. Cooke, *Memoirs of Charles Macklin, Comedian*, pp. 94-95.

8. Scouten, Vol. II, p. 1088.

9. Forster, p. 352.

10. Charles Lee Lewes, *Comic Sketches; or the Comedian his own Manager* (London, 1804), p. 189, states: "His performance of Othello was such a masterpiece of burlesque that it never yet had been forgotten by those who saw it." This remark, however, came long after Foote had become famous for his comic roles, and it is unlikely that it is based upon this performance of Othello.

11. The *Daily Advertiser,* February 21, 1744, stated that "the Gentleman who perform'd the character of Othello receiv'd Universal Applause." Cited by Scouten, Vol. II, p. 1090.

12. Kirkman, Vol. I, pp. 292-293.
13. Scouten, Vol. II, pp. 1088-1105.
14. He did occasionally play Shylock but undoubtedly as a farcical figure. Lewes, p. 190, has an amusing transcript of a deliberate hash Foote made of *Hamlet* playing the lead role for his benefit at Bath [Foote to Laertes]:

> What is the reason that you use me thus?
> I loved thee ever—but 'tis no matter.
> Let Hercules himself do what he may,
> The dog will mew—No, no!

> No, no! that's wrong—the cat will bark—Oh no! that's the dog—the dog will mew—No—that's the cat—the cat will—No! that's the dog again—the cat—the dog—the dog—the cat—the dog—the cat—Pshaw—Pish—Pox—'tis something about barking, mewing, and caterwalling, but, as I hope to be saved, Ladies and Gentlemen, I know nothing about the matter.

15. Robert Hitchcock, *An Historical View of the Irish Stage* (Dublin, 1788), Vol. I, p. 147. This view is also supported by Genest, Vol. X, p. 324.
16. Forster, p. 353, states that Foote began his acting in Dublin in the 1745-1746 season.
17. Scouten, Vol. II, pp. 1189 ff.
18. Cooke, *Memoirs of Charles Macklin, Comedian*, pp. 150-151.
19. Anon., *The English Aristophanes*, p. 8, mentions Foote as wishing to leave the stage, "not having the success he wanted in acting." Forster, p. 355, quotes Foote's rueful comment, "If they won't have me in tragedy, and I am not fit for comedy, what the deuce am I fit for."
20. *The Letters of David Garrick*, ed. David M. Little and George M. Kahrl (Cambridge, Mass., 1963), Vol. I, p. 81. A footnote to this letter (n. 1, pp. 83-84) states that Foote had decided to become a mimic and was not vacationing at Cheltenham, but working to perfect his new art. Even though he does mention Foote as being part of the resort's facilities along with the balls and the assemblies, Garrick did not express himself clearly in his letters; and Foote's insistence that he had renounced the stage forever directly contradicts the footnote. I have written to Professor Kahrl about this point, and even though he still maintains the same point of view, he also wrote that he had no evidence other than this letter to support his statement. My own opinion is that Foote was merely on vacation. In addition to Foote's renouncement of the stage, I find it unlikely that Garrick would not comment in some way on Foote's ability as a professional mimic.
21. This essay is not dated, but a rejoinder was printed on March 19 (see the description in Scouten, Vol. II, p. 1296), and Foote makes slighting references to Garrick's farce, *Miss in Her Teens* (presented at Covent Garden, Jan. 17, 1747), in his work. Since the great popularity of the

farce did not become evident until the end of January, Foote probably wrote the essay in February.

22. Samuel Foote, *A Treatise on the Passions*, (n.d.), p. 24.

23. Scouten, Vol. II, p. 1299.

24. Samuel Foote, *The Roman and English Comedy Consider'd and Compar'd. . . .* p. 10.

25. *Ibid.*, pp. 38-39.

26. Scouten, Vol. II, p. 1269.

27. No cast is listed for December 4. The advertisement merely states, after listing Foote as Othello, "The Other Parts by Young Actors." (See Scouten, Vol. II, p. 1269.)

28. *Life*, Vol. II, pp. 154-155.

29. A farce, *The Credulous Husband*, pieced from Congreve's *Old Batchelor* was also offered, with Foote playing the part of Fondlewife; but here Foote could shine as an *outré* character and not clash with the less farcical elements which undoubtedly had been cut out.

30. *Daily Advertiser*, April 20, 1747; cited by Scouten, Vol. II, p. 1305.

31. Cited by Scouten, Vol. II, pp. 1305-1306. It is possible that Henley was paid by Foote to make this ineffectual protest. Mary Megie Belden, *The Dramatic Work of Samuel Foote* (New Haven, 1929), p. 55 and n. 16, states that Henley engaged Foote this season on the Haymarket boards in scurrilous battles of buffoonery.

32. Quoted in full by Belden, p. 7; and partially cited by Genest, Vol. IV, pp. 225-226, and Scouten, Vol. II, p. 1306.

33. They knew how effective he could be having smarted at his mimicry when he performed Bayes at Drury Lane. Garrick was the first to introduce mimicry, especially of rival actors, in *The Rehearsal* when he began his acting career at Goodman's Fields. Even though he stopped this practice when he came to Drury Lane, his enemies blamed him for the success of mimics such as Foote and Tate Wilkinson. T. Cibber, in particular, complained that *The Rehearsal* was no longer a satire on authors, but was used against actors: "Instead of critically pointing out their [the actors'] want of Taste or Judgement,—he [Garrick] cruelly turn'd the whole Artillary of his Mockery against their natural Defects, or such Particularities of Voice, which did not misbecome them; nor met with Reproof, 'till his Vice of taking off, as it is call'd, became the foolish Fashion;—and taught School-Boys to be Critics." (*Theophilus Cibber to D. G. Esq. with Dissertations on Theatrical Subjects* [London, 1759], pp. 44-45.) Even though Garrick did stop mimicking actors, he continued to use this device in his farce, *Miss in Her Teens* (Covent Garden, Jan. 17, 1747) where "it is said he mimics *eleven* men of fashion." (Little and Kahrl, *The Letters of David Garrick*, Vol. I, p. 88.)

34. *Thespian Dictionary* (London, 1802), p. 103, and Tate Wilkinson, *Memoirs of His Own Life* (York, 1790), Vol. I, pp. 23-24.

35. Cited by Scouten, Vol. II, p. 1307; and see Belden, p. 9.

36. Arthur H. Scouten, "On the Origin of Foote's Matinees," *TN*, VII (January-March, 1953), 28-31.

37. Scouten, *The London Stage,* Vol. II, p. 1308.
38. This version is in Cooke, *Memoirs of Samuel Foote,* Vol. III, pp. 113-129; Tate Wilkinson, *The Wandering Patentee* (York, 1795), Vol. IV, pp. 237-256; and in *The Dramatic Works of Samuel Foote,* ed. Jon Bee Esq. [pseud. for John Badcock] (London, 1830), Vol. I, pp. lvii-lxv. All subsequent quotations from Foote's plays are taken from this edition.
39. This farce is in Wilkinson, *The Wandering Patentee,* Vol. I, pp. 285-298. Genest, Vol. IV, p. 611, also refers to the farce as the *Modern Tragedy.*
40. Badcock, Vol. I, p. lvii. This statement is true for the performances given in Drury Lane during the 1757-58 season.
41. Belden, p. 60.
42. Johnson characterized him as a fine instance of how far impudence will carry ignorance (*Life,* Vol. III, p. 390).
43. Cooke, *Memoirs of Samuel Foote,* Vol. I, pp. 53-55; and also in Wilkinson's *Memoirs,* Vol. I, pp. 25-26.
44. *The London Stage, 1660-1800, Part 4,* ed. George Winchester Stone, Jr. (Carbondale, Ill., 1962), Vol. I, p. 13. This is Stone's first listing of this season for Foote, but it seems likely that the thirty-sixth performance, which is not listed, was given a few days earlier.
45. Emmet L. Avery, *Congreve's Plays on the Eighteenth-Century Stage* (New York, 1951), pp. 91-92. Avery states that the odds against Rich were so great that the actors frequently played to empty houses.
46. Stone, Vol. I, pp. 13 ff.
47. Genest, Vol. IV, p. 247.
48. Wilkinson, *Memoirs,* Vol. I, 82-83, states that "his mimickry at Covent Garden consisted of a whimsical teaching of stage pupils, the Puppets, —the Chevalier Taylor and a Dr. Heberden." In the *Orrery Papers,* ed. Countess of Cork and Orrery (London, 1903), Vol. II, pp. 20-21, one source states that Foote did prepare mimicry for his Covent Garden appearance but was forbidden by the Licensor.
49. Genest, Vol. IV, p. 248.
50. *Exshaw's Magazine,* January, 1748, p. 50.
51. Genest, Vol. X, p. 359.
52. Arthur P. I. Samuels, *The Early Life, Correspondence and Writings of the Rt. Hon. Edmund Burke, LL.D.* (Cambridge, 1923), p. 319.
53. Letitia Pilkington, *Memoirs of Letitia Pilkington, 1712-1750* (New York, n.d.), Vol. III, p. 347.
54. Stone, Vol. I, p. 103.
55. Stone, Vol. I, p. 46.
56. He was easy to caricature because he was notorious for his campaigns against houses of prostitution. Hogarth had a chamber pot emptied on his head in *Night* from *Times of the Day.*
57. W. L. Cross, *The History of Henry Fielding* (New Haven, 1918), Vol. II, p. 89.
58. *Jacobite's Journal,* February 6, 1748.
59. The identity of Madam de la Nash and the satirical purpose of the

puppet theatre have been discovered by Martin C. Battestin, "Fielding and 'Master Punch' in Panton Street," *PQ,* XLV (January, 1966), 191-208.

60. *General Advertiser,* March 30, 1748. The puppet shows were given from March 25 through June 2.
61. *General Advertiser,* April 14, 1748. Cited by Battestin, p. 201.
62. M. P. Willcocks, *A True-Born Englishman, Being the Life of Henry Fielding* (London, 1947), p. 195.
63. *General Advertiser,* April 21, 1748. See Battestin, p. 201; and Stone, Vol. I, p. 48.
64. *Daily Advertiser,* April 23, 1748. Cited by Battestin, p. 203.
65. *Jacobite's Journal,* April 30, 1748. Partially cited by Belden, pp. 56-57; and Battestin, p. 204.
66. Battestin, pp. 204-205.
67. *Daily Advertiser,* May 4, 1748. See Stone, Vol. I, p. 53.
68. Battestin, pp. 205-206, describes how little alteration would be needed in this burlesque to satirize Foote.
69. Stone, Vol. I, pp. 46 ff.

CHAPTER III

FARCE AND MARRIAGE, 1749-1753

Foote returned to London at the height of the theatrical season and gave his *Auction of Pictures* eighteen times between December 1 and February 18.[1] He had spent part of his vacation in Cornwall during the summer months and had become acquainted with three members of the rural gentry. Their eccentricities inspired him to write a two-act farce, *The Knights,* a play with little plot but containing broad strokes of caricature. Since the play needed polishing and rehearsals, and Foote undoubtedly needed money for rent, costumes, and his company, he began presenting *Auction* during December. It is clear that he did not intend to settle down for a long run with his old material, for he advertised that December 24 would be the last performance of *Auction.* However, Foote continued to stall for time; he said the twenty-eighth would positively be the last performance, and on January 2 advertised *Auction* again as a benefit for the Locke Hospital.[2] Perhaps Foote decided his new play was not quite ready for the public. At any rate, the rapidity with which he seized at his next object of satire shows how unformed his plans were. On January 2, 1749, Garrick revived his farce, *Lethe* (Drury Lane Apr. 15, 1740). Garrick's prompter, Richard Cross, noted in his "Diary" that "this farce of Lethe was wrote some years ago and play'd with Success, & was reviv'd this Night with great Alterations, & was but indifferently receiv'd by the Audience." [3] In a short time, however, public reception became more cordial,[4] and therefore worthy of Foote's notice. From past experience Foote knew he could not keep playing his old material and hope to draw audiences. *Lethe* was a godsend. A new and popular farce by Garrick would annoy Foote at any time, but at this moment his contemptuous ire at Garrick's popularity as dramatist and actor could be put to practical use on his stage, and not waste at the Bedford.

Part of the cast of *Lethe* consisted of Garrick in the roles of a Poet, Frenchman, and Drunken Man; Woodward as a Fine Gentleman; and Yates as a Tailor.[5] Foote advertised for his performance on January 7 that he would include in *Auction* a "Poet, Beau, Frenchman, Miser, a Taylor, a Sot, two young Gentlemen, and a Ghost." [6] It was easy for Foote to satirize a bit of froth, which *Lethe* was, and he must have taken special satisfaction in his parody of Garrick as Frenchman and Sot. For Garrick's role as Poet, Foote found a butcher of Clare-Market who greatly resembled the actor and dressed him in poet's clothing.[7] What could be more piquant than representing the great Roscius as a butcher turned poet? Woodward's role of the Finely Gentleman was so negated by Foote that he "made the Part the Beau appear, as he said, Nothing." [8] For once, Garrick retaliated and allowed Woodward to rewrite one of his speeches in *Lethe*. When asked for an account of himself, Woodward, as Beau, answered:

> Sir, by Birth, Title, Travel, and Education, I lead the Fashions; I am principal Connoissour at all Auctions, except that of the Haymarket and there indeed is an impudent Fellow of an Auctioneer who makes nothing of me; but I' Gad I'll be even with him; for I intend to bribe Woodward the Actor, who has almost as much impudence as himself, and he shall treat him with the same Ease and Familiarity as he did in Dublin, where he drove him out of the Kingdom with a dish of his own Chocolate.[9]

The theatrical battle that these words were to evoke was temporarily deferred in favor of another theatrical rout held at the Haymarket. On January 16 an announcement appeared trumpeting an amazing conjuring feat to be seen that night at the Haymarket:

> To be seen, a Person who performs the most surprizing Things . . . he presents you with a common Wine bottle, which any of the Spectators may first examine; this Bottle is placed on a Table in the Middle of the Stage, and he (without any Equivocation) goes into it in Sight of all the Spectators, and sings in it; during his Stay in the Bottle, any Person may handle it, and see plainly that it does not exceed a common Tavern Bottle. The Performance continues about Two Hours and a Half. These Performances have been seen by most of the Crowned Heads of Asia, Africa, and Europe, and never appear'd anywhere in Public but once.[10]

The most graphic account of what happened at the Haymarket that fateful evening was given by Charles Adams, who described Foote's dissection of *Lethe* in the same letter:

> I come now, Sir, to the Affair which principally for this Week past has ingross'd every Person's Attention—We have come to Town a Conjurer; a Thing very rare, Sir, you know in England; his Performances exceed human Thought, and I have sent inclos'd the Advertisement. Last Night was the expected Hour of Action, the Theatre was crowded (at near double Prices) by five o'clock; at Seven the House was lighted up, but during the whole Time not a single fiddle appear'd, or any diversion to amuse the Company, save Catcalls and knocking of Canes, which Musick was play'd for three Hours; when every Bodys Patience was tir'd, and all like to be in confusion, a Person came before the Curtain, and, bowing, promis'd if Mr. Conjurer did not arrive in half an Hour, their Money

should be return'd this they quietly submitted to; but after near an Hour, their Passions grew predominant, and a Gentleman in the Box snatch'd a Candle lighted, and in Violence threw it on the stage; this was the Signal for the Onset of Battle; and in a Moment such a confus'd Jargon arose, which by much exceeded that of Babel—The Boxes, Seats, Glasses, Scenes, Chairs, Machinery, and all the Furniture of the Playhouse, were in less than ten Minutes carried into the Street; the Curtain display'd on a Pole, was erected as a Triumphal Flag; there amidst Curses, Hootings, Noise, and Uproar, an excellent Bonfire was made of the Materials of Mr. Foote's Auction Room—Hats, Wigs, Swords, Snuffboxes &c were as plenty as the Pick Pockets could wish; and I am mightily deceiv'd if the Audience were [not] as agreeable entertain'd by this Riot, as they would have [been] if Mr. Conjurer had kept his Word; the chief Dissapointment, I fancy, was to the Partizans for Miracles, who crowded in Numbers, in Hopes by the Affair of the Bottle, to convince their incredulous Enemies, that Miracles were not ceas'd—A Party of Guards were sent for, and came just Time enough to solace themselves with the Ale, which they drank as they stood warming them by the Fire —Various are the Conjectures on this Account—some say the Managers of both Play houses contriv'd it to hinder Foote's going on—others imagine that Foote himself is at the Bottom of it, to elude the Performance of his Promise in granting a Benefit to his Company—from what Source it sprung I know not; but it may put a [Pe]riod to the Auction, till the Theatre can be refitted; for [suc]h a Devastation, so ruinate a Place never did my eyes behold.[11]

Foote, of course, was accused of perpetrating the hoax despite a letter he sent to the papers pleading innocence.[12] John Potter, the owner of the theatre, was accused of negligence in renting it to the conjurer. He responded that he had been prepared to return their money to the audience if they were displeased but that some of the mob broke into the box office and took all the money. He hoped that those who were responsible for the damage to the Haymarket of over £4,000 would make some restitution.[13] When tempers cooled, the Bottle Hoax became a staple of merriment, and it provided lively conversations and conjectures for many years.

One reasonable answer as to who was responsible for the hoax was given in a gossip column long after the event:

> This was a scheme planned by the late Duke of Montague, in company with the Duke of Richmond, and other noblemen of distinguished taste and humour; who conversing upon the credulity of the English Nation, the first of these noblemen offered a wager of 100 guineas that if an advertisement was publish'd setting forth that on such a day a man would get into a bottle, the inhabitants of the metropolis would flock to pay for being spectators of an impossibility. The event confirmed his Grace's opinion, and, of course, won him the bet; but it was fatal to the proprietors of the House in the Haymarket, who sustained considerable loss from the resentment of the audience at being imposed upon, as no such exhibition was attempted.[14]

It is difficult to determine the extent of Foote's financial losses due to the damage done to the Haymarket. The destruction looked worse than it actually was, because nine days after the riot Foote was again performing his *Auction*. The theatrical rivalry between Foote and Woodward continued even though Foote stopped performing after February 18 to prepare his new play, and *Lethe* had finished its run for the season. Woodward reopened the feud by advertising *Tit for Tat, or One Dish of his own Chocolate* as an afterpiece for his benefit to be given March 18. This time, Foote was angry enough to write an open letter to Woodward in the *General Advertiser* of March 10:

Oh! ho! is it come? What at your Irish tricks again?—
No my Dear, they won't do; I am too well establish'd here;
Do you think we have so soon forgot your H........n Puffs:
you defeat *me* in Ireland! Very likely; as if we did not
know you!—but what *you* (or the whole Town) could
mean by propagating such a report, the Devil take me if
I know; unless you have taken an antipathy to the Irish,
and found out this method to damn their judgement at
once. Which by the Bye, Hal, would be a little ungrateful,
considering how you profited by their ignorance. But let
what will be the motive, if it produces a piece of Dullness
equal to your last, I shan't quarrel at the means, or be uneasy now than then, Yours F. (From my Auction Room).[15]

Woodward was unabashed by the letter and presented his *Tit for
Tat* which was described by Cross as being "a bam in mimickry
upon Mr. Foote given by Woodward for his own benefit." [16] It
was received well, and Woodward played it, with revisions, six
more times through April.

Foote planned revenge, but at the moment his first concern
was for his *Knights*. Finally, Foote advertised his new performance
for April 3: "First time of performance. The Company to be
waited on by two Knights, from the Land's End, and a Brace of
Cats from Italy. The Ladies and Gentlemen are desired to leave
their Lapdogs and Spaniels at home because of the Cats. To begin
exactly at twelve." [17]

Foote played the *Knights* twenty times from April 3 through
June 1.[18] This was Foote's first regular dramatic venture, and, as
can be seen by his advertisement, it was far from regular. The
cat-duet performed by Shuter and "Cat" Harris was an unsubtle
dig at Italian opera [19] and served as a conclusion to a play which
had nothing to do with opera at all. But, seeing that this novelty
did not gain the acclaim hoped for, after three performances Foote
substituted a traditional conclusion in place of the duet.[20]

The cast consisted of Foote as Hartop, Shuter as Sir Gregory
Gazette, and Costollo as Tim. The actors who played the other
characters, Jenkins and Miss Sukey, were not listed in the original

cast.[21] The play is about a young wastrel, Hartop, who tries to cancel his debts to Sir Penurious Trifle by marrying his daughter, Miss Sukey. On route to Sir Penurious's estate to ask for his daughter's hand, Hartop meets Sir Gregory Gazette and his son Tim. Unfortunately for Hartop, Sir Gregory wants Miss Sukey for Tim and indeed has the match already arranged. Hartop, by impersonating Sir Penurious, who never actually appears on stage, and by playing on Sir Gregory's passion for news, tricks Miss Sukey into marrying him. In the meantime, Tim runs off to marry his Mally, a farm servant.

The plot is flimsy, but the real humor lies in the characterization of Sir Gregory and Sir Penurious. Sir Gregory's passion for news leads him to believe Hartop's most outrageous lies. He is told that England is concluding a secret treaty with the Pope. The terms are that England is to give up part of the *Terra Incognita,* both the Needles, the Scilly-Rocks, and Lizard Point, on the condition that the Pretender takes over the government and the Bishop of Greenland is anointed Pope. Though England may seem to be the loser by this arrangement, the Bishop being a Protestant will issue a bull commanding all Roman Catholics to convert. Since they believe the Pope to be infallible, all Europe will soon be of England's mind. Sir Gregory is overcome with joy. "Good lack, good lack! rare news, rare news, rare news! . . . Why, then, when this is finished, we may chance to attack the great Turk, and have holy-wars again, Mr. Hartop. . . . Ah! good now! you see I have a head! politics have been my study many a day. Ah, if I had been in London to improve by the newspapers!" [22]

Sir Penurious, who is impersonated by Hartop, is characterized by his miserliness and a penchant for telling long, rambling stories.[23]. The role as acted out by Foote must have succeeded greatly. Foote was especially skillful in seizing upon a peculiar turn of phrase and by repetition and grimace making it an outstanding feature of the character. The effect was to make a general trait, such as miserliness and a love of stale stories, seem singular to the character because these traits were always expressed in terms of the character's peculiarities. The plot serves only to set the characters in motion and put them on exhibit. Subtlety of characterization is impossible under these conditions, but Foote wanted the immediate response of laughter from the galleries, not the approbation of the pit. Despite his subsequent disclaimers,[24] Foote's first step as a dramatist pointed squarely to his ultimate direction as a writer of farces.

In the meantime, Foote was not allowed to forget Woodward, who continued his *Tit for Tat* and even took aim at the *Knights* on April 8: "As the Auctioneer gives *Tea* tomorrow at Covent Garden, Mr. Woodward (by particular desire) on Saturday next will present him with a dish of his own chocolate, with an addition of one mew at his cats." [25] Foote, having revised the conclusion of his play, responded: "The Company may depend upon having an Additional Treat of Chocolate, but vastly different from that lately distributed by Harry the Smuggler. As the Italian Cats would not do for the Haymarket he has dispos'd of them to Drury Lane." [26] On April 15, Foote reinstated his *Auction* as an afterpiece to the *Knights* and prominently displayed Woodward as one of his portraits. He continued his retaliations, with occasional revision,[27] until he closed his doors on June 1.

Although the summer put an end to theatrical hostilities, Woodward, perhaps feeling worsted in his battle with Foote, decided to strike again the following season. He let it be known that in his role as Malagene in Otway's *Friendship in Fashion,* scheduled at Drury Lane, January 22, 1750, he would mimic Foote completely, even to the point of dressing like him. Foote was furious and dashed off a letter to Garrick threatening him with retaliation if he did not prevent Woodward from carrying out his plans:

> Sir,
> It is impossible for me to conceal a piece of intelligence that I have received this minute from either a friend or an enemy.
> I am told, that on the revival of a comedy called "Friendship in Fashion," a very contemptible friend of yours is to appear in the character of Malagene, habited like your humble servant. Now, I think it is pretty evident

that I have as few apprehensions from the passive wit of Mr. Garrick, as the active humour and imitation of Mr. Woodward; but as we are to be in a state of nature, I do conceive that I have a plan for a short farce that will be wormwood to some, entertaining to many, and very beneficial to, Sir,

Yours,
Samuel Foote.

If your boxkeeper for the future returns my name, he will cheat you of a sum not very contemptible to you, viz. five shillings.[28]

Garrick must have been amused and delighted at Foot's predicament but was sufficiently frightened by his threat not to answer in kind:

Sir

I am very much surpriz'd to find you so uneasie & hurt at ye Intelligence given you last night, but as you were doubtfull whether you receiv'd it from a Friend or an Enemy, I think, in prudence, you shou'd have consider'd twice before you had put pen to paper. . . . I assure you I never *have* nor *will* set my Wit to yours, either in y^r Active or passive sense, for I confess myself incapable of engaging with you, at your usual weapons— . . . but pray, Sir, wou'd you have me . . . interfere in the Affair while there is a Mimical War betwext you, & first declar'd on y^r side? if I did, wou'd he not justly complain of unfair treatment, & say, that I am holding his hands, while you are beating him? But shou'd he dress at you in the Play, how can you be alarm'd at it, or take it ill; the Character of Malagene (exclusive of some little Immoralities which can never be apply'd to you) is that of a very smart, pleasant, Conceited fellow, & a good Mimic . . .[29]

Garrick's letter was no comfort to Foote, who saw that Woodward was not be deterred. As a last resort, he published an open letter to Woodward, a curious compound of arrogance, silly rationalizations, and special pleading:

> Sir,
>
> After the many defeats you have already suffer'd in the Mimical War between us, to which Ireland as well as England have been laughing witness; I was greatly surpris'd to hear that you again intended to provoke my future vengeance, by dressing at me in the character of Malagene, which you are to perform in the reviv'd play *Friendship in Fashion*. Whatever you may think, Mr. W——d, these public exhibitions of particular persons by no means become the dignity of the stage, & though a disorder in my Finances may occasionally have urged me to some Pleasant attacks in this way, yet give me leave to say, I was never abandoned enough to think 'em justifiable . . . Your intended attack on me . . . as the character you are to represent is . . . indeed not that of the most nice Morality; who knows but that . . . some may cry, "Tis he from head to Foot." As you are sensible this would be doing me great Injustice, & in my present circumstances might be particularly injurious to me, I expect you will alter the Design.[30]

If Foote wrote this letter, it is impossible to guess what his "present circumstances" were that would make this rather mild spoof so unpalatable. It is possible that Woodward had written this letter to embarrass Foote and mock his protestations, for no one could take its contents seriously.

The fateful day of January 22 came, and the surprising turn of events exceeded even Foote's fondest hopes. Cross, who became inadvertently involved, described the reversal: "Mr. Woodward did ye part of Malagene in which he took off Mr. Foote & would have many of the Actors, but the Audience grew so outrageous, that he forc'd to desist ye 4th and 5th Acts were much hooted. . . .

It was given out again, wch so enraged the Audience yt they call'd loudly for Garrick, but as he was not this Night at the House, they pull'd up the Benches, and tore down ye Kings Arms. . . ." More damage would have been done, but Lacy calmed the mob by telling them that the prompter, Cross, was at fault for giving out the same play. He announced that the *Provoked Husband* would be played next and so pacified the angry crowd.[31] Foote, who had finally won his battle in unexpected but decisive fashion, could not contain his glee. On January 26, he gloated from the pages of the *Daily Advertiser:*

> We hear from Drury Lane that on Monday night Harry the Smuggler, who was tried and convicted last summer at the Haymarket, was found hanging in one of the cells of that prison: It seems he had long had a Design to make way with himself and at several times procured poison from Foppington, Harry Wildair, Tom Thimble, &c. but the Quantity, though it made him exceeding sick, not being sufficient to dispatch him, he at last tack'd himself up in his own *Tit for Tat*. When he was cut down he look'd very ghastly, and great groanings were heard in the prison before, at, and after his committing the Fact. . . . It is very remarkable that he had on the very coat, which, in Conjunction with one Abel Drugger, not yet taken, he stole from Sammy the Auctioneer; but from the diligent search made after Drugger, it is believed he will soon be brought to justice.[32]

This was the last word the public was to hear from Foote for some time. He left the stage after his last performance at the Haymarket on June 1, 1749, and did not return to regular acting until his reappearance as part of the Drury Lane troupe in October, 1753. According to most of his biographers, Foote had inherited his third fortune at about this time and was actively engaged in spending it, mostly abroad. Perhaps this was the reason he so resented Woodward's 'dressing at" him as Malagene. To Foote,

Woodward was striking an underhanded blow at a gentleman who was no longer in a position to retaliate and, indeed, had a reputation to lose. Like many controversialists of his time, Foote took his works, his pedigree, and his education very seriously. Even though he was the first to mock these pretensions in others. he refused to be treated as a mere player.

Foote's inheritance relieved him temporarily from the cares of work, and considerably less detail is available about his activities during these years. Much of his time was spent with his dearest friend, Francis Blake Delaval. Delaval, seven years Foote's junior, probably came to know Foote while still at college, about the time of Foote's Haymarket debut. Delaval was forced to leave Oxford in 1747 after he and a group of school mates killed a college servant in rough play.[33] Delaval sincerely regretted the incident, but it characterized his irresponsible and crude nature. As heir to the Delaval fortune, he was to come into £7,000 a year, yet he dissipated much of this even before his father's death. Tall, fair, and strikingly handsome, he epitomized the eighteenth-century rake. The complications and entaglements of his many amours were frequently explicated in the newspapers and in the letters of gossips.

Delaval, like Foote, loved to play ourageous practical jokes with complicated mechanical devices and devious stratagems. After his father's death, Delaval took over Seaton Delaval, a huge and cumbrous mansion built by Vanbrugh, and appointed Foote the Minister of Entertainment.[34] With Macklin and Angelo, famous fencing-master, as cadre, visitors were victimized by ingenious pranks and outrageous practical jokes:

> The assiduous host and his friends, candlesticks in hand, passed from bedroom, stifling their laughter as they made things comfortable for their unsuspecting guests. Ducks and hens were put between the sheets, a tub of water beneath a remarkable bed that let down in the middle by means of pulleys, mannikins like ghosts of ancient Delavals were set up in clothes closets, and a sleepy housemaid was pinched awake to take in the seams of a jilted baronet's

suit of clothes so that when he awoke he would think love had given him a dropsy. One guest was kept in bed three days by persuading him that it was still night, and at times these masters of the revels vanished right out of the house and mysteriously appeared somewhere quite else by means of a secret underground passage.[35]

But, unfortunately, life is not all fun and games, and Delaval was getting bored of seeking sanctuary in Paris to escape his creditors. One obvious solution to a prodigal's dilemma was portrayed by Hogarth in his *Rake's Progress:* marriage to a wealthy widow. By the greatest of coincidences, when Foote was acting at the Haymarket, he had captivated Lady Isabella Pawlett, a reputedly wealthy widow was almost twice his age. A proven dupe, Lady Isabella seemed the answer to all of Delaval's financial problems. Foote agreed to deliver the lady for an agent's fee of ten percent of her total fortune, and Delaval, delighted, gave a bond to Foote for £12,000, dependent on the success of his services.[36] Everything was settled; all that remained were the stratagems necessary to persuade Lady Isabella to shift her affections from the married Foote to an aristocratic and handsome bachelor. It would have been very simple to arrange an introduction and let the nature of a vague, half-mad old woman, only too eager to marry, take its course. But deep planning and dark strategy were psychological necessities to Foote, and, true to the bent of his imagination, he prepared a farce.

In the past, Foote and Delaval had amused themselves at fortune-telling. Disguised with turbans and beards, they practiced their craft in a large darkened room. The conjuror, seated on an ottoman, looked wise and gesticulated as his assistant struck a huge drum and accepted questions from the visitants. The assistant, by interpreting the conjuror's signs, gave startling revealing answers. Of course, Foote's and Delaval's knowledge of their visitors was prodigious, fed as it was by a network of spies and servants. Last minute information was elicited from bribed servants who were waiting for their masters outside the conjuror's room and was whispered through tubing connected to the huge drum

inside.[37] Drawing on past experience, Foote decided to replay this
old game, but with a new conjuror, Jemmy Worsdale, whose
ability as a mimic and actor was established, as was his predilic-
tion to roguery.[38] Luring Lady Isabella to see the new conjuror
was no difficult task for Foote, and Worsdale, properly primed,
described in closest detail the man she would meet and later
marry.[39]

The affair succeeded, as it would have without all the riga-
marole. Both parties wanted marriage. And Foote, undoubtedly
anticipating many easy years before him, took a pleasure trip to
Paris. He saw Voltaire's new play, *Rome Preserved,* and, as he
wrote back to Delaval, was further confirmed in his theory that
it is more important to please the public than the critics:

> Feb. 18 [1750]
> Nothing new at Paris but a tragedy of Voltaire called *Rome
> Preserved.* The subject was chosen in direct opposition to
> Crebillon, but if crowded houses and universal applause
> are testimonies of merit,Voltaire must be allowed infinite.[40]

Foote's vacation was short lived, however, and he was forced to
sail back to England to secure his fee. Kelynge, Delaval's lawyer,
refers to this difficulty in his bill of particulars: "My attendance
upon Lady Isabella with Mr Foote in order to scatter Terrors
alias Humbug; and the good Effect that my first Interview had
with her Ladyship, so as to determine her to marry you the next
day." [41] It seems that Lady Isabella's relations were extremely
anxious that she not remarry, and great pressure was put on the
lady to call off the wedding. Foote warned her that her relations
were trying to get her declared *non compos mentis* in order to
control her fortune. A double revenge, Foote suggested, would be
marriage: "First by . . . marriage, and secondly by having children
her relations would be cut off from succession." [42] This flattering
reference would not help but further the cause. Lady Isabella
capitulated, and the nuptials were held March 8, 1750.

But the ironic pen of comedy altered the farceur's hoped-for conclusion. Before the wedding bells had stopped echoing, Mr. Nuttall, the Pawlett's family lawyer, informed Delaval that of the £110,000 Lady Isabella had only £23,000 at her disposal. The remainder was held in trust for her daughter and could not be touched.[43] As might be expected, money became an issue between the newly married couple, and the disillusioned bride fled Delaval to seek solace and protection from the man she really loved, Foote. He did his best to console her, and, seeing his payment from Delaval endangered, Foote retained Mr. Nuttall to hold Delaval to the letter of the bond.[44] Delaval, who was able to squeeze only a few thousand pounds from his bride's securities,[45] was forced once more to go to Paris to avoid having judgment placed against him. However, Kelynge got Foote and Nuttall to agree to deliver up the judgment for £12,000, and Delaval was free to return and have a reconciliation with his bride.[46] In return for giving up his claim, Foote undoubtedly settled for a smaller sum, one that Delaval could pay.[47] Delaval was disillusioned by Foote's mercenary attitude, and their friendship, though never broken, suffered a cooling period for several years.

Foote remained absent from the stage until his production of *Taste* was given at Drury Lane, January 11, 1752. Not yet pressed for cash, Foote played the gentleman scribe and did not plan to act or profit financially from the piece.[48] He charitably gave his author's profit to Jemmy Worsdale, probably for his help in the Delaval-Pawlett marriage, and for Worsdale's assistance in creating Lady Pentweazle, the most memorable character in the play.[49] Worsdale, a very clever mimic who might have been responsible for first inspiring Foote to use mimicry, also acted the role of Lady Pentweazle.

Shortly after production, on January 25, Foote had *Taste* printed and dedicated it to Francis Blake Delaval. He named Francis and his brother John as his benefactors, acknowledging their help in his early productions, "when necessity listed me in the service of the public." [50] In this dedication Foote insists on lifting his two-act piece to the dignity of comedy, arguing that his characters do not go beyond nature as in farce, and that "with the aid of a love-plot, I could have spun out the piece to the extent of five acts." [51] Most amusingly, Foote felt it necessary to

defend his image from detractors who might not take his theories
on comedy seriously: "I once intended to have thrown into this
address, the contents of many of our [Foote's and Francis Delaval's] conversations on the subject of *comedy,* for in whatever
dissipations the World may suppose our days to have been con-
sumed, many, many hours have been consecrated to other subjects
than generally employ the gay and the giddy." [52]

But Foote's reputation preceded him to the playhouse, and
the house filled as soon as it opened with an audience impatient
for a farce written by the gay and giddy Foote. The prompter,
Cross, writes that the audience clamored and wanted the farce
before the play. They applauded the main piece, *Revenge,* but
they "wish'd it over."[53] They got their money's worth. The cast
originally consisted of Palmer as Carmine; Yates as Puff; Shuter
as Lord Dupe; Taswell as Alderman Pentweazle; Costollo as Calib;
Cross as Brush; Blakes as Novice; Worsdale as Lady Pentweazle;
and Master Cross as Boy.[54] But Foote did not like Yates as Puff, so
he got Garrick to say that Yates was sick and that Foote would
take his role. Foote then piously recited his apology to a surprised
and delighted audience: "Gentlemen: I have left the Stage some
time, nor have I any hopes of profit from this Piece, but as a
performer is taken ill, I had rather appear myself, than have so
many people whom Curiosity has drawn together, be disappointed." [55] With great applause the play began.

Taste illuminates the mysteries of the auction room. Foote
satirizes the fraud of the seller but directs his heaviest fire at the
ignorant dupes who pretend to taste and scholarship, but who
value disfigured and fragmented works of art because they have
been represented as foreign and old. Here, only "broken" English
is recognized as the authentic voice of connoisseurship. The prologue, written by Garrick,[56] was delivered by that actor dressed
as an auctioneer who, ironically, defends himself against Foote's
charges:

> If we should fall—to you it will be owing;
> Farewell to *arts*—they're *going, going, going;*
> The fatal hammer is in your hand, oh town!
> Then set *us* up—and knock the *poet* down.[57]

The first act reveals Carmine, the painter, and Puff, the promoter, preparing to defraud an all too willing public. Carmine prides himself as a true artist but sighs that "Family Connections, private recommendations, and an easy, genteel method of flattering" are necessary for a painter to succeed. Puff, angry that Carmine so underrates the art of public relations, reminds him forcibly of his mean origins:

> Why, thou post-painter, thou Dauber, thou execrable white-washer, thou—Sirrah, have you so soon forgot the wretched state, from whence I dragged you. The first time I set eyes on you, rascal! what was your occupation then? Why, scribbling, in scarce legible letters, coffee, tea and chocolate on a bawdy-house window in Goodman's-fields. . . . Pray, how high did your genius soar? To the daubing diobolical angels for alehouses, dogs with chains for tanners yards, rounds of beef and roasted pigs for Porridge-island. . . . From that contemptible state did not I raise you to the Cat and Fiddle in Petticoat-Lane; the Goose and Gridiron in Paul's Churchyard; the first live things you ever drew, dog? [58]

Seemingly chastened, Carmine greets his waiting client, Lady Pentweazle, who has commissioned him to paint her portrait. Her ladyship, a *nouveau riche* matron, née Molly Griskin, is eager to be flattered by the oil of Carmine's brush and tongue. This scene was undoubtedly the most successful part of the play. Her simpering acceptance of Carmine's flattery and her idiotic descriptions of her family's beauty and taste go below satiric caricature to the level of incongruous whimsical farce where laughter exists for its own sake:

> Why all my Family by the mother's side were famous for their eyes: I have a great aunt among the beauties at Windsor; she has a Sister at Hampton-court, a *perdigious*

fine woman—she had but one eye, indeed, but that was a piercer; that one eye got her three husbands—we were called the gimblet-eyed family.[59]

In the second act Carmine is disguised as a French importer of old and delicate curiosities of high price that are to be sold to a group of foolish faddists. Puff, acting as a shill, is disguised as a German connoisseur who is a buyer for royalty and therefore can expertly support Carmine's extortionate demands for the junk that is to be sold. Puff is found out by Lady Pentweazle's boy Caleb, who penetrates his disguise. Carmine, traitorously saving his own neck, disclaims all knowledge of Puff. But Puff, in revenge, exposes Carmine and threatens the dupes with the extreme mortification of revealing their gullibility to society if they dare to bring legal action against him.

The audience greatly enjoyed the first act, especially Lady Pentweazle, and they loudly applauded Wordsdale. The second act was hissed, and the play ended with shouts of "No more," and "Encore." *Taste* was altered slightly and given out four more times that month, but opposition grew, and finally the play had to be dropped.[60] The reviews, however, were generally favorable, one stating that the subject was too "abstract and singular" for popular consumption but that the play would make a good reading piece.[61] Foote agreed with this verdict in his dedication,[62] and most of his future productions of *Taste* were given with a different second act, usually various burlesque scenes, and called the collations *Modern Tragedy, Tragedy à la Mode,* or *Diversions of the Morning.* But no matter what changes were made, the favorite role of Lady Pentweazle was retained and became one of Foote's most popular roles.

Again, Foote left the theatrical scene after his performance in *Taste* and continued to spend his remaining money on various pleasure jaunts. Undoubtedly, the most magnificent of these was planned by Frank Delaval shortly after his father's death on December 9, 1752. Delaval and Sir Richard Atkins had a yacht built, ostensibly for the purpose of sailing to Corsica so that Delaval could fill the vacant throne. But pleasure took precedence over these practical affairs of state, and, among others, Foote and Worsdale were invited for their wit, and the Misses Roach and Murray, notorious women of the town and mistresses of the new yachtsmen, were invited for their beauty. A magazine gives a lyrical description of this affair:

> The yacht was equally elegant and convenient, there being every accommodation that could be suggested. It was launched at Deptford, in the presence of numerous spectators, and the party who were to sail attended, when a very elegant repast was provided, and a band of music. It were needless to say that the bottle circulated very briskly, and at every toast being drunk, there was a discharge from the yacht of six guns, which was re-echoed from the shore of six more. The evening passed in great harmony and conviviality, and concluded with a ball, which continued till morning.
>
> But how transitory are the events of this world!—At this very critical juncture, when there was such a glorious perspective of pleasure, and the gratification of almost unlimited ambition, Sir Richard Atkins was carried off with a violent fever. The whole project was laid aside, the yacht was sold, the provisions given to the poor, the cooks, confectioner, and musicians were dismissed, and sung small indeed! [63]

By January, Foote was back in town with a play that reflected his travels, *The Englishman in Paris*.[64] At this time Foote seemed to be on fairly good terms with John Delaval and kept him in touch with the latest news from London, including this new theatrical venture:

Mar. 13 [1753]

> In the North, what do ye do in the North? When you are wanted in the West[.] On the 24th instant appears a Farce of your H[um]ble Servants, which without the

powerful aid of such friends as Mr Delaval will I fear
encounter a most disastrous destiny. . . .

There is no news but what the papers will bring you,
but we have long and pompous accounts of the tilts, tourne-
ments, flings & Bull baitings at London. Your Uncle Price [65]
says that Mr Pelham had hired the two dancing Bears to
transmit to your Brother by way of keeping him in the
Country till the Parliament is up. . . . You must expect
the wits to be arch, but I don't know how to take your
calling me one in your last, as I know in what light you
men of Business regard that Character, but I give you leave
to think of me as you please in every other respect, provided you do me justice in one article; that I am & ever
shall be

Dear Mr Delaval
Yr Most obligd & obdt Servt [66]

This time, Foote flippantly dedicated his play, printed on
April 21, 1753, to his bookseller, Mr. Vaillant, because, "I have
no obligations to any great man or woman in this country, and
as I will take care that no production of mine shall want their
patronage, I don't know any person whose good offices I so much
stood in need of as my bookseller's." [67] This was not strictly true,
for Foote felt obligations to Macklin, his old tutor, though he was
not a "great man." Accordingly, Foot completed his afterpiece
in time for Macklin's benefit on March 24, 1753, and he also
revised the ingenue's role of Lucinda to reflect the various abilities
of Maria, Macklin's daughter. Macklin went to great expense to
give his daughter every educational advantage that would add
to her grace and charm as an actress. She became fluent in Italian
and French, could sing, dance, play musical instruments, and,
supposedly, had a wide knowledge of belles-lettres. But, though
competent and reliable, Maria lacked the emotional vitality so
necessary to an actress, and consequently attracted no great following. Macklin despaired of her future and prevailed on Foote to
write the role of Lucinda so that Maria's expensive education
could be seen to its greatest advantage. The cast, dominated by

the Macklin family, had Maria as Lucinda, Macklin as Buck, and
Mrs. Macklin as Mrs. Subtle.[68]

The Englishman in Paris, as the title indicates, satirizes the
English blood who refuses to modify his natural rowdiness even
when visiting a country with delicate and effeminate tastes. The
play was very well received, as Francis Delaval noted in a letter
to his brother John: "I am just come from Mr. Foote's farce, which
went off with applause. Miss Macklin danced a minuet, played
on a 'pandola' and accompanied it with an Italian [sic, French]
song, all which she performed with much elegance." [69] Foote's
letter to John a week later reaffirms the success of his farce, but
Macklin's acting grated him:

> 5 Apr. 1753
>
> The *Englishman in Paris* has been better received
> than I expected. Garrick and all the Delicae of the Theatre
> say kinder things of it than modesty will permit me to re-
> peat. Upon the whole it was damnably acted, Macklin mis-
> erably imperfect in the words and in the character (oh
> stain to comedy). You might have seen what I meant. An
> English Buck, by the powers of dulness instantaneously
> transformed into an Irish Chairman. . . . The piece will
> be printed the 25th instant which I will inclose to you.
>
> I set out for foreign parts the first of May, and shall
> petition for the continuance of our correspondence. . . .[70]

The play became a standby in both Drury Lane and Covent
Garden, and was regularly played for more than twenty years.
Foote, however, after appearing in the role frequently at Drury
Lane during the 1753-54 season, rarely played it again. Perhaps
he became aware of the inadequacy of the piece. Except for a
few bright spots in the first act with Buck, Foote's play is stodgy,
dull, and heavily didactic. Fortunately for Foote's future works,
this was only an occasional failing. Perhaps it was a need to
justify the usefulness of his satire as a vehicle to correct folly,

for, as we have seen, Foote could take himself too seriously. His genius lay in outrageous caricature of rogues and fools, and when he departed from this technique his characters became not only unnatural and stiff, but completely undifferentiated. Foote was a master of the many tongues of roguery, but knew only one heavy monotone for virtue.

NOTES

1. Stone, Vol. I, pp. 79ff.
2. *Ibid.*, pp. 83, 85, 86.
3. *Ibid.*, p. 86.
4. On the next night Cross wrote: "Great applause to ye Farce, some little Hiss" (Stone, Vol. I, p. 87). *Lethe* went on to become one of Garrick's most popular farces.
5. Stone, Vol. I, p. 86.
6. *Ibid.*, p. 87.
7. A unique account of this travesty is found in an exchange of letters discovered and published by Alan D. Guest, "Charles Adams and John Gilbert-Cooper," *TN*, XI (July-September, 1957), 138.
8. *Ibid.*
9. *Ibid.*
10. Stone, Vol. I, p. 90.
11. Guest, p. 139.
12. *General Advertiser*, January 18, 1747.
13. Stone, Vol. I, p. 91.
14. *Town and Country Magazine*, September, 1772, p. 457.
15. Cited by Stone, Vol. I, p. 103.
16. Stone, Vol. I, p. 103. See also Stone, "The Authorship of *Tit for Tat*, A Manuscript Source for 18th-Century Theatrical History," *TN*, X (October-December, 1955), 22-28.
17. Stone, *The London Stage*, Vol. I, p. 108.
18. *Ibid.*, pp. 108ff.
19. Thomas Davies, *Dramatic Miscellanies* (London, 1783-4), Vol. I, p. 212.
20. Cooke, *Memoirs of Samuel Foote*, Vol. I, p. 60; and Stone, *The London Stage*, Vol. I, p. 110.
21. Stone, *The London Stage*, Vol. I, p. 108.
22. Foote, *The Dramatic Works*, Vol. I, pp. 18-19.
23. *Ibid.*, pp. 31-35.
24. In his dedication to *Taste*, I, v-vii, Foote insisted that his short pieces were really comedies and not farces. "As the Follies and Absurdities of Men are the sole Objects of *Comedy*, so the Powers of the Imagination (Plot and Incident excepted) are in this kind of Writing greatly restrained. No unnatural Assemblages, no Creatures of the Fancy, can

procure the Protection of the *Comic* Muse; Men and Things must appear as they are."

25. Stone, *The London Stage*, Vol. I, p. 103.
26. *Ibid.*, p. 110.
27. On May 15, Foote advertised. "To conclude with a new Smuggling Epilogue, called *Tit for Tat; or, The Smuggler foil'd at his own weapons*" (Stone, *The London Stage*, Vol. I, p. 120).
28. *Private Correspondence of David Garrick*, ed. James Boaden (London, 1831-32), Vol. I, pp. 54-55.
29. *The Letters of David Garrick*, Vol. I, pp. 141-142. This affair seems to have been complicated by various accusations made by Woodward and Lacy as well as Foote. Contrary to what one might have expected, Garrick was far from delighted with Woodward. In a letter to Lacy, he describes the actor as "a disconted Spirit & in order to please ye Persons about him or indulge his Spleen, has resorse to ye last refuge of low Minds; Tale-bearing & Mischief-making. He has had my confidence it is true, but I am as little affraid of his betraying it, as I am certain he w^d if he could gain Sixpence by it—Therefore, if you please, first to ask him, whether he Acknowledges what Mr. Foote has been pleas'd to relate concerning You." (*The Letters of David Garrick*, Vol. I, p. 140, n. 5.)
30. Stone, *The London Stage*, Vol. I, p. 169.
31. *Ibid.*, pp. 169-170.
32. *Ibid.*, p. 171.
33. *The Correspondence of Horace Walpole*, ed. W. S. Lewis (New Haven, 1937-   ), Vol. XIX, p. 387, n. 13.
34. Cooke, *Memoirs of Samuel Foote*, Vol. II, p. 70.
35. Francis Askham, *The Gay Delavals* (New York, 1955), p. 78.
36. Delaval MSS, DE/38/4, at Northumberland Record Office. This manuscript contains a bill of particulars in which Kelynge, Delaval's lawyer in the ensuing proceedings. lists his services in detail and asks for £500 "over and above what I have received from you." In this futile attempt to blackmail Delaval, Kelynge states that Foote had Delaval's bond for £12,000. Also see Askham, pp. 51-52.
37. Edgeworth, pp. 84-85.
38. See Belden, pp. 59-60, for an interesting account of his life.
39. Askham, pp. 49-50; and *Town and Country*, August-September, 1771, p. 421.
40. *Historical Manuscripts Commission, Eleventh Report, Pt. VII. The Manuscripts of the Duke of Leeds* . . . (London, 1888), p. 79.
41. Delaval MSS; and see Askham, p. 51.
42. *The English Aristophanes*, pp. 16-17.
43. Askham, p. 51
44. *Ibid.*, p. 56.
45. Delaval MSS; and Askham, pp. 57-58.
46. In the Delaval MSS Kelynge insisted on being reimbursed "For my transacting all your Affairs during your prudent retreat to Paris, which for some Months engrossed all my time and Attention; Numberless

Attendences upon Messrs. Foote and Nuttall and others until matters were compromized & you returned to England in safety, by Foote and Nuttall first agreeing to deliver up the said Judgment, which was accordingly done at our Meeting at the Cardigan-head Tavern."

47. Most of Foote's memoirs claim that Foote received his full fee as marriage broker in an annuity which he quickly sold and as quickly spent. It is interesting to note that even though this fantastic story of Foote's involvement with the Delaval-Pawlett marriage was faithfully repeated in all contemporary accounts of Foote's life, few subsequent biographers could believe the story. Forster, p. 71, n. 1, disbelieved the story entirely, and Belden does not even mention the affair at all. Factual evidence was discovered by Francis Askham when he sifted through the Delaval papers, then at the Central Library at Newcastle-upon-Tyne, in search of material for his biography of the Delaval family.

48. Foote claimed in his preface, I, viii, that he did not write the play for money, but to help out a good friend, Worsdale, "to whom, on the Score of some late Transactions, I think the Public vastly indebted."

49. Cooke, *Memoirs of Samuel Foote*, Vol. I, p. 64; Murphy, Vol. I, pp. 213-214.

50. Foote, *The Dramatic Works*, Vol. I, p. 53.

51. *Ibid.*

52. *Ibid.*, p. 55.

53. Stone, *The London Stage*, Vol. I, pp. 284-285.

54. *Ibid.*, p. 283.

55. *Ibid.*, pp. 284-285.

56. The prologue was not completed until Worsdale's benefit one week later (Murphy, Vol. I, pp. 213-214).

57. Foote, *The Dramatic Works*, Vol. I, p. 59.

58. *Ibid.*, pp. 62-64.

59. *Ibid.*, p. 67.

60. Stone, *The London Stage*, Vol. I, p. 287.

61. *Monthly Review*, January, 1752, pp. 77-78. See also Stone, *The London Stage*, Vol. I, p. 284.

62. Foote, *The Dramatic Works*, Vol. I, p. 56.

63. *Town and Country*, November, 1777, p. 597.

64. *Historical Manuscripts Commission, Thirteenth Report, Pt. VI, Delaval Manuscripts* (London, 1893), p. 200. In a letter dated January 17 [1753] Foote writes to John Delaval that, "I am writing the *Englishman at Paris* for Macklin's benefit."

65. Price was later ridiculed as Cadwallader in Foote's farce, *The Author*.

66. Hyde Collection.

67. Foote, *The Dramatic Works*, Vol. I, p. 91.

68. Stone, *The London Stage*, Vol. I, p. 360.

69. *Historical Manuscripts Commission, Delaval Manuscripts*, p. 201.

70. Folger Shakespeare Library, MS, W.b.472.

CHAPTER IV

THE ENGLISHMAN RETURNED FROM PARIS
—A DISPUTED SEQUEL, 1753-1756

After leaving England in May, Foote again took to the continent and enjoyed a long vacation. He met Garrick who was also vacationing in Europe [1] and probably secured an agreement to act the following season at Drury Lane. Upon his return to London in mid-August, Foote became acquainted with the widely-spread rumor that he had been condemned for some crime and executed near Bordeaux.[2] Delighted by the story, Foote got Garrick to write a new prologue for *The Englishman in Paris* that, by capitalizing on the rumor, would reintroduce him to the London stage:

> Whene'er my faults or follies are the question,
> Each draws his wit out, and begins dissection.
> Sir Peter Primrose, smirking o'er his tea,
> Sinks, from himself and politics, to me.
> "Paper! boy." "Here, Sir, I am." "What news today?"
> "Foote, Sir is advertised." "What! run away?"
> "No, Sir; this week he acts at Drury-lane."
> "How's that?" (cries feeble Grub). "Foot come again!
> "I thought that fool had done his devil's dance;
> "Was he not hang'd some months ago in France?" [3]

The 1753-54 season was far more successful than Foote's last attempt at Drury Lane, in 1745-46. His first four engagements averaged £160 a night. His new farce, played seventeen times between October 20 and February 22,[5] was particularly success-ful,[6] and he even achieved praise in his acting of Fondlewife in Congreve's *Old Bachelor*. His friend Arthur Murphy lauded him: "Mr. Foote has again drawn together a very splendid and numerous Audience, by his appearing in the Character of *Fondle-wife*, which whole Incident is represented by this Performer and *Mrs. Pritchard*, with as much Pleasantry as was known on the stage." [7] Even Davies, who disliked Foote, personally, gave him grudging and partial praise: "[Foote] had luckily remembered that great master of acting, Colley Cibber. In the course of the first scene he drew the attention of the audience, and merited, and gained much applause; but, in the progress of the part, he forgot his exemplar and degenerated into buffoonery." [8] When Foote played Ben in *Love for Love* he was less successful. Murphy wrote that Foote acted "with great Pleasantry" and "shewed by his Manner and his Looks, that he has entered into the Secret of the character, tho' it was visible at the same Time, that his Powers were greatly suppressed by his Sollicitude for his first Appearance in a new Character." [9] Davies thoroughly damned Foote's acting in this role: "It will scarce be credited, that for three nights the boxes were crowded, to see Foote murder the part of Ben; for his acting bore no resemblance to nature and char-acter. He was even destitute of what no man could suppose him to want, a proper confidence in his own abilities; for sure his Ben was as lifeless a lump of insipidity as ever a patient audience was presented with; it was not even a lively mistake of humour." [10] This view was supported by Cross, who noted that "Foote could not sing ye *Song* in Ben, so said two or three times, I can't do it & upon a little Hissing said Gentlemen I have no talents for sing-ing—ye whole play Hum [dull]." [11] He also had little success with Sir Courtly, appearing in the role only twice. Cross thought "Foote very indifferent—so all ye play." [12] *Tea* seemed to promise more, and its first appearance brought in £200, but the farce was not liked and drew only £80 on the second and last night.[13] After Foote's *Englishman from Paris* had sated his audience, his old pieces no longer drew crowds. *The Knights* was revived toward the end of Foote's stay, but the farce was hissed and brought no large audiences.[14]

By the time Foote gave his last performance on Feb 22, 1754, he had exhausted his great initial popularity. A scene-stealer [15] and prima donna, Foote was a disruptive force in a repertory company. And, of course, harmonious relations with Garrick could only be a sometime thing. After leaving Drury Lane Foote appeared as Hartop in benefits at Covent Garden. In acting the prologue to *The Knights* at Bellamy's benefit, Foote gave an imitation of Garrick,[16] and undoubtedly this humorous thrust reflected Foote's antagonism on parting.

After Foote left Covent Garden in April, probably with an agreement to return the next season, he acquired a new summer residence in Blackheath, about five miles southeast of London. He spent considerable time there that summer entertaining his friend Arthur Murphy [17] and giving him instruction in the art of acting. Murphy believed Garrick had encouraged him to think that his new farce, *The Apprentice* (Drury Lane, Jan. 2, 1756), would be put on during the 1753-54 season. Garrick wrote him that he mistook a "maybe" for a "yes" and that it was because of Foote's engagements that there was no room for new plays at Drury Lane that year.[18] Murphy, who had recently been disowned by his wealthy uncle, was £300 in debt and bitterly blamed Garrick for taking away his opportunity to become solvent.[19] In desperation he turned to Foote, who, having profited himself by going on the stage, told him to do the same. Although reluctant at first because of family objections, Murphy finally agreed. He accompanied Foote to his new summer home, and in addition to room and board Foote gave the impoverished Murphy acting lessons. Murphy was an apt pupil, and arrangements were made for his debut with Rich at Covent Garden. Foote refers to some of these activities in a letter to Francis Delaval: "I have fixed my abode at Blackheath. . . . I have been to a ship launching at Woolwich, where we had the Royal Family and Miss Roach . . . Murphy promises greatly, both as an author and actor. We have Woffington, etc. etc. so that on the whole I fancy Rich will make a powerful opposition next winter." [20]

The summer passed pleasantly for the two friends, and Murphy so enjoyed Foote's merry hospitality that he allowed Foote to dissuade him from going into town to ready his *Gray's Inn Journal* for the press. Taking up a copy of *Le Journal Littéraire,* Foote told him, "You need not go on that account. Here is a French magazine, in which you will find a very pretty oriental tale; translate that and send it to your printer." [21] Murphy liked the tale well enough to save himself the trip, and, as he never grew tired of repeating, to the consternation of the Great Cham, that was how he first met Samuel Johnson. As Murphy found out when he did get to London, he had retranslated Johnson's *Rambler* No. 190,[22] and his apology to Johnson led to their subsequent friendship.

Despite Foote's rosy anticipation for the new theatrical season, he did poorly at Covent Garden; Murphy, however, gained a modest success. A blurb in the *Entertainer* heralded Murphy's debut: " A brilliant wit [Murphy] will appear some time next month in this house [Covent Garden] in the character of Othello, attended by Mr. Foote who will perform the part of Iago, and Desdemona by Miss Bellamy."[23] Fortunately for Murphy, Foote backed out of the role, and Iago was played by Ryan, a regular member of the cast. Murphy was well received contrary to Charles Churchill's spiteful ridicule in his *Rosciad,*[24] and he continued to act leading roles throughout the season. But Foote appeared only twice in mainpieces, and later in the season he performed in three of his afterpieces for actors' benefits.[25]

After November 12, Rich must have decided that he could do without Foote, and the comic was stranded in mid-season, undoubtedly needing funds. Fortunately, he had not far to cast for opportunity. His one-time mentor, Macklin, had played his last performance on December 20, 1753,[26] and at that time formally announced his retirement from the stage. To support himself in his old age, Macklin decided to open a tavern and school of oratory. Confident of success, Macklin leased a former gambling den near Covent Garden for twenty-one years and spent over £1900 renovating the building.[27] When he first heard of Macklin's plans to retire from the stage and open a tavern, Foote prophesied, "First he will break in business, and then he will break his word." [28] The words proved accurate, but Foote, to some extent, was responsible for making them come true.

Macklin opened his tavern in March of the following year, and by November additional rooms were added so that Macklin could give his lectures on oratory. Some idea of the grandiose range of these lectures is given through Macklin's advertisements:

The British Inquisition

This Institution is upon the plan of the plan of the ancient Greek, Roman, and Modern French and Italian Societies of liberal investigation. Such subjects in Arts, Sciences, Literature, Criticism, Philosophy, History, Politics, and Morality, as shall be found useful and entertaining to society, will there be lectured upon and freely debated; particularly Mr. Macklin intends to lecture upon the Comedy of the Ancients, the use of their masks and flutes, their mimes and pantomimes, and the use and abuse of the Stage. He will likewise lecture upon the rise and progress of the modern Theatres, and make a comparison between them and those of Greece and Rome, and between each other; and he proposes to lecture also upon each of Shakespeare's Plays; to consider the original stories from whence they are taken; the artificial or inartificial use, according to the laws of the drama, that Shakespeare has made of them; his fable, moral character, passions, manners will likewise be criticized, and how his capital characters have been acted heretofore, are acted, and ought to be acted. And as the design of this inquiry is to endeavour at an acquisition of truth in matters of taste, particularly theatrical, the lecture being ended, any gentleman may offer his thoughts upon the subject.[29]

Macklin's opening night was a huge success as curiosity drew almost eight hundred people to the tavern.[30] But in time, curiosity satisfied, his audience came to heckle and ridicule the presumption of an ignorant, self-educated actor who lectured on this grand scale. Unemployed and having little better to do, Foote came to lead the hecklers, and his witty sneers became a greater attraction than Macklin's oratory. On one occasion, Macklin, annoyed by Foote's chatter, tried to silence him. "Pray, young gentleman, do you know what I am going to say?" "No, sir," Foote mocked. "Do you?" [31] On another occasion Foote interrupted Macklin's weighty lecture on duelling in Ireland by asking him the time. "Nine-thirty," was the puzzled and irritated reply. "Very well," said Foote. "About this time of night every gentleman in Ireland than can possibly afford it is in his third bottle of claret, and therefore in a fair way of getting drunk; and from drunkenness proceeds quarrelling, and from quarrelling duelling, and so there is an end of the chapter." [32] The audience was so satisfied with this abridgement that they did not allow Macklin to continue his lecture.

Foote's most amusing deflation occurred when Macklin tried to exhibit his powers of memory. The old actor challenged his audience to jot anything down on paper and then claimed he could memorize its contents at a glance. Foote waited until Macklin was through boasting and handed him the following nonsense:

> So she went into the garden to cut a cabbageleaf, to make an apple pie; and at the same time a great she bear, coming up the street, pops its head into the shop. "What! No soap?" So he died, and she very imprudently married the barber; and there were present the Picaninies and the Joblilies and the Garcelies, and the Grand Panjandrum himself, with the little round button at the top; and they all fell to playing the game of catch as catch can, till the gunpowder ran out at the heels of their boots.[33]

Poor Macklin was caught again and again had to close up shop early.

Foote did not continue to give his wit away gratis at Macklin's tavern. Seeing that there was a large audience willing to pay to laugh at Macklin, Foote rented the Haymarket to start a series of comic lectures ridiculing the *British Inquisition*. War was formally declared in the *Public Advertiser* of December 13, 1754: "At the Little theatre in the Haymarket Monday next a Write of Inquiry will be executed on the Inquisitor General By Mr. Foote. The Members of the Robin-Hood are summoned to the Jury." [34] Macklin responded the next day:

> At the request of most of the Wits, Witlings, Smarts, Laughers, Jokers, Critics, Sneerers, and other Choice Spirits of this Metropolis, on Monday next, At Mr. Macklin's Great-Room in Hart Street will come on before the Inquistor General, the Trial of the egregious Sam. Smatter, alias Would-be, alias Mimic, alias Buffoon, alias Critt, alias Wit, alias Beau, alias fine Gentleman, and vulgarly called Esquire, for a public Cheat and Imposter. The whole Public are summoned to be on the Jury. . . .[35]

Foote gave six performances [36] satirizing Macklin, Dr. Rock, a quack, and "Tiddy-Doll," a gingerbread merchant noted for his foppery.[37] Each person was to contend for the right to be Inquisitor General. Within this framework, Foote mocked Macklin's pretensions to learning:

> I shall here, Gentlemen, take an opportunity to explain to you the Meaning of the Word—Learning—Learning as I take it to be, is that Knowledge, that Instruction, that sort of Science which the more ignorant Individual imbibes from the more knowing one: now whether the Ancients excelled the Moderns in the Point, or not, is what lays on me to clear. By the bye, I must here remark that the world has all along called themselves Moderns, and the people who went before them, Ancients; now, Gentlemen, (if I am wrong, I hope some ingenious Gentleman will correct me; I hope, he will; nay, I am sure somebody will:

for give me leave to say, I always look upon your disapprobation of what I advance as a Great Honour) now,
Gentlemen, I say it is my Opinion, and *I do insist on it,*
that as the world is now older by 1600 years than it was
in the time of Augustus and the 6th Harry that *we* ought
to be termed the *Ancients.*[38]

He also flayed Macklin's vanity as dramatist and actor, mimicking
him in the role of a teacher:

"Well, Sir,—did you ever hear of Aristophanes?"—
"Yes, Sir,—a Greek dramatist, who wrote"—
"Aye, but I have got twenty comedies in these drawers
worth his 'Clouds' and stuff.—Do you know anything of
Cicero?"
"A celebrated orator of Rome, who, in the polished
and persuasive, is considered a master of his art."
—"Yes, yes; but I'll be bound he couldn't teach
elocution!"
—"Perhaps not, Sir."—
"Perhaps, then, you have heard of one Roscius, whom
Cicero praised?"—
"Certainly, Sir,—a very celebrated actor."—
"Stuff! he couldn't have played Shylock!"[39]

Foote's exhibition became the talk of the town, and Macklin
became so curious that he went to the Haymarket to see what
was being said about him. It was a mistake. Macklin grew more
and more furious at seeing himself the object of all this ridicule.
But, barely containing himself, Macklin watched Foote begin an
exhortation to his "pupil":

Now, Sir, remember; I, Charles Macklin, tell you,
there are no good plays among the ancients, and only one

great one among the moderns, and that's the "Merchant of Venice," and there's only one part in that, and only one man that can play it;— now, Sir, as you have been very attentive, I'll tell you an anecdote of that play: when a Royal Personage, who shall be nameless, (but who doesn't live a hundred miles from Buckingham House) witnessed my performance of the Jew, he sent for me to his box, and remarked, "Sir, if I were not the Prince—ha—hum—you understand—I should wish to be Mr. Macklin!" Upon which I answered "Royal Sir, being Mr. Macklin, I do not desire to be the———."

At this point Macklin could no longer hold himself back and in fury shouted, "No, I'll be damned if I did." [40] The delighted audience turned and hooted him out of the house. By the time the audience had tired of the vituperation, Foote had profited by some £500 [41] and Macklin was forced into bankruptcy. [42] Strange to say these incidents did not completely rupture Foote's friendship with Macklin. According to one report, the two rivals, meeting by chance, began to blackguard each other with such scurrility that their embarrassed friends took to cover. Finding themselves without an audience, Foote and Macklin marched arm in arm to the nearest tavern to share a bird and a bottle. [43]

During the summer, Foote again spent considerable time in the company of Arthur Murphy, but the friendship this summer was not as satisfactory to Murphy as it had been the first time. Murphy conceived the idea of writing a sequel to *The Englishman in Paris* in the summer of 1756 and, naturally, told his good friend and fellow dramatist of his plans. According to William Cooke, Foote not only used Murphy's idea, but cynically drew Murphy out so that he could plagiarize considerable portions of the play for his own sequel, *The Englishman Returned from Paris.* [44] Up to this time, Murphy's manuscript of his sequel (the play was never printed) had been thought lost, and the extent of Foote's plagiarism had been open to conjecture. Fortunately, the play was recently discovered in the Newberry Library, and the manuscript makes it clear that Foote was not guilty of Cooke's

charges. He did betray Murphy's confidence by secretly writing
his own sequel after Murphy told him of his plans, but his plot
and characters differ considerably from Murphy's; his dialogue
is superior and his story moves with better pace. Unfortunately
for Foote's reputation, it was Cooke's opinion that influenced later
writers of theatrical history.[45] An earlier version of the incident
was written by Tate Wilkinson who states that he saw Murphy's
play when it opened.[46] Even though Wilkinson does not state his
opinion on this point precisely, he indicates that Murphy "informed" Foote of his plans in writing a sequel. "It [Murphy's
information] caused his [Foote's] genius to set to work and finish
a farce in two acts on the same plan." [47] And Wilkinson further
stated that Foote's actual experience in France made him a better
judge than Murphy on the topic of the play.[48] However, these
statements did not clear Foote of the more serious charge of
extended plagiarism, for Wilkinson only vaguely recalled the
incident, and his account was not specific enough to provide
Foote with a defense.

Cooke, whose version seemed authoritative because of its
specific statements, probably did not see the play, and he might
very well have derived his information from Murphy himself.
Cooke states in his preface to his biography of Foote that an "old
friend" helped considerably. A subsequent review of the book
indicates that the "old friend" was probably Murphy,[49] who as
a familiar of Foote's was particularly well qualified for the task.
Certainly Murphy was deeply chagrined at Foote's duplicity,
and he had every reason to put him as much in the wrong as he
could. Murphy could hold a grudge, as Garrick well knew, and
even after a life-long friendship with Foote, his anger was still
capable of bursting out anew. This sketch was found in Murphy's
effects after his death: "Foote gives a dinner—large company—
characters come one by one:—sketches them as they come:—each
enters—he glad to see each. At dinner, his wit, affectation, pride;
his expense, his plate, his jokes, his stories; all laugh;—all go,
one by one—all abused, one by one;—his toadeaters stay;—he
praises himself in a passion against all the world."[50]

Despite Foote's desire to keep secret his plans for putting
on his *Englishman Returned from Paris* to insure that it would

come out first, the information had to leak out to Murphy when plans were made for rehearsal. Murphy's first printed reaction, a two-act farce that was never acted, *The Spouter: or, the Triple Revenge,* was published anonymously,[51] probably in late January, a week or two before Foote's production. The plot is of no great consequence here, for it seems mainly to have been written, with the aid of Garrick,[52] to satirize Theophilus Cibber, who was trying to break the monopoly of the London stage held by the patentees of Covent Garden and Drury Lane. The farce seems too personal to have been written for the stage, yet I am convinced that Murphy meant to have it acted but was so furious when he wrote it that he lost his sense of proportion.[53] The *dramatis personae* were Patent (Garrick), Lun (Rich), Slender (Dr. Hill), Squint-Eyed Pistol (T. Cibber), and Dapperwit (Foote). The first three were lightly satirized, and it was typical of Garrick to hide his hand by satirizing himself. Though the real point of the play was to ridicule Cibber, Murphy's personal ire was directed at Foote. He lashed out at his former friend with the spite and intimate knowledge that can come only through close acquaintance. He ridiculed Foote's pretensions as a scholar, his personal habits, his backbiting, his mimicry, his use of opium, his jokes, his attempt to show culture by singing French songs and using Latin tags, and his insistence on reading his plagiarized farces to any audience, even weary waiters. He even brought in Foote's ill-fated ventures as a seller of small beer and his first attempt at tragedy in *Othello:*

> Dapperwit alone, plucking his Beard; one Foot against the Chimney, greasy Night-Cap on, his Nails overgrown . . . [speaks] Mr. ———, Bond-Street, two Barrels of Small Beer, Mr. ———, in Pall Mall, two Half Barrels. Half a Barrel return'd because the servants could not drink it.— Damn the Small Beer—I was humm'd then. It won't do.
> "I was a Wight, if ever such Wight were"
> To do what
> "To suckle Fools and chronicle Small Beer."
> O, damn the Small Beer. But here's a Reviver—A

New Farce—that is—a New Comedy. It's true a Gentleman
told me of the Subject first; and in Confidence too! by
way of consulting my Judgment—"Thus do I ever make
my Fool my Purse"—To consult me!—A Blockhead!—He
might have known me better. There will be a great Burst
when this appears—I'll change the name of the Piece. Yes,
but won't that be like the *Irishman,* that deserted from his
Regiment; and when he was taken afterwards, said to his
Friend, "By my Shoul, myself did not think I would be
taken, for I went by another Name."—Never mind that
tho'. I wish I could have got it done at Drury Lane; but
damn it, I was rejected there—But I'll do it at the other
House: It's true, it's not in much Repute, but I'll take
my chance.[54]

In one passage Murphy publicly accused Foote of betraying
their friendship, but at this time he did not charge Foote with
the pillage of which Cooke said he was guilty. Murphy, of course,
did not want to exonerate him in any way, so that he did not
make it explicit that, except for the idea of a sequel, Foote's
play was his own. Murphy's bitterness led him to state his charges
so ambiguously that more could be inferred. It would seem likely
that Murphy's private statements were not so carefully couched,
and that he probably influenced Cooke to believe that Foote
stole considerable detail from his play. Certainly Cooke had no
ulterior motive of his own nor any other source of such biased
information.

Contemporary reviews of Murphy's farce defended Foote
by way of attacking *The Spouter.* One stated that few would
understand it because of its personal satire,[55] and another accused
Murphy of writing and publishing "this motley performance"
to gratify Garrick at Cibber's expense. "Nothwithstanding all the
virulence he has spit at Pistol and Dapperwit, he may spout till
his sides ake, before he can rival the one in acting, or the other
in wit." [56] Theophilus Cibber also defended Foote by accusing
Murphy of ingratitutde to a good friend. Among other personal
remarks about Murphy, Cibber also stated "that he had calum-

niated . . . one of his best Friends, who oft supplied him with Lodging, Food, Raiment, Cash, and all Necessaries for many Months." [57]

Foote, as might be expected, did not answer Murphy's charges. He was busy rehearsing his play which opened at Covent Garden on February 3, 1756, shortly after the publication of *The Spouter*. Murphy's attacks did not harm Foote and merely gave extra publicity to the play. It proved very successful and was performed nineteen times that season and played regularly on the Covent Garden stage until 1760.[58] The critical notices on the new play were generally favorable,[59] and Foote was highly gratified in every way. Foote's farce, unlike Murphy's, was a real sequel, for he could build upon the characters that proved so successful in their first outing—Buck and Lucinda.

Finally, exactly two months after Foote's opening, Murphy chose his benefit night, April 3, 1756, to present his sequel. A large audience paid £240 [60] to see Murphy's farce, but the play did not go off very well—Foote's sequel was obviously superior. Stone quotes from the "Cross Hopkins Diary" that Murphy's play "went off well." [61] But Wilkinson, who probably saw the play, says that except for Murphy's remarks on Foote's duplicity, which "occasioned a great roar," it was the only such outburst "I remembered to have heard during the farce, unless to Mrs. Clive." [62] Murphy, who did not act in his play, spoke the prologue which contained the first hit at Foote:

> Shall he consult his friends?—when once 'tis shown
> If some friends like, they make the hint their own.[63]

One of the other hits which brought out the roar that Wilkinson heard is not in the manuscript and was obviously inserted at the last minute. Here, perhaps at the end of the play, Buck, who is not in the *dramatis personae* of the play, appears, undoubtedly accoutred like Foote's Buck, to say: "O Yes! I grant you there has been an imposter about town, who with easy familiarity and assurance, has stolen my writings, &c; and not only thus treacher-

ously robed, but impudently dared to assume my very name even
to my face; but I am the true Charles Buck, I assure you."[64] It
was probably this reference to Buck that misled later critics to
think that Murphy based his play on Foote's characters, but the
dramatis personae show how completely different the characters
are.

Murphy's play centers on the sentimental conversion of Jack
Broughton, the fop from Paris. Because of his affected airs, he
stumbles through a series of unhappy incidents with his former
friends, his father, and his future father-in-law. Jack finally
decides to convert back to plainer ways when his disgusted father
threatens to marry Harriet, a girl he has chosen to be Jack's wife.
The fear of being disinherited by a younger brother is enough to
bring him back to his English senses. In Foote's play the general
situation is similar. Buck returns from France, and he too is
made an object of ridicule because of his exaggerated French airs.
But here the similarity stops. Buck's father dies leaving his friend,
Crab, executor of his will. The will has the stipulation that if
Buck refuses to marry Lucinda she gets £20,000 from the estate,
and if she refuses to marry him, only £5,000. When Buck returns
from Paris, instead of marrying Lucinda, he tries to induce her
to become his mistress. But since he dislikes the idea of parting
with £20,000 by publicly refusing marriage, he tells Lucinda that
his father did not mention when he had to marry, and unless
Lucinda gives in to his proposals she will not get a shilling.
Lucinda, with the aid of Crab, who overheard Buck's proposal,
deceives Buck into thinking that his tea has been poisoned. Crab,
by pretending he has the antidote, forces the "dying" Buck to
renounce Lucinda, and for good measure he also has Buck dismiss
his French servants and destroy his French clothing and cosmetics
before telling him that his pains are imaginary.

As one can see, despite some fortuitous coincidences unavoid-
able because of the similarity in plot, the plays are different.
Murphy's play does have a few humorous situations, but on the
whole is obvious and trite. The repartee is lame, and the sentimental conversion of Jack is far too abrupt and poorly motivated
even for popular taste. It is no wonder that Murphy never had
this play printed, for it has all the earmarks of a hastily con-

structed potboiler written to cash in on the popularity of the original. And despite the fact that Foote's sequel does not measure up to the excellence of his best farces such as *The Mayor of Garrat*, it does have outrageous and whimsical dialogue that is almost always irresistible. It is, of course, unfair to use these two plays as a springboard to compare the two dramatists. *The Englishman from Paris* was probably Murphy's poorest dramatic effort, and he went on to write far better plays with interesting characters and sparkling dialogue. Perhaps Murphy fails because his piece falls somewhere between farce and comedy. Only Lady Betty Mockmode remains on the outrageous farcical level, and she did draw roars of laughter. To allow for the audience's acceptance of the conversion Jack and his friends undergo at the conclusion, the playwright never permits their behavior to get out of hand. Jack, then, is a harmless, simpering fop whose immoral bragging is like his French clothes and bogus accent: all pure affectation and to be put away at the first sign of pressure. He was not a real fop; he was only pretending to be one because he was momentarily attracted to a basically uncongenial style.

Foote's Buck is quite another matter. He is the man. He revels in every last article that belongs to the fop. Buck is harmless because he is stupid and easily outwitted; his intentions, however, are malicious and in keeping with his character. Foote, as always, allowed himself great scope for humorous and farcical byplay, not only in his dialogue, but in his characters and plot. The morally upright characters in his play are fully justified in taking extreme measures to correct the perverted actions of an unfeeling fop, and had the full approval of the galleries. Murphy's play might have failed even without Foote's competition. But with Foote's farce as example, the audience was educated to the farcical possibilities of a former English blood turned fop, and Murphy's sequel was doomed by the comparison. Murphy, perhaps recognizing Foote's claim to his own sequel, soon was on good terms again with his old friend,[65] and even though Murphy never wholly forgave Foote for his treachery, he remained on intimate terms with him until Foote's death in 1777. And about six weeks before Murphy died, he had written these last words on Foote: "If I have health enough, my intention is to write the

life of Samuel Foote; a man to whose company I owe some of
the greatest pleasures of my life, and whose memory I now esteem
and value." [66]

NOTES

1. Forster, p. 381.
2. Murphy, Vol. I, p. 242.
3. *Gentleman's Magazine*, October, 1753, p. 493; and Foote, *The Dramatic Works*, Vol. I, p. lxxxvi.
4. Genest, Vol. IV, p. 380.
5. Stone, *The London Stage*, Vol. I, pp. 385 ff.
6. Even after Foote quit Drury Lane, Woodward continued as Buck for five more performances (*Ibid.*, pp. 387 ff.).
7. *Gray's Inn Journal*, November 3, 1753.
8. Davies, Vol. I, p. 190.
9. *Gray's Inn Journal*, January 19, 1754.
10. Davies, Vol. I, p. 190.
11. Stone, *The London Stage*, Vol. I, pp. 402-403.
12. *Ibid.*, p. 389.
13. *Ibid.*, p. 392.
14. Stone, *The London Stage*, Vol. II, p. 408. It is interesting to note that Foote again had difficulty with Yates, for though *The Knights* was originally scheduled for February 5 as part of Miss Macklin's benefit, Foote changed the date to February 9, because Yates was not ready for his role.
15. John O'Keefe, *Recollections of the Life of John O'Keefe* (London, 1826), Vol. I, p. 329. O'Keefe states that Foote took all the attention by facing the audience while keeping the other performers in profile.
16. Wilkinson, Vol. IV, p. 184.
17. Murphy was one of his oldest friends. Foote got to know him during his stay in London from 1744 to 1747. Murphy had just graduated from college and stayed in London until he was sent to Cork to study business with his uncle (Dunbar, p. 2). While waiting in Bristol for the ship to take him to Cork, Murphy was despondent about leaving London until (as he writes his brother) Foote came to wish him farewell:

> While I am writing this, Foote is grinning at me from a
> corner of the room—He arrived here yesterday, about the same
> time I did, about one o'clock, with splendid equipage, and very
> handsomely dressed. We have had Punch already; and his com-
> pany has lifted my spirits into some degree of cheerfulness, and
> that is what makes me run on at this rate. (J. Foot, p. 25)

18. *The Letters of David Garrick,* Vol. I, pp. 203-204.
19. Dunbar, p. 8.
20. *Historical Manuscripts Commission, Eleventh Report, Pt. VII, The Manuscripts of the Duke of Leeds* (London, 1888), pp. 78-79.
21. Boswell, *Life,* Vol. I, p. 356.
22. This appeared in *Gray's Inn Journal* No. 39 (folio) on June 22, 1754 (Dunbar, p. 7).
23. No. 4, September 24, 1754. The theatrical essays in the *Entertainer* are attributed to Murphy by Arthur Sherbo, ed. *New Essays by Arthur Murphy* (Michigan State University Press, 1963), p. 8.
24. See Dunbar, p. 16 and n. 73, and pp. 106-121.
25. Stone, *The London Stage,* Vol. I, pp. 445 ff.
26. Foote played Buck for Macklin's benefit that night.
27. Appleton, pp. 98-99, 101.
28. Knight, p. 141.
29. *The Public Advertiser,* No. 21, 1754.
30. *Gentleman's Magazine,* October, 1754, p. 532.
31. Cooke, *Macklin,* p. 208.
32. *Ibid.*
33. Belden, p. 15.
34. See Stone, *The London Stage,* Vol. I, p. 458.
35. *Ibid.*
36. December 16, 18, 23, 27; January 1, 3 (Stone, *The London Stage,* Vol. I, pp. 458-461). After Macklin declared bankruptcy, Foote gave three *Comic Lectures* on April 12, 24, and 16 (*Ibid.,* p. 479).
37. Belden, pp. 15-16 and notes 6 and 7.
38. Anonymous, *Macklin's Answer to Tully* (London, 1755), pp. 17-18. This pamphlet and an earlier one, *An Epistle from Tully in the Shades to Orator M—n in Covent Garden* (London, 1755), also anonymously written, were attacks on Macklin's effrontery and contain information pertaining to Foote's satire.
39. John Bernard, *Retrospections of the Stage* (London, 1830), Vol. II, p. 122.
40. *Ibid.,* pp. 123-124.
41. Foot, pp. 93-95.
42. Appleton, pp. 100, 107. Macklin pleaded bankruptcy on January 25, 1755. Foote, however, was not completely responsible for his failure. Macklin found it difficult to refuse credit to his fellow actors, and his inexperience as host allowed his staff to fleece him unmercifully.
43. John Taylor, *Records of My Life* (London, 1832), p. 252.
44. Cooke, *Foote,* Vol. I, pp. 72-73.
45. Genest, Vol. IV, p. 467, dismisses the play by accusing Foote of taking the tea trick from Mrs. Centlivre's *Artifice,* and "Foote seems to have stolen the rest of his farce from Murphy." Genest also quotes Cooke's account on pp. 456-457. Fitzgerald, p. 107; Beldon, p. 70; and Dunbar, p. 32, despite their varying suppositions basically accept Cooke's version of the incident.
46. Wilkinson, Vol. II, p. 71. Wilkinson is not always reliable, but his

account of Clive's acting and the audience's reaction to the play seems accurate and would indicate that he had seen the play or was told about it by an observer.

47. *Ibid.,* p. 70.
48. *Ibid.,* p. 71.
49. *Critical Review,* November, 1805, p. 314. Dunbar, p. 31 and note 58 also supports the view that "Cooke may have gotten his account from Murphy."
50. Foot, p. 172.
51. *Biographica Dramatica,* Vol. III, p. 296, attributes the farce to Murphy as do modern commentators: Dunbar, p. 27 and notes 44, 45; and Emery, p. 29. But see *CBEL,* Vol. II, p. 478.
52. Genest, Vol. IV, p. 461; Dunbar, p. 26.
53. Emery, p. 29, supports this view, but Dunbar, p. 26, believes that Murphy never intended to have it performed.
54. *The Spouter: or, the Triple Revenge* (London, 1756), pp. 18-19.
55. *The Monthly Review,* January, 1756, p. 67.
56. *Critical Review,* March, 1756, pp. 146-147.
57. *Dissertations of Theatrical Subjects, As they have several Times been delivered to the Public (with General Approbation) By Mr. Cibber. With an Appendix Which contains several Matters relative to the Stage, not yet made Public; and in which the Laws relative to the Theatres are considered* (London, 1756), 2nd Dissertation, p. 16.
58. Stone, *The London Stage,* Vol. II, p. 494, *passim.*
59. *Monthly Review,* March, 1756, p. 269, liked it but said that it played better than it read. *Critical Review,* January-February, 1756, p. 83, praised it highly and thought it superior to his *Englishman in Paris. Biographica Dramatica,* Vol. II, p. 105, was of the same opinion as the *Critical Review.*
60. Stone, *The London Stage,* Vol. II, p. 536.
61. *Ibid.*
62. Wilkinson, Vol. II, pp. 71-72.
63. *Literary Magazine,* March 15-April 15, 1756, p. 29.
64. Cooke, *Foote,* Vol. I, pp. 74-75; Wilkinson, Vol. II, pp. 71-72.
65. Foot, p. 463, quotes from Murphy's diary which has Murphy dining frequently at Foote's during October and November, 1758. In *The Letters of David Garrick,* Vol. I, p. 295, Garrick accuses Murphy of intimacy with Foote in a letter dated December 4, 1758.
66. Foot, p. 18.

CHAPTER V

"THOSE DAMNED EXOTICS":
FOOTE'S AND WILKINSON'S MIMIC WAR
ON ACTORS, 1756-1759

During the summer of 1756, Foote amused himself by dramatizing a theatrical battle between Peg Woffington and George Anne Bellamy. In the previous January, both actresses had performed in Lee's *Rival Queens* at Covent Garden. Barry acted Alexander; Woffington, Roxana; and Bellamy, Statira. Bellamy, just back from a shopping trip to Paris, returned with two new gowns in the latest fashion. Donning a deep yellow one over which she wore a purple robe, she paraded proudly in the Green-Room just before the performance. Woffington, in pale yellow, took one look at the gorgeously attired actress and begged, "Madam, I desire you will never more upon any account wear these clothes in the piece we perform tonight." Bellamy cunningly agreed, and all went well the first night. But the second night, Bellamy, keeping to the letter of her word, put on her other gown which was even more spendid than the first. Furious at the trick, Woffington bided her time until the fifth act, when Roxana is to kill the new favorite, Statira. Though armed only with a wooden dagger, Woffington drove Bellamy from the stage. "Though I despise revenge, I do not dislike retaliation," was Bellamy's smug statement. "I therefore put on my yellow and purple once more." The effect was predictable. The air turned

blue with the recriminations and uncharitable accusations made
by the angry actresses.[1] Although no copy of this farce survives,
Foote could scarcely have exaggerated the original incident. He
called it *The Green-Room Squabble or a Battle Royal between
the Queen of Babylon and the Daughter of Darius.*

In the fall, Foote negotiated with Garrick for the 1756-57
season. His roles in the main pieces were kept at a minimum,[2]
but Garrick probably engaged him because of interest in his new
farce, *The Author.* This season, like others, began badly for
Foote, who clearly needed new material to attract audiences.
Despite contradictory critiques of his acting,[3] it is certain that
Foote took in little money at the box-office. *The Englishman
Returned from Paris* was hissed, and on November 1 Cross
morosely commented that "Mr. Foote brings sad houses." [4] However, it seems likely that Foote did not take on this engagement
without being in the process of preparing a play for the stage.
Foote gave his last performance for the year on November 1,
partially, no doubt, in deference to his "sad houses," and also in
order to have more time to polish and rehearse his new play.

The Author opened February 5, 1757, and was a complete
success. The plot, subsequently used by Sheridan and Goldsmith,
is that of the wealthy guardian or parent who pretends to be dead
so that he can spy on his ward. In this play the guardian is the
father to Young Cape, an apparently poor, but expensively educated young man, who tries to make ends meet by literary hack-
work. Despite his many assignments, payment is so inadequate
that young Cape cannot escape his grinding poverty. He has two
possible means of escaping a military life: a hopefully successful
comedy that he is writing for the stage, or marriage to Arabella,
a wealthy and spirited girl who loves him, but whose brother,
Cadwallader, is so purse and pedigree proud that he will not allow
his sister to marry a poor poet. After the usual complications,
the senior Cape reveals his identity and the lovers are allowed
to marry.

Even though the ostensible satiric point of the play is to
ridicule the sly tricks of the booksellers and to deplore the decline
of literary patronage among the aristocracy, the great attraction
of the play was the role of Cadwallader as acted by Foote. Though

Foote felt it necessary to deny that the role was based on any real person,[5] this gratuitous declaration merely served to confirm what was only suspected. This newspaper reaction is typical:

> This piece is truly of the farcical kind; the principal Characters being so whimsical, that we can hardly believe that they have anywhere a real Existence; and yet as the Author was obliged to advertise that his Satire was not directed at any particular person, we must imagine it bears resemblance to some living Prototype, otherwise there would have been no room for the Suspicion.[6]

Foote, in fact, had chosen as his models for Mr. and Mrs. Cadwallader Francis Delaval's aunt and uncle Apreece (or ApRice).[7] In Foote's defense, it may be added that this incredible man had actually asked Foote to portray him on stage. After Foote's death, an anonymous writer with an intimate knowledge of Foote's affairs described the incident:

> The late Mr. Ap . . . ce, who was a very singular man, told Foote one day at dinner that the ministry had quite overlooked him and that he thought if Foote would bring him upon the stage, he was sure government would certainly take notice of him. Upon this hint Foote wrote the *Author*, and Ap . . . ce was so much resolved that his own character should be known in that of Cadwallader, that he lent the mimic a suit of clothes he had been very conspicuous in at court. Somebody hinted that he did not use his friend well, thus to expose him. "You are quite mistaken, I do it at his own request, in order to make his fortune." [8]

Foote certainly satisfied Apreece's urge for notoriety. In putting on his victim's clothes, Foote assumed all the nervous mannerisms of the original. Taking on a broad unknowing stare, Foote "made him to look and walk absurdly. His voice was loud, his manner of speaking boisterous; his words were uttered rapidly and indistinctly, while his head was constantly undulating to his left shoulder, as if to recall what he had inadvertently spoken." And from time to time, he would bring his wrists to his mouth and make loud supping noises.[9] The mind was closely correlated to the portrait; nonsense constantly flowed from his mouth: he scolded his wife for not carrying his pedigree about; boasted of his innate brilliance unhappily undeveloped for lack of an education; and, wanting the company of a poet, urged his wife to invite the writer to his home:

> Hey, ecod, do, Cape, come and look at her grotto and shells, and see what she has got—well, he'll come, Beck,—ecod do, and she'll come to the third night of your tragedy, hey! won't you, *Beck?*—isn't she a fine girl? hey, you; humour her a little, do;—hey, *Beck;* he says you are as fine a woman as ever he—ecod who knows but he may make a copy of verses on you?—there, go, and have a little chat with her, talk any nonsense to her, no matter what; she's a damn'd fool, and won't know the difference.[10]

Becky, as played by Mrs. Clive, was no less ridiculous than her husband. A scatter-brained hoyden, she is only too ready to cuckold her husband in the scene where young Cape tries to flatter her by pretending to be smitten by her charms:

> Cape: . . . zooks you are too hasty; the pleasure of this play, like hunting, does not consist in immediately *chopping* the prey.
> Mrs. Cad: No! How then?
> Cape: Why, first I am to start you, then run you a little in view, then lose you, then unravel all the tricks and doubles you make to escape me.

You fly o'er hedge and stile,
I pursue for many a mile,
You grow tired at last, and *quat,*
Then I catch you, *and all that.*

Mrs. Cad: Dear me, there's a deal on't! I shall never be able to hold out long; I had rather be taken in view.
Cape: I believe you.
Mrs. Cad: Well, come, begin and start me, that I may come the sooner to *quatting*—Hush! here's sister; what the deuce brought her? *Bell* will be for learning this game too, but don't you teach her for your life, Mr. *Poet.*[11]

The Author drew good houses, and the reviews were generally favorable. One reviewer found it difficult to reconcile his enjoyment of the farce with the knowledge that Foote was making game of an individual: "I read the farce before I could see it performed; the judgment I then passed on it was not in its favor, and the exhibition did not make any material alteration in my way of thinking. I laughed indeed much more than I had done in reading it, but on recollection I was not a little displeased to find that I was laughing at an individual not at a species." [12] But another reviewer decided that the point of farce is humor, and by that standard he considered the play a success:

However, real or imaginary, . . . there are such Strokes of Bizarre throughout the Farce, that nobody can be present at it without being highly diverted. . . . Mr. Foote's own performance has great Merit; the extravagance of Cadwallader's Mind and Manner, together with the whimsical Circumstances of his Dining with the Princes, his Pedigree, and his Enquiry into the Poet's Amour with his Wife, all come very properly within the Province of Farce, and happily answer the End of that Kind of Writing, which

is to raise a Laugh, and send the Audience Home in
Good-Humour.[13]

The most interesting review of *The Author* praised Foote's
ability as a colloquial and witty writer and argued the difference
between comedy and farce: "Farce is to Comedy what the *carica-
tura* is to the just and regular designs of portrait painting."
Features may be allowably exaggerated, but the person caricatured
must remain recognizable. The critic admits that "these touches
of bizarre imitation" may sometimes appear even in comedy; "it
is not difficult to remember lineaments extended beyond their
boundaries, without turning over the pages of *Joseph Andrews*
and *Tom Jones.*" The point, however, is that these "lapses" are
exceptional in true comedy but remain the rule in farce. Foote
"has not lost sight of nature," but he has exaggerated its limits.
After all, the critic is forced to confess that "such a man as
Cadwallader may be easily conceived to exist in human life."
The conclusion, therefore, is that Foote's play is a farce. "It does
not anywhere descend to low buffoonery, commonplace characters,
indelicate vulgarisms and hackney'd worn out conversation . . .
but there is novelty in the humor, an original turn of ridicule
in many passages of the dialogue, and pleasantry in the situations:
inasmuch that, though we cannot agree with Mr. Foote in calling
it a *comedy* of two acts, yet we must on the whole, declare it to
be a very good *farce* of two acts." [14]
     Though Foote had been favored with laudatory critical re-
views in the past, his productions up to and including *The
Englishman in Paris* had been only intermittently clever. Mimicry
and highly seasoned dialogue served him well, but characterization degenerated into whimsy, especially in *Knights* and *Taste;*
and his plots were either non-existent, as in his *Diversions of the
Morning* and his *Tragedy à la Mode,* or flimsy outlines as in
The Knights and to a lesser degree *The Englishman in Paris* and
its sequel. But *The Englishman Returned from Paris* was able to
sustain characterization of Buck and others without faltering into
didacticism and, aided by superior dialogue, succeeded as the
earlier version did not. *The Author,* too, deserved the favorable

critical notice it received, for the play sustained Foote's salty and humorous dialogue and maintained greater unity of plot than his previous plays. No doubt, the knowledge that Cadwallader was really Apreece titillated the theatre-going public. But the play's theatrical history proves how little this scandal contributed to its success in a twenty-year span. The play was performed eighty-four times on London stages in the period between 1769 and 1776,[15] long after Apreece's death.

The season over, Foote took a well-earned vacation and returned to Drury Lane on October 15 and played through February 1, 1758.[16] He had an agreement with Garrick that he was to perform *The Author* for about a week, then go to Dublin for two months to act with Sheridan's troupe and return to Drury Lane to revive *The Author* again.[17] A week before Foote left for Ireland, he accidentally met Garrick returning to the greenroom after a performance. When the conversation turned to mimicry, a talent both actors practiced on and off the stage, Garrick mentioned one Tate Wilkinson, a player he had just hired that season.[18] Armed with a letter of introduction from Lord Mansfield, Wilkinson, in desperate need of a job, gained a reluctant audience with Garrick. The young actor tried to ingratiate himself with Garrick by imitating Foote. This was done with such genius that Garrick delightedly hired him on the spot at the princely wage of thirty shillings a week.[19] Garrick in his conversation with Foote recalled this prodigy and claimed that he was superior in mimicry to them both, smugly adding, "He has tried to resemble me, but that will not do." "Damn it," said Foote, "I should like to hear him." Wilkinson was quickly sent for and entertained Foote and Garrick with remarkably accurate imitations of the leading actors of the day: Barry, Sparks, Woffington, Ridout, and Sheridan. Foote was so impressed with the exhibition that he persuaded Wilkinson to accompany him to Dublin. As incentive, Foote promised to pay traveling expenses, fix terms with Sheridan, play Iago to his Othello, and, most necessary, get the needed permission from Garrick. Wilkinson, tempted by stardom, eagerly agreed and cursed Garrick who "thought me only fit for his Hobby Horse in the *Rehearsal*." [20]

On October 20 Wilkinson took the trip with Foote to their

point of embarkation at Holyhead. On the way Foote gave his
protégé lessons in traveling. Though he met with aristocratic and
wealthy company on the road who wished Foote to travel with
them, Foote politely but consistently refused to accompany them.
He told the puzzled Wilkinson that such important people expect
the best accommodations on the road, and even if they were so
kind as to allow them to be given to a mere author, he in all good
manners could not accept the favor. Therefore, Foote told him,
it was better to travel a half-day's journey behind or ahead of
such company so that one could get the best rooms for one's self.[21]
On reaching the boat Wilkinson found there were no beds on
board, even for Foote. As night came Wilkinson was beyond being
cheered. The long trip and seasickness lowered Wilkinson's resist-
ance, and the result was a very high fever, probably pneumonia.
Foote, an experienced traveler, seemed unconcerned by the lack
of beds and cheerily walked the deck most of the night. When
they finally arrived at Dublin, Foote took to his reserved lodgings,
leaving the sick and frightened Wilkinson to his own devices.
Wilkinson never forgot or forgave Foote for this display of
callousness, even though he later collaborated with him on many
occasions.[22]

Foote played his usual roles with Sheridan: Ben, Brazen,
Fondlewife, Paul Plyant, Lord Foppington, and Bayes, in which
he was not particularly successful. But in his own plays, as Buck
and as Cadwallader, "he stood alone, and his original acting, good
or bad, set criticism at defiance." [23] In early December, shortly
before he was to return to London, Foote visited the almost recovered Wilkinson and apologized for his neglect, saying he could
not afford to be ill and that he was afraid of catching the fever.
The angry Wilkinson sneered at "my most anxious friend," but
Foote lived up to his earlier promises. He arranged a dinner with
Sheridan and suggested that Wilkinson appear on stage with him
before they both had to return to London.[24] Sheridan agreed, and
Foote took Wilkinson on as one of the pupils in his *Diversions
of the Morning*.[25] A terror stricken Wilkinson appeared barely in
time for the performance. When called, "I trembled like a frightened clown in a pantomime: which Foote perceiving, good nat-
uredly took me by the hand and led me forward. Foote perceiving

I was not fit for action, said to his two friends on the stage, 'This young man is really a novice on the stage; he has not yet been properly drilled. But come, my young friend, walk across the stage; breathe yourself and shew your figure.' " The friendly audience applauded the novice, and Wilkinson gained the courage to do his imitations. By the end of his act he was nervy enough to take off Foote himself to ringing applause and laughter. This was Wilkinson's moment of revenge, and he gleefully reports that Foote affected to be pleased, for he was forced by the crowd's reaction to swallow his rage. But, added Wilkinson, since the audience liked it, "Foote may be said to have pocketed the affront." Thus *The Diversions* (or *Tea*) was acted in regular succession to large audiences until Foote had to leave for London. He promised Wilkinson that he would get Garrick's permission to allow him to stay in Dublin and cash in on the popularity of his imitations.[26]

However, it seems that while Wilkinson was imitating Foote and threatening his manager, Sheridan, with the same treatment,[27] Foote had not quite finished milking Dublin of all he could get. According to a letter quoted in a London newspaper, Foote had gone into business for himself:

> I suppose you have heard of the famous Comedian Mr. Foote. He is at present in this town [Dublin]. He is a Man of much Humour. He took it into his Head to take a private Lodging in a remote Part of the Town, in order to set up the lucrative Business of Fortune-Telling. After he had got his Room hung with Black, and got his dark Lanthorn, with some People about him that knew the People of Fashion who live in this City, he gave out Hand-Bills, to let them know there was a Man to be met with at such a Place, who wrote down People's Fortunes, without asking them any Questions. As his Room was quite dark (the Light from his Lanthorn excepted) he was in less danfer of being discovered: So that he went on with great Success for many days; insomuch that it is said he cleared at least Thirty Pounds a Day at half a Crown a Head.[28]

When he finally arrived in London in late January, he obtained Garrick's permission for Wilkinson's extended leave and started playing Cadwallader again, relieving Yates who had been playing it in his absence. But this time there was opposition to the play. Poor Apreece, who naively had thought that it would be good fun to become known through Foote's play, found himself and his wife becoming objects of ridicule for the town. He begged Foote not to portray him anymore. Foote, of course, could see nothing wrong with his play—after all, the man had asked for it. And even earlier, using apt metaphor, Foote had defined the humorist as being the natural victim of the satirist: "The Man of Humour . . . is always joyous and pleasant; the Humourist is his [the satirist's] Food; like the Carrion and the Crow, they are never asunder; it is to the Labour and Pleasantry of the former [the satirist], that you are indebted for all the Entertainment you meet with in the latter.[29]

Finding that he could get no satisfaction from Foote, Apreece, in desperation, broke into the rehearsal on January 30 and complained to Garrick about Foote's play.[30] Garrick, characteristically, disclaimed responsibility, emphasizing that he and Foote had a business contract and that Foote was at liberty to choose his own plays. According to one story, Apreece then considered challenging Foote to a duel, but Garrick dissuaded him with a warning. "My dear Sir, don't think of doing any such thing; why, he would shoot you through the guts before you had supped two oysters off your wrists." [31] Apreece would still not leave rehearsal and insisted that The Author be dropped from the Drury Lane repertory. To silence Apreece for the moment, Garrick agreed that they would all meet and continue the argument at the Rose Tavern that night. The trio argued the matter, Foote was particularly abusive to his former friend, and no final agreement was reached. But after Foote had given his February 1 performance, Garrick did not offer the play again that season.[32]

This action left Foote stranded in mid-season again, and this time there was no Macklin to profit from. But since Foote did not attempt any novelties or comic lectures, it can be assumed that his pockets were filled from his Irish venture. An any rate, no more is heard of him until the following season. Wilkinson too found himself in similar straits when he returned to Drury Lane in April.[33] Thinking to be put on the payroll when he returned, Wilkinson found out that his temporary release from Drury Lane did not terminate until the new season and that Garrick, probably deliberately, had neglected to inform him. Only briefly dismayed, Wilkinson continued to make his living from Foote. In the summer, he appeared at Bath and other resorts treating "Mr. Foote with a Dish of his own *Tea.*" [34]

Foote had no prior agreement with either of the major houses for the 1758-59 season, nor did he have a new play to offer them. Possibly he might have been forced to turn to less prestigious stages, but luckily, his one time protagonist in the lists of theatrical battles, Woodward, was unable to come to monetary terms with Garrick. Barry had solicited Woodward as a partner in a new theatrical venture at Dublin, and Woodward decided to leave Drury Lane for Ireland on September 16. Before leaving, he angrily told his side of the story to Foote. "Why," said Foote, "you play in Farce as well as Comedy almost every night?" "Yes," replied Woodward. "You invent Pantomimes?"—"Yes."—"You play the Harlequin in them?"—"Yes." "You take leaps of great height, and you descend through trap doors?"—"Yes."—"You journey over mountains and valleys?"—"Yes."—"You make trips to the moon?"—"Yes; he makes quite a *Hackney* of me." "Why then," said Foote, "you have a just right to every shilling you ask; you have earned it all, either by the time or by the distance." [35]

Foote was probably right. Woodward was the second most important actor at Drury Lane. He played leading roles in all comedies when Garrick did not act and was his chief support when he did. It was in the pantomime, however, that Woodward was indispensable; he wrote, produced, and acted all of them. Undoubtedly he was worth the extra money. But Garrick probably resented his airs and his impudences and, perhaps, was glad to get rid of the troublesome actor.[36]

The loss of Woodward and other actors whom he took with him to Ireland led Garrick to revise his schedule for the new season. Unable to find suitable replacements at this late time, he was forced to produce new roles and to cast around for some substitute for Woodward. Though it went against the grain, Garrick had to turn to Foote, and this time Foote had the advantage. Before coming to any specific terms with Garrick, Foote decided to bring Wilkinson into his act, knowing how profitable his extraordinary imitations had been in Dublin. Wilkinson still bore his grudge against Foote, however, and he also resented the great profits that went to Foote while he received only salary, though it was his talent that was being exploited. But he was not happy with Garrick either. Still smarting from Garrick's rebuff the previous spring, Wilkinson continued to find the manager displeased with him. Garrick kept him at the minimal salary at which he was first hired, and, to mortify Wilkinson further, who still heard the applause of Dublin ringing in his ears, refused to give him any parts.[37] While in his unhappy situation, Wilkinson found himself hailed by a smiling and friendly Foote. Like Murphy, Johnson, and Delaval, Wilkinson could not resist Foote's gaiety and charm: "It would certainly have appeared very rude not to have complied with so smiling and earnest a summons and after ten minutes conversation all my slights and wrongs were forgot and forgiven; and sure if ever *one* person possessed the talents of pleasing more than another, Mr. Foote was certainly the man." [38] Later that evening over dinner, Foote proposed that Wilkinson make his first acting appearance at Drury Lane as Bounce in *Diversions of the Morning*. He assured Wilkinson that despite Garrick's antipathy, he could exert the proper influence to change the manager's mind:

> If you give me permission to ask for your first attempt on his stage and to be in my piece the hound will refuse the moment I mention it; and though his little soul would rejoice to act *Richard III* in the Dog Days, before the hottest kitchen fire for a sop in the pan; yet I know his mean soul so perfectly, that if on his refusal, I with a grave face tell him, I have his figure exactly made and dressed as a puppet in my closet, ready for public admiration, the fellow will not only consent to your acting, but

what is more extraordinary, his abject fears will lend me money, if I should say I want it.[39]

Foote was as good as his threat, and before the middle of October Foote settled preliminaries with a cornered Garrick for his "two damned exotics," as he exasperatedly called them.[40]

Foote next went about praising his co-mimic to all of his friends and acquaintances to build up an audience for this unknown genius who had not yet been exhibited on the London stage.[41] Of course, Wilkinson's dreaded talent was not unknown in the acting profession. Peg Woffington, who had already suffered at his hands in Dublin, frenziedly tried to forestall the mimic. She got her lover, Colonel Caesar, to warn Garrick on the threat of challenge to restrain Wilkinson. Garrick wholeheartedly agreed, and the day before *Diversions of the Morning* was to be acted, he called in his two exotics and told them he would not allow his actors to be humiliated in his house. Surprisingly, Foote and Wilkinson acceded to the demand without argument.[42]

On the first night, the first act of *Taste* went well. The second act, in which Foote as Puzzle runs an acting school, satirizing and mimicking T. Cibber, Sheridan, and Macklin, also went off very well—especially the part when Foote as Macklin instructs Wilkinson as Barry in the art of acting Othello.[43]

> Puz.: Advance, *Bounce* . . . Now catch at me, as you would tear the very strings and all—keep your voice low —loudness is no mark of passion—mind your attitude.
> Bounce: "Villain!"—
> Puz.: Very well!
> Bounce: "Be sure you prove my love a whore!"—
> Puz.: Admirable!
> Bounce: "Give me the ocular proof,"—
> Puz.: Lay your emphasis a little stronger upon oc— oc—oc.
> Bounce: "Oc-oc-ocular proof,"—

Puz.: That's right.

Bounce: "Or, by the worth of my eternal soul, thou had'st better been born a dog"—

Puz.: Grind *dog* a little more—"Do-o-o-g, Iago."

Bounce: "A do-o-g, Iago, than answer my wak'd wrath."—

Puz.: Charming! now quick. (*Speaking all the time as the recital goes on.*)

Bounce: "Make me to see it, or, at least, so prove it that the probation bears no hinge or loop to hang a doubt upon—or woe"—

Puz.: A little more terror upon *woe*—wo-o-e, like a mastiff in a tanner's yard—wo-o-oe. (*They answer each other—wo-o-oe, &c.*)

Bounce: "Upon my life, if thou dost slander her, and *torture me*"—. . .

Puz: (*Imitating Macklin.*) Sir, do you consider the mode of the mind—that a man's soul is lost, and lost crost, and his entrails broiling on a gridiron—bring it from the bottom of your stomach, sir, with a grind, as "To-r-r-r."—

Bounce: "Tor-r-torture me!"

Puz.: That's my meaning.[44]

Despite being amused by this passage, the audience felt that they had been promised something not performed and they grew uneasy. Foote had puffed Wilkinson too well. When Bounce left the stage and Puzzle began to work with his puppets, the crowd began to call for Wilkinson. To quiet the shouts, Garrick hastily allowed Wilkinson to give his imitations. To the delight of the unruly audience, he gave a rapid series of imitations including Sparks, Barry, and concluded with Foote. It was a great success for Wilkinson.[45]

The following nights people came to see Wilkinson's imitations. The approval of the audience emboldened the mimic to include Garrick and other actors in his repertoire, so that by the fifth night some members of the troupe were ready to tear

Wilkinson limb from limb. One of the maligned actors, Sparks, complained to Garrick that his livelihood was being destroyed, for no one would take his acting seriously again. In his hesitating manner, Garrick tried to reassure him: "Why now hey, Sparks! why now, hey, this is so strange, now hey, a—why Wilkinson and be d——d to him, they tell me he takes me off, and he takes Foote off, and so, why you are in very good company." "Very true Sir," said Sparks, "but many an honest man has been ruined by keeping too good company." [46] Garrick, who in truth detested Wilkinson and his imitations, called in the tormentor and ordered him to give no more imitations on the penalty of a £300 fine. At this tense moment, Mossop, a tremendously pompous actor, took it on himself to second Garrick. Entering with slow, purposeful steps, hand on sword, "breathing as if respiration were honor," Mossop accosted Wilkinson. "Mr. Wilkinson! phew! Sir, —Mr. Wil-kin-son, Sir, I say—phew!—how dare you, Sir, make free in a public theatre, or even in a private party, with your superiors? If you were to take such liberties with me, Sir, I would take my sword and run it through your body, Sir! you should not live Sir!" The tension was released as all the actors broke up with laughter. At this appropriate moment, Foote entered and was promptly told by Garrick that there would be no more imitations. Foote acquiesced again, and the relieved company prepared for the evening's performance.[47]

But despite Garrick's determination, the audience was all powerful. They continued to call for Wilkinson and his imitations.[48] Foote came forward and apologized to the audience, explaining that some performers had complained so that the imitations were to be omitted, but "as for being taken off himself he had no Objection to it, as he was always glad to contribute to their Entertainment." [49] His explanation had no effect; he was hooted down, the calls mounting for Wilkinson. Even after Garrick told him to go on stage, Wilkinson still had fears of paying the fine. Foote and Garrick finally had to push the "unwilling" mimic on stage. To great applause he ran through his repertoire, beginning with Foote and ending with Garrick.[50] He did try to leave out Sparks, but the audience would not let him go until Sparks too was done, and then, finally, they released him to thunderous cheers.[51] After this night, Garrick and the actors realized the futility of their protests, and all appeals to Wilkinson were dropped. The imitations went on night after night. Of course, Wilkinson was still dissatisfied; he was the great attraction, but Foote profited from the crowds.[52]

There were no serious reviews of *The Diversions of the Morning*, but the following descriptive comment in the *London Chronicle* is interesting, for it shows the attitude of the intelligent theatre-goer to such scrappy fare, and it refers to a new opening scene that was never printed:

> Booksellers who have a mind to play the rogue, sometimes steal five pages from one book, and ten from another, clap a fresh title page to them, and publish it so as it may be taken for new. Now this is just the case with the above *Diversions*, which is no other in the first act, than a scene about we don't know what, and between we don't know who, with which it opens; and this is followed by a very humorous one, indeed taken from the author's farce called *Taste* in which he acts the part of Lady Pentweazle inimitably.
>
> The second act is a strange *Impromptu* in which Mr. Foote appears in the Character of Mr. Theophilus Cibber, at the theatre in the Haymarket, where we are to suppose he has set up a theatrical school under the name of Project. His insruction of his pupils was very justly hissed; however, we at last found out that all this was done only to introduce one Mr. Wilkinson, a very excellent mimic: the man with two voices is nothing to him. He gave us Foote, Garrick, Barry, Woodward, almost all in a breath; and to a person well acquainted with theatrical personages, was undoubtedly amusing. However I can't help saying, that whatever those Diversions might be in a Morning, in an Evening they are, in my opinion, mighty indifferent.[53]

Even if his *Diversions* did not gratify the spectators in the pit, Foote was compensated by other considerations: money, and critical appreciation of Gomez, one of his favorite roles: "Gomez is the representative of a character very common in human life; he is a mixture of archness, cowardliness, and covetousness; and nobody can show the part to more advantage than the agreeable Mr. Foote. His looks are so sly, his manner of speaking so bitter; and he is enabled by his great talent at mimickry to put on the old fellow in his voice and gestures with such a ridiculous propriety, that it looks as if either he had been made for the part, or the part for him." [54]

With his benefit approaching on December 18, Foote cooked up something special to draw a large audience. He decided to play Shylock and to top off the evening with *The Author*, which had not been played for a year. To add some spice, he wrote a new scene just for Wilkinson.[55] But on the morning of the eighteenth, the Lord Chamberlain, Duke of Devonshire, intervened at Apreece's request and forbade any performance of *The Author*.[56] Apreece had taken Garrick's advice regarding the only way to stop the performance, and what friendship, pleas, and threats could not perform, money and influence could. Foote was stunned at this last minute edict, not only because of his benefit night, but also because he wanted to use *The Author* as an attraction for the second half of the season. Foote had to substitute *The Diversions of the Morning*, and in a speech to the audience he apologized for the hasty substitution and defended his good name against any imputations that might be made because of the prohibition. Fortunately, the audience took all this in good humor.[57]

His contract with Drury Lane concluded, Foote spent the Christmas holidays at his country home in Blackheath with his friends, among whom were Murphy and John Cleland of *Fanny Hill* fame.[58] George Anne Bellamy, for whom Foote had performed several benefits, also came to add to the holiday spirit. She commented that Foote at a later time asked her to join him at the Haymarket. Her refusal is an interesting explanation of why Foote was rarely able to engage head-liners at his theatre: "Had the Haymarket been then upon the plan it now is, I know not a performer, if they were able to go through the fatigue, but would gladly have accepted of an engagement. Mr. Colman [59] is indefatigable and spares no expense to indulge and entertain the town. The former manager depended mostly upon his own strength, and his own pieces; which gave but very few opportunities for a performer in any capital line to make a tolerable figure." [60]

Though the holidays were soon over, Foote's Christmas spirit was not. He continued to hold parties at the Thatched House and the Bedford Arms and by January had squandered all his profits. His situation became precarious, for his *Author* was banned and his *Diversions* was used up; it "would not even produce tea for breakfast." [61] Inspired by his desperate state, Foote wrote to Callender, the theater manager at Edinburgh, to see if he could perform there. Callender was overwhelmed; no known performer from London had ever gone to Scotland. He replied that he would be proud of Foote's assistance. The matter agreed; Foote packed, rode off—and recalled he had no money for coach fare. Too proud to face Garrick directly, he begged Wilkinson to ask for him. Garrick patiently obliged for £100, and when Wilkinson returned with the money, Foote's spirits were so elevated it seemed that he would remain in the tavern and tell all his jokes about Garrick. But prudence won out for once, and Foote finally set off to make theatrical history at Edinburgh.[62]

The Edinburgh *Courant* carried a notice that Foote had arrived on March 15, 1759, and that on Tuesday, March 20, he would put on *The Author,* which was banned only in London and its environs.[63] He later played his *Diversions* and *The Englishman Returned from Paris,* which were new in this part of the country and also acted Shylock, Gomez, Bayes, and Sir Paul Plyant. In addition, he gave what Dibdin says "was in all probability the first morning performance of a play in Scotland," on Friday, March 30, at noon.[64]

His pockets filled, Foote seems to have left Edinburgh shortly after his noon performance, for on April 21 he was bolstering Murphy's courage at the Rose Tavern near Drury Lane. A party was being held in celebration of Garrick's production of Murphy's *Orphan of China.* After years of hesitation, Garrick had finally agreed under coercive circumstances to produce it. The play was to open that evening, and Murphy had every reason to be apprehensive: Mrs. Cibber, the female lead had no faith in the play and fell "sick" just before performance. Fortunately, Murphy had foreseen this possibility and had privately rehearsed Mrs. Yates for the role. She knew the lines but had almost no experience with the role on stage. As Murphy squirmed in the tavern, Mrs. Cibber, who would have loved nothing better than to see her rival fail and her judgment of the play vindicated, hypocritically sent him a note wishing him luck and assuring him that "I shall offer up my prayers for your success." Foote then asked the company if she were not a Catholic, gravely adding, "They always pray for the dead." [65] Foote's joke broke the tension, and, happily, the play went off brilliantly. As one critic put it, "Mrs. Cibber lost a capital part, gained a new rival, and received an answer to her prayers." [66] Murphy then describes Foote's response to the good news: "It must not be omitted that Foote, who loved his friends, though he would never lose his joke, came at the end of the play to congratulate with the author; he ran to embrace him, but a gush of tears choaked his utterance, and he sat down unable, for a short time, to utter a word." [67] Foote's response was not so uncharacteristic as it seemed. A highly emotional man, his spontaneous empathy to a situation often led to a generous and noble response. Even though he made many enemies through contentiousness and a biting wit, he rarely held a grudge for long. Murphy, Wilkinson, Macklin, Woodward, Johnson, and even Garrick at times, though they frequently gave as good as they got, resumed their long friendships with Foote once the battles were over.

At the start of the 1759-60 season, Foote's financial position worsened. Neither major house would employ him; his old works were stale, and his new piece was not yet completed. Fortunately for Foote, Barry and Woodward, who had begun their theatrical venture at the Crow-Street Theatre in Dublin in October, 1758, were finding greater opposition from the Smock-Alley Theatre in 1759. The new owners wanted Foote as a counter attraction, and they hired him to play his *Diversions* and his new play, *The Minor*.[68] It is not clear whether Foote actually played with Barry and Woodward in September and October, but if he did, it could only have been for a few times. Foote found himself short of money and went back to London to give a comic lecture at the

Haymarket on November 9. Garrick, perhaps still holding Foote accountable for Wilkinson's imitations, sent Wilkinson to spy for him. The first part of the lecture hit at Rich and Garrick, and, though the material was thin, Foote's delivery struck fire. The second part of the lecture proved so poor that Foote stopped it midway. Darkening the stage, Foote sat at a table illuminated by two candles and began to read *The Minor*. The audience remained unmoved. Foote stopped his reading, apologized to his followers, and promised alterations for the next performance.[69] Shaken and disappointed by this lack of response, Foote returned to Dublin the next day.[70]

Wilkinson quickly reported to Garrick the good news of Foote's failure. But Garrick, thinking perhaps of his £100 loan, was too angry at Foote's attack at him to be mollified by its failure. Garrick soon found out that Foote was engaged with Barry and Woodward in Dublin and, giving to Wilkinson a letter of introduction addressed to Brown, the manager of Smock-Alley, he sent the mimic to Dublin to compete with the Crow-Street Theatre. Wilkinson was given special orders not to come to terms with or act for Barry and Woodward.[71] The point of Garrick's move was not only to even a score with Foote, but also to hurt Barry and Woodward, with whom he had had differences in the past.

Wilkinson left immediately and arrived in Ireland on December 26, 1759. Brown welcomed him warmly, for Wilkinson had many connections in Dublin from his last appearance and was a greater attraction than Foote in bouts of mimicry.[72] The opposition, alerted to his presence and divining his purpose, tried to sign him, but Wilkinson virtuously reports his refusal, remembering his instructions from Garrick. Waiting for Foote's next performance of *The Diversions*, advertised for January 4, Wilkinson gave his performance of the piece on the same day, aping Foote's mannerisms throughout. He was going to include Barry and Woodward among his imitations but decided to desist, thinking he might need employment from them some day. Foote, in great financial difficulties, tried to warn off his tormentor. Wilkinson with great glee persisted in the competition, but prudently avoided Foote socially for fear of being humiliated by his stinging tongue.[73]

On January 28, 1760, Foote finally unveiled *The Minor,* a two-act satire on Methodism. He also got back at Wilkinson by introducing him as Shift, an unprincipled mimic. But, though Foote aimed at sensation and scandal, the play was not successful. Supposedly, Woodward, who played the bawd, Mother Cole, was partially to blame for the failure; he acted the role too broadly, and the play was damned after his appearance. Foote did not attempt *The Minor* again, and, after his unsuccessful benefit on February 11, he left Ireland.[74] The trip was a disaster; Wilkinson's great popularity left thin audiences at Crow-Street; *The Minor* failed; Foote was forced to share his few profits with Macklin, who was also hired on the same basis as Foote. His financial situation now desperate, Foote could no longer wait for the opening of the winter theatres to produce a play that seemed to have little chance of success.[75]

NOTES

1. George Anne Bellamy, *Apology for the Life of . . . Late of Covent Garden* (London, 1785), Vol. II, pp. 205-211.
2. Stone, *London Stage,* Vol. II, pp. 560 ff.
3. Davies hated Foote's low style of acting in the *Double Dealer,* (Vol. I, p. 191), but *A General View of the Stage* (London, 1759), pp. 273-274, by Thomas Wilkes, states that Foote's acting was so "striking, without trick or grimace, that he not only commands the applause of the judicious, but of the *million.*"
4. Stone, *London Stage,* Vol. II, p. 562.
5. Foote placed the following advertisement in the *Public Advertiser* the day before performance, February 4, 1757:

> Whereas it has been represented to the managers of Drury-lane Theatre, that Mr. Foote in his new Farce call'd the *Author,* intends introducing the Character of a gentleman for whom he has the greatest Esteem and Regard, he thinks it incumbent on him to assure the Public, that all the Personages in the Piece are fictitious and general.

6. *London Chronicle,* February 15-17, 1757, and see Stone, *London Stage,* Vol. II, p. 580.
7. Foote had mentioned Apreece's family pride in *The Knights* and commented on "your Uncle Price" in a letter to John Delaval quoted here on p. 60. In another letter to Delaval, written October, 1752,

Foote wrote, "The town is as empty as your Aunt Price's head." (Askham, p. 67.)

8. *Town and Country Magazine,* November, 1777, pp. 599-600. Davies, Vol. I, p. 201, also gives a similar version of this story.

9. Cooke, *Foote,* Vol. II, p. 42; Davies, Vol. I, p. 193.

10. Foote, *The Dramatic Works,* Vol. I, p. 198.

11. *Ibid.,* pp. 209-210.

12. *Theatrical Review,* (London, 1758), p. 48, cited by Stone, *London Stage,* Vol. II, p. 620.

13. *London Chronicle,* February 13, 1757.

14. *Literary Magazine,* February 15-March 15, 1757, pp. 76-79. Arthur Sherbo reprints this article in his *New Essay by Arthur Murphy,* pp. 117-122, and by internal evidence, but no real proof, tries to show that Murphy is the author of this and other reviews. It is my opinion that Murphy did not write this highly favorable piece. There is no evidence to show that Murphy had resumed his friendship with Foote at this time. The earliest proven date for their resumption of relations is October, 1758. It seems unlikely to me that Garrick would make a point of Murphy's intimacy with Foote if their quarrel had been over for two years.

15. Stone, *London Stage,* Vol. II, p. 551, *passim.*

16. *Ibid.,* pp. 557, ff.

17. Wilkinson, Vol. I, p. 146.

18. *Ibid.,* p. 147.

19. *Ibid.,* pp. 125-127.

20. *Ibid.,* pp. 147-150.

21. *Ibid.,* p. 152.

22. *Ibid.,* pp. 153-161.

23. Hitchcock, Vol. I, p. 290; and Wilkinson, Vol. I, p. 164.

24. Wilkinson, Vol. I, p. 169.

25. See p. 26 above for a description of this play.

26. Wilkinson, Vol. I, pp. 172-178.

27. *Ibid.,* p. 187.

28. *London Chronicle,* January 17-19, 1758. Though this tale may have been merely rumor, we have seen that Foote was particularly attracted to playing the conjuror, and furthermore he had the time to do it. He gave his last performance as Brazen in Dublin on December 7 (Hitchcock, Vol. I, p. 292), yet did not return to the London stage until January 26.

29. *The Roman and English Comedy Consider'd and Compar'd,* p. 12.

30. Stone, *London Stage,* Vol. II, p. 644.

31. Forster, p. 395.

32. Stone, *London Stage,* Vol. II, p. 644.

33. Wilkinson, Vol. I, p. 207.

34. *Ibid.*

35. Foot, p. 186.

36. See p. 62, n. 29 above.

37. Wilkinson, Vol. I, p. 231.

38. *Ibid.*, p. 233.
39. *Ibid.*, pp. 238-239.
40. Wilkinson, Vol. II, p. 5.
41. *Ibid.*, p. 17.
42. *Ibid.*, pp. 13-15.
43. *Ibid.*, p. 17.
44. Foote, *The Dramatic Works*, Vol. I, pp. lxi-lxiii.
45. Wilkinson, Vol. II, pp. 18-19.
46. *Ibid.*, pp. 26-27.
47. *Ibid.*, pp. 29-31.
48. *Ibid.*, pp. 32-35.
49. Stone, *London Stage*, Vol. II, p. 690.
50. Wilkinson, Vol. II, pp. 37-40.
51. Stone, *London Stage*, Vol. II, p. 690.
52. Wilkinson, Vol. II, p. 40.
53. *London Chronicle*, October 19-21, 1758.
54. *London Chronicle*, November 14-16, 1758. This review is also cited by Sherbo, pp. 91-92, as coming from Murphy's pen.
55. Wilkinson, Vol. II, p. 54. The additional scene appeared in the *Monthly Mirror*, VII (1759), 39-41.
56. Stone, *London Stage*, Vol. II, p. 701; and Wilkinson, Vol. II, pp. 54-55.
57. Wilkinson, Vol. II, p. 56; Stone, *London Stage*, Vol. II, p. 701; Genest, Vol. IV, p. 542.
58. Bellamy, Vol. III, p. 90.
59. George Colman bought the Haymarket from Foote in 1777 and ran it upon the conventional lines of the patent houses.
60. Bellamy, Vol. IV, p. 206.
61. Wilkinson, Vol. II, pp. 67-69.
62. *Ibid.*, pp. 67-76.
63. Cited by James C. Dibdin, *The Annals of the Edinburgh Stage* (Edinburgh, 1888), p. 105.
64. Dibdin, p. 107.
65. Dibdin, pp. 62-64; and Murphy, Vol. I, pp. 340-341.
66. Dunbar, p. 64.
67. Murphy, Vol. I, p. 341.
68. Hitchcock, Vol. II, p. 8.
69. Wilkinson, Vol. II, pp. 133-138.
70. Stone, *London Stage*, Vol. II, p. 755.
71. Wilkinson, Vol. II, p. 140.
72. Hitchcock, Vol. II, p. 27.
73. Wilkinson, Vol. II, pp. 167-175.
74. *Ibid.*, pp. 183-187.
75. Cooke, *Foote*, Vol. I, p. 97.

CHAPTER VI

A *MINOR* VICTORY AT THE HAYMARKET, 1760-1762

Foote's troubles were not over when he returned to London. Someone, perhaps Murphy, had spread the story that he had been horsewhipped by an apothecary whom he had imitated on stage and that a group of London's choicest literary wits, Johnson, Garrick, Burke, and Murphy, had gravely discussed the situation: "But I wonder," said Garrick, "that any man would show so much resentment to Foote: . . . nobody ever thought it *worth his while* to quarrel with him in London." "And I am glad," said Johnson, "to find that the man is *rising* in the world." When Foote heard the story he vowed to impersonate Johnson on the stage.[1]

When Johnson heard of Foote's threat, he asked Davies, the bookseller, the price of an oak stick. On being told six-pence, Johnson asked for one that cost a shilling. "I'll have a double quantity; for I am told Foote means to *take me off*, as he calls it, and I am determined the fellow shall not do it with impunity." Johnson then gave Foote notice "that, the theatre being intended for the reformation of vice, he would go from the boxes on the stage and correct him before the audience." [2] Foote hastily dropped the idea.

But in a short time Foote's financial troubles, his Dublin failure, and the maligning wisecracks directed at him were forgotten in the revivifying air of London. Filled with his Irish venture, Foote probably began telling the Irish jokes for which he was famous. One of his favorites has him dining at a public table in Dublin where the company was giving patriotic toasts. One young man who sat by a priest began to tease him by proposing impudent toasts. The priest ignored the insults until it came to his turn, when he asked his neighbor what the preceding toast had been. "The Glorious Revolution, Doctor; match it if you can." "Was it a good one?" asked the priest drily. "Oh, most excellent!" "Why then, my honey, I'll give you *Another of Them.*" [3]

Holding forth in the Bedford, Foote found his old friend Francis Delaval and made a new one, Laurence Sterne. Sterne had first appeared in London just before Christmas, when he came for a short time to look over his two new volumes of *Tristram Shandy.* They succeeded greatly when they appeared at the beginning of the year, and he hurried back to London in March, to be welcomed by fashionable society and literary wits, especially Foote and Delaval.[4] One serious gentleman wrote of Sterne's deterioration with great dismay.[5] Foote certainly set a poor example for Sterne of sobriety and prudence, but, undoubtedly, that gentleman needed no guide for bawdy wit and prodigality. Foote enjoyed his company, but after reading *Tristram Shandy* complained that "with all his *Stars* he was but an *obscure writer.*" [6]

Accounts of Foote's liveliness at the coffee houses reached Murphy's ear, and his description of Foote's holding forth gives a good account of Foote's style: "I have not seen the comical fellow, Mr. Foote; indeed, I do not go much to the Bedford, but am tempted to drop in there, to hear him dash away at everybody, and everything. 'Have you had good success in Dublin Mr. Foote?' 'Poh! damn 'em. There was not a shilling in the country, except what the Duke of Bedford, and I, and Mr. Rigby have brought away. Woodward is caterwauling among 'em and Barry like a wounded snake; and Mossop sprawling about his broken arms with the rising of the lights.' " [7] It seems that by this time even the Irish disaster had become a great success.

Perhaps his improved humor reconciled him to Wilkinson once more. Wilkinson finally left Ireland in March, after a good season, only to find that Garrick again refused to pay him on his return to London. He now suspected that Garrick's revenge extended not only to Barry, Woodward, and Foote, but to himself as well.[8] Earning no salary at the moment, Wilkinson busied himself by setting up an acting debut for Mrs. Weir, a former mistress of Francis Delaval's. Invited to Delaval's house to talk business, he found to his horror that Foote was among the guests. But after the introduction, Foote behaved with his usual good humor and began to praise the Irish hospitality he had experienced on his trip. Delaval disagreed, and briefly stepped into an adjoining room. Foote turned to the company and said, "Did you ever hear such a hound as this?—talking of the elegancies of the table; and here I have been seven days together dining with him on a greasy loin of pork. By God I'll not dine here again these three months; for I suppose he means to run his loin of pork against *The Beggar's Opera.*" Delaval returned, and overhearing Foote's last statement, remarked, "What, Foote! at my loin of pork still?" "No," said Foote, "your loins of pork have been *at me;* and if you don't *take them off,* in another week I suppose I shall be as full of bristles as Peter the wild man." [9]

But even though Foote seemed gay and lighthearted, time and money were running out quickly. He had to gamble on *The Minor* succeeding as a summer entertainment at the Haymarket. Among other revisions, he lengthened the play to three acts by adding an epilogue and the part of Shift.[10] Increasing the odds against success, he was forced to recruit a rag-tag company, some of whom had never performed before. *The Minor* opens with a rehearsal type of introduction to acquaint the audience with some of his difficulties. Two young bucks walk into the Haymarket to persuade Foote to satirize their relatives. Foote appears in his own person to chide them by reminding them that the last time he did that the play was banned. Indirectly, and perhaps untruthfully, Foote seems to claim that Delaval gave him Apreece and then did not use his influence to prevent the prohibition. Giving the bucks "laws for laughing," Foote claims that he satirizes only those who set up to be what they are not fit for. He then invites them in to see a rehearsal of his new piece, asking them to allow for the inexperience of his cast. And, amusingly, he prepares the audience for seeing a man take the part of Mother Cole by having the prompter say, "Mrs. O'Schohnesy has return'd the part of the bawd; she says she is a gentlewoman, and it would be a reflection on her family to do any such thing. . . . If it had been only a whore, says she, I should not have minded doing it; because no lady need be ashamed of doing that." Foote then remarks that he will do the character himself.[11] He had originally intended the part to be played by a man, and after Woodward's failure perhaps he did not want to take the chance of letting anyone else do it. Foote also played the mimic, Shift, who impersonates Smirk and Squintum.

The main plot of *The Minor,* similar to that of *The Author,* is that of the young rake reclaimed. Sir William Wealthy disguises himself as one of a gang of parasites who are despoiling his son, George, of his wealth. The father also employs a mimic, Shift, to impersonate an auctioneer, Smirk, through whom the son tries to raise money. The boy reveals his basic goodness of heart when he shelters an innocent girl who was being forced into prostitution by Mother Cole. Listening to the girl's pleas, George exposes Mother Cole and is taken back by his father, who he had thought was dead. The girl turns out to be his cousin who was disowned by her merchant father for refusing to marry the man of his choice. The merchant repents of his hard heart, and the young couple go off to marry.

This unexciting plot was bolstered by the appearance of Mother Cole, the bawd who tried to interest George in her wares. She, no doubt, was immediately recognized by the theatregoers as Mother Jennie Douglas, a notorious London procuress, who had already been satirized by Hogarth.[12] Foote probably 'took off" the old woman, wearing her clothes and imitating her speech and gait. To complete the portrait, he has Mother Cole act the part of an enthusiastic convert to Methodism who constantly mouths pieties while trying to tempt young George with one of her girls. She gives the credit for her reformation to Mr. Squintum, a popular name for George Whitefield. The famous Methodist preacher had a cast in his eye, and even though he does not appear in the play, he is mimicked by Shift in the epilogue. Foote as Cole constantly quotes Whitefield, using his speech mannerisms: "born again," "regenerate," "new creature," and "her time not being yet come."

Nor did Foote forget Wilkinson, whom he impersonated as Shift. But though he satirizes his background, the takeoff is whimsical and humorous rather than vicious, and Wilkinson, who seemed to take offense at almost everything, did not object to this. In having the breezy Shift explain how he came to his unusual profession, the laugh is directed as much against Foote as against Wilkinson:

> . . . As I was saying, sir, nothing came amiss to my master. Bipeds or quadrupeds; rationals, or animals; from the clamour of the bar, to the cackle of the barndoor; from the soporific twang of the *Tabernacle* of Tottenham-court, to the melodious bray of their long-ear'd brethren in Bumhillfields; all were objects of his imitation and my attention. In a word, sir, for two whole years, under this professor, I study'd and starv'd, impoverish'd my body, and pamper'd my mind, till thinking myself pretty near equal to my master, I made him one of his own bows, and set up for myself.[13]

Shift also imitates Smirk, the auctioneer, an impersonation of Abraham Langford, a well known auctioneer and a successor to Cock, who had been taken off by Foote many years earlier. Smirk mourns his passing:

> O dear me! You did not know the great man—alike in everything. He had as much to say upon a ribbon as a *Raphael*. His manner too was inimitably fine. I remember, they took him off at the play-house, some time ago; pleasant but wrong. Public characters should not be sported with—They are sacred.[14]

The play was far more successful than even Foote could have anticipated. Beginning June 28, it ran for 35 performances.[15] The crowds were so great that when Wilkinson, who looked upon all of Foote's pieces as his own, came to London he had to wait a number of days before he could see a performance.[16] After the eighth night, Foote gave performances on Mondays, Wednesdays, and Fridays, but the press for seats was so great that Foote, whose license for the Haymarket showing expired in September, showed performances every night beginning the eighteenth of August.[17] Even Garrick, who would not hire Foote the previous seasons, came to terms with him on July 22 so that *The Minor* could be seen at Drury Lane for the 1760-61 season.[18]

The furor set off by *The Minor* was remarkable. Letters, exhortations, additional scenes to *The Minor,* and other written controversy, pro- and anti-Methodism, filled the air. (A good summary of the literature occasioned by *The Minor* can be found in Miss Belden's book, pp. 86-106). Foote himself ignored much of this controversy and condescended to answer only one anonymous letter, probably by Martin Madan,[19] a minister and writer of hymns. Its full title, *Christian and Critical Remarks on a Droll, or Interlude, called The Minor. Now acting by a Company of Stage Players in the Hay-market; and Said to be acted by Authority. In which The Blasphemy, Falsehood, and Scurrility of that Piece is properly considered, answered, and exposed. By a Minister of the Church of Christ,* is properly antagonistic. Like most of the pieces reproving Foote, it is totally devoid of humor, completely self-righteous, and usually beside the point. He defends Whitefield's theatrical mannerisms and pious tales as the only means of reaching a Godless and low audience. Foote retorted that Whitefield in using real examples was no different from Aristophanes, and though there was no chorus, "yet a melodious nasal twang produced by an orchestra of old women, who surrounded the actor, ably supplied that deficiency." [20] His play was merely a response in kind. The Methodist attack, in general, was so inept that the *Critical Review* stated that "this waggish comedian had hired a set of dunces for whetstones to his wit." [21] Supposedly Whitefield had punned that the devil would make a football of Foote,[22] and there is a reference to this pun in *The Minor's* epilogue.

The character of Mother Cole and her jumbling of both worlds gives the impression that the Methodists would allow anyone into their church who professed belief; that Methodists preached piety but did not let religion interfere with business; that personal spiritual experiences were frauds; that George Whitefield was a hypocritical, canting charlatan who practiced his oratorical craft for money and secretly despised the fools who listened to him; that the lay parsons were idle, ignorant fellows who, having forsaken their craft, lived by cheating others. It seems that Foote's play came at that time in English history when such a satirical point of view could be publicly displayed and applauded. With nerve and skill Foote was able to capitalize on his sense of the public's mood. Foote reflects the popular prejudices and opinions concerning the Methodist movement rather than exposing real abuses made by them. Umphrey Lee in tracing the background of Methodist enthusiasm brings out some interesting theories that help explain many of these prejudices. He claims that the enthusiast traditionally "insisted upon an inner light or a divine seed in all men, not in the elect alone, and upon an inner authority to preach which depended neither upon human learning nor ordination." [23] An ordained clergy could see only chaos resulting from this, and frequently refused to let lay preachers use their churches. This was certainly one of the reasons that led Whitefield and Wesley to become itinerant preachers to crowds in the fields. Lee also sees a connection in the popular mind between enthusiasm and the reign of Cromwell. Because of this, Methodism was also associated with dangerous political and social movements that threatened the status quo.

Simultaneous with these fears was the growing sense of decorum, taste, and skepticism in the eighteenth century which held the ideal of religion to be a moderate piety. Most people resented any display of religious emotion. "Polite society learned to laugh at the ill-breeding of enthusiasts, instead of trembling at supposed plots of the inspired to cut the throats of disbelievers," [24] and Foote was a member of polite society. Thus a preacher, lit by the divine spark of inner light, was ridiculed by polite society and provided an irresistible subject for Foote; his presentation was an hilarious confirmation of the prejudices of the crowds that forced their way into the Haymarket.

In the fall of 1760, while preparing *The Minor* for Drury Lane, Foote began to find considerable opposition against the production. Lady Huntington, Whitefield's patroness, used her influence on the Lord Chamberlain, the Duke of Devonshire, to suppress the play. He was polite but told her it was too late to withdraw the license. She also applied to Garrick, who delicately professed offense at the play, but implied that the decision was now out of his hands.[25] The Archbishop of Canterbury, Thomas Secker, also tried to have the play suppressed, but the Lord Chamberlain refused and agreed only to alter those passages pointed out by the Archbishop. But his Grace was too canny for that. He complained that "Foote would publish the play as *corrected* and *prepared* for the press by his Grace the Archbishop of Canterbury." [26] Foote, annoyed by this interference, declared he would take out a license to preach, Sam Cant against Tom Cant. (The abbreviated official signature of the Archbishop was Thomas Cant.) [27] Though Foote apparently overcame this attempt to suppress *The Minor,* he was only a partial winner. The Lord Chamberlain, despite his statement to Garrick that little alteration would be necessary,[28] was moved to action by a letter signed Anti-Prophanus, probably by Madan again:[29] *A Letter to David Garrick, Esq.; Occasioned by the intended Representation of the Minor at the Theatre-Royal in Drury Lane. The Minor* was to have opened on October 25, but because of the death of George II on that day, all theatres were closed for three weeks. Madan's letter appeared in this interim, and Joseph Byrnes points out that, though some of his sillier suggestions were ignored by the Lord Chamberlain, almost all of his more serious objections were sustained, that even the famous epilogue was gutted, and that *The Minor* as presented at Drury Lane that year contained very little to offend anyone.[30]

As Foote prepared his play under these constrictions, a final obstruction was placed in his way. Wilkinson was engaged by Rich at Covent Garden that season and, carrying with him a pirated copy of *The Minor,* he talked Rich into presenting it in opposition to the official version at Drury Lane. Of course, Wilkinson would act Mother Cole, Shift, and Smirk in Foote's manner. When Foote got wind of the plot, he angrily sped to Covent Garden and shouted great threats to Rich:

> Damn it, you old hound! if you dare to let Wilkinson, that pugnosed son of a bitch, take any liberty with me as to mimicry, I will bring you yourself, Rich, on the stage! If you want to engage that pug, black his face, and let him hand the tea-kettle in a pantomime; for damn the fellow he is as ignorant as a whore's maid! And if he dares to appear in my characters, in the *Minor,* I will instantly produce your old stupid ridiculous self, with your three cats, and your hound of a mimic altogether, next week at Drury Lane, for the general diversion of the pit, boxes, and galleries; and that will be paying you, you squinting old Hecate, too great a compliment! [31]

Wilkinson commented that though Rich feared for his cats, he did not give in to the threats. The real difficulty for Wilkinson was that the Covent Garden troupe needed some weeks to properly prepare the play, and Drury Lane had already advertised it for October 25. Fortunately, the closing of the theatres gave Wilkinson the necessary time. The theatres did not open again until November 17, and this time *The Minor,* with Foote acting the roles of Mother Cole, Smirk, and Shift, was advertised for November 22.

Wilkinson obtained seats for the first night and, noting that "Foote was received, as usual, with great eclat by a most brilliant and crowded audience," he saw the need for great haste in presenting his version lest the right moment escape.[32] By working long hours, the Covent Garden company was able to put on *The Minor* on November 24 and continued through the month to compete with Drury Lane, giving performances on November 25, 26, 27, 28, and on December 3 and 18. In his first performance, Wilkinson gave his imitations and, though noticing Garrick seated before him in the pit, did not refrain from taking him off as well. That piece of bravado infuriated Garrick, who never spoke to Wilkinson again.[33] Though this competition could not help Foote, it probably did him little harm. Wilkinson's performance was only a burlesque of Foote's; to enjoy the copy, presumably one had to see the original.

Foote did not work in March of 1761, but he had little leisure time. *The Rosciad,* a satire on actors by Charles Churchill, was published that month. Blasting all other wits and actors, Churchill gave unreserved praise only to Garrick and Robert Lloyd, a poet and close friend of Churchill's. A poem by Lloyd, *The Actor,* had appeared the previous year, and its success encouraged Churchill to write his poem on a similar topic.[34] Though Churchill was a newcomer to London and seemed to have had little time to form connections, Dunbar gives good evidence to show that parts of *The Rosciad* were politically motivated. "The triumvirate" of Churchill, Colman, and Lloyd, aided by Garrick and by Bonnell Thornton, editor of the *St. James's Chronicle,* sought to discredit Murphy as unofficial playwright for Drury Lane and to replace him with George Colman.[35] Though Murphy was probably unaware of Garrick's involvement, he knew who his other enemies were. Though fully capable of fighting back on his own,[36] Murphy found in his friend Foote a willing ally against the triumvirate. Churchill had resumed Lloyd's attack on Foote, repeating his friend's argument but with sharper words:

> By turns transform'd into all kinds of shapes,
> Constant to none, F[oo]te laughs, cries, struts,
>   and scrapes:
> Now in the center, now in van or rear,
> The Proteus shifts, Bawd, Parson, Auctioneer.
> His strokes of humour, and his bursts of sport
> Are all contain'd in this one word, Distort.
> Doth a man stutter, look a-squint, or halt?
> Mimics draw humour out of Nature's fault:
> With personal defects their mirth adorn,
> And hang misfortunes out to public scorn.[37]

Foote ordinarily might have ignored this attack as he had ignored
Lloyd's poem, but he probably felt that he had been singled out
by the triumvirate as a close friend of Murphy's. A contemporary
satire confirms the view that Foote would take sides in the battle.

> Foote, with a troop of apes and bears,
> Mimicks call'd, and strolling play'rs,
> Sent down his aid de camp to know,
> If he shou'd wait in Butcher-row,
> And act as a reserve brigade,
> Should General Murphy want his aid.[38]

Avenging Murphy as well as himself, Foote revised the second
act of the *Modern Tragedy* [39] for the purpose of satirizing Churchill, Lloyd, and Colman,[40] and he acted the farce at Drury Lane
on April 6. There is little in the manuscript of the piece that can
be interpreted as an attack on anyone, except for some innocuous
comments on Manly's (Churchill's) bearlike appearance and,
ironically, his great devotion to his wife:

> Townley [commenting on Manly's determination to
> leave London and return to his wife]:
> My stay as short as possible! What a various unaccountable
> creature is Man. What a fellow absorbed in all the Dissi-
> pations & Pleasures of this Town should at once Plunge
> into the deepest solitude with no other temptation than
> the ravashing Delights of a Wife and six children!
> *(Enter Manly)*
> Manly! impossible! hey, yes faith it is; what a ridicu-
> lous transformation! why thou art as rugged and shaggy
> as a Beast of my own Breeding after a hard Winter. . . .
> What brings thee to London; to rub off thy Rust I reckon,
> to be well curry'd and get a fresh coat.[41]

According to Weatherly, Townley represents Colman and Fus-
tian represents Lloyd, but there is nothing in the manuscript to

indicate this; the evidence is indirect. Foote advertised the play
as having "three performers who never appeared on any stage." [42]
In June, 1761, *The Critical Review* in reviewing *The Church-
illiad,* a prose attack on Foote and Murphy, stated: "As for the
Third Being [Churchill], he was convinced of the justice of Mr.
Foote's satyr in a little piece, where he exhibited Three New
Performers, with wooden bodies as well as heads." It is clear
then that Foote's satire consisted mainly of puppet caricature and
that he did not greatly revise the play. It was totally unsuccessful,
however, for the audience probably found it too personal. The
"Cross-Hopkins Diary" records that the play was greatly hissed
and almost damned.[43] Though the play was performed again on
May 15, Foote was too sensible to continue the battle with such
a formidable adversary, and he let the matter drop.

Foote became involved in yet another broil before the season
was over. He had acted the Scotchman in *The Register Office,*
a farce by Joseph Reed, on April 25, 1761. When Reed published
the play later that year, he claimed in his preface that Foote used
Mrs. Snarewell, a character in *The Register Office,* as a prototype
for Mother Cole. Reed claimed to have given Foote a copy of the
play in August, 1758, well before *The Minor* had been performed.
Foote was also accused of this plagiarism in *An Additional Scene
to The Minor,* which was anonymously published three months
before *The Register Office* appeared. As has been pointed out
by Joseph Byrnes [44] and Miss Belden,[45] the lack of definite proof
makes it impossible to make a firm judgment, especially since
there are other similarities that Reed could have claimed as his
own but did not. The earliest copies of *The Register Office* were
printed or written at least six months after *The Minor's* appearance, so Reed theoretically would have had ample opportunity
to revise his play. However, it is possible that Foote risked the
accusation of plagiarism and presented this farce because he had
to repay a financial debt. Reed might have felt the necessity to
keep quiet all this time to insure the eventual production of his
farce. Because of these doubts, I suspect that Foote did appropriate
the character of Snarewell from Reed. Reed's charge, after all,
would bring him no profit, nor would an accusation of this kind
really discredit Foote.

When the summer came, Foote tried to rent the Haymarket but found that it had already been leased. Foote then, perhaps jokingly, complained to Murphy that a trained dog act had preceded him to the Lord Chamberlain's office and proposed that Murphy join him in a partnership to lease Drury Lane from Garrick and Lacey for the summer.[46] Although there is no record of any dog act at the Haymarket that summer, Foote may have been referring sarcastically to the Italian burlettas that did play there. Murphy, who had been burned once by Foote, probably agreed to the proposal because he wanted to further the career of Ann Elliot, a young actress he had met earlier in the year.[47] According to Murphy's account, the terms were simple; they were to produce three new pieces each.[48]

When Garrick was approached, he agreed to rent the theatre for one fifth of their profits on the conditions that there would be no other co-manager but Foote and that Drury Lane would have the option of producing any new plays that Murphy staged that summer.[49] Murphy agreed to these moderate demands and opened the season on June 15 with *All in the Wrong*, a five-act comedy with a prologue written and recited by Foote. Although Murphy had supplied a sparkling comedy and two good farces, *The Citizen* and *The Old Maid*, the season was not successful, especially for Murphy, who might have made far more money had he released his new pieces in the winter. Dunbar states that the bad season was due to too large a theatre, that few theatregoers remained in town, and that theatrical competition was offered at Vauxhall, Ranelagh, and Sadler's Wells.[50] This was all true; but Foote, though playing in a smaller house, made considerable profits playing summer theatre in London for the next fifteen years. Perhaps the winter house did make some difference, for in addition to its unneeded size, it made theatregoing seem too much like a continuation of the regular season, and perhaps the patrons wanted a change. At any rate, Drury Lane played only about half of the forty-eight nights it was rented, and it closed for the summer on August 8. The disappointed co-managers each netted only a little over £300 for the venture.[51]

When the season was over, Murphy complained because Foote had not contributed three new plays to their venture as he had done; in fact, Foote's only written contribution was the prologue to *All in the Wrong*. And though Murphy good-naturedly stated, "Of what use was it to be angry with him, when within five minutes, he would have laughed me into a good humor: no, I could never be angry with Foote;"[52] it still seems that Murphy did not actually tell the truth about their agreement. Despite Foote's undoubted ability to charm Murphy, it is very unlikely that he would not have shown some anger at Foote's failure to fulfill his part of their agreement. Furthermore, Murphy had his three plays ready before the summer project began, and it would have been a simple matter, since he had good reason to mistrust Foote, to see at that time what plays Foote actually had in hand. Did he suppose that Foote, though acting in the plays and directing a raw company, would be able to quickly scribble three new pieces in as many weeks?

Foote was preparing one three-act comedy, *The Liar*, for the later weeks of the summer production, but his plans were forestalled by the necessity of putting on Richard Bentley's play *The Wishes; or, Harlequin's Mouth Opened*, by royal command.[53] The play did badly; though part of the blame, by Walpole's account, can be attributed directly to inexperience and lack of talent on the part of the acting company they had so hastily recruited.[54]

After this unsatisfactory summer, Foote made arrangements with Rich to produce his new play, *The Liar*, at Covent Garden in the fall. He made what seems to have been his usual transaction of taking one fourth of the receipts over £60 for acting in his own pieces, in addition to a benefit.[55] Foote's new play came out rather late in the season, January 12, and it is likely that Rich's death on November 26 delayed production. The new manager was John Beard, who, as a son-in-law of Rich, shared in the patent rights as well.

The Liar, was written as a three-act comedy, though it was later played as an afterpiece. Young Wilding is the lying hero of the piece. Just come from Oxford, he has decided to plunge himself into the delights of London without his father's knowledge. Seeking the advice of Papillon, his French servant, on how to best conquer London, he finds out that his valet is really an

Englishman who has been forced to disguise himself as a Frenchman in order to find decent employment among his style-conscious
countrymen. Papillon, despite his new-found loquaciousness, is
of little use to Wilding, for he cannot hope to even keep up with
his master's outrageous lies and schemes. Wilding continues to
lie himself into incredible complications and is finally taught a
lesson when his father and friends pretend to take his lies seriously.

Foote claimed in his prologue to have based his plot on a
play by Lope de Vega. Belden, however, points out that Foote is
mistaken. Corneille's *Menteur* is the immediate source for *The
Liar,* and because Corneille mistakenly ascribed his debt to de
Vega, Foote also thought he could point to the original source.
The real source of Corneille's play is *la Verdad Sospechosa* by
Don Juan de Alarçon. Steele's *Lying Lover* was an earlier adaptation of Corneille's play, but Foote used little of Steele's play,
for "all the main elements of plot and character that originate
with Steele are omitted by him." [56] Belden also suggests the possibility that since Foote was working on an edition of transla-
tions of French comedy,[57] he was probably familiar not only with
Corneille's *Menteur* but with an anonymous translation of the
play as well: *Mistaken Beauty, or the Lyar, a Comedy acted by
their Majesties Servants at the Royal Theatre, London, 1685.*[58]

The Liar, the least representative of Foote's plays, was poorly
received at Covent Garden when Foote acted the leading role,
but it had an extremely successful stage history when Foote was
not in the play. John Palmer, a young and graceful actor, took
over the role and acted it for many years at Drury Lane and at
the Haymarket. According to Cooke, Foote, "from a clumsiness
of person, and an exuberance of *grotesque,* failed in giving that
easy, familiar, unabashed manner, which so happily distinguished
the late John Palmer."[59] Uncharacteristically, the play contained
very few topical allusions, which probably accounts for its successful revival in 1879 when it played at the Olympic Theatre
for more than one hundred nights.[60] Although the gentility of
the play shielded Foote from the adverse criticism he received
when caricaturing Apreece, Whitefield, Douglas, Langford, Wilkinson, *et al.,* the play brought Foote little money since its long
history of performances depended on the author's absence from

the stage. Financially, Foote was not encouraged to use *The Liar* as a model for future writing.

Perhaps in reaction to the blandness of *The Liar,* Foote's next play, *The Orators,* reveled in topical satire, caricature, and formlessness. Indeed, it was no play, but an exhibition on the topics of the day. But these supposed handicaps drew partons in such numbers to the Haymarket that Foote was encouraged to give thirty-eight performances of *The Orators* out of the fifty-nine he gave during the season.[61]

The Orators as printed consists of three acts: a long exordium on oratory; a mock trial of the Cock-Lane ghost; and a satire on the Robin Hood Society, an amateur debating club. The device that provides some sense of unity to these unrelated scenes is cleverly introduced when the play opens. Two young dandies enter a side-box, arguing loudly whether it is worth their time to stay and listen to a dreary discourse on oratory. However, on finding their whores in the audience, they halloo to them across the theatre and ask the candle-snuffer what is to be shown on stage. The snuffer refuses to divulge stage secrets, so they insist on seeing the proprietor, Foote himself. Foote enters and assures them that they will see enough to divert them. But from the opposite box, one Ephriam Suds, a soap-boiler, wants a guarantee that he will learn to give speeches. Foote assures him that he too will get what he came for. Through this exchange it is learned that Foote heads a school of oratory so proficient that even the most burr-tongued Scotsman can learn to speak brilliantly on any topic. After Foote's opening lecture on the principles of the art, he will allow his students to practice what they have learned in various contrived situations. This framework not only provides unity but, like the prologue in *The Minor,* provides an excuse for poor performances; in one situation the actors are rehearsing, and in the other they are merely beginning students. This device was obviously necessary, for the inadequacy of the actors was long remembered, especially by Charles Lewes: "There are numbers living who remember the orators produced by Aristophanes in 1762, when he collected a company who would have been rejected by Old Noll, Carr, or his rival Linnet." [62]

Foote originally advertised his production as a *Course of*

Comic Lectures on English Oratory and added the following descriptive comments:

> 1. Oratory in general. 2. Its Utility demonstrated from its Universality. 3. Destinct species of Oratory. 4. The present practice of Oratory peculiar to the English. 5. Necessity of an Academy for the Promulgation and Inculcation of modern Oratory. 6. The Propriety of appointing the Author perpetual Professor. The whole to be illustrated in apt Instances by a Set of Pupils long trained in the Art, one of which is an amazing Proof of the Force of Genius when properly cultivated.[63]

As might be guessed, these formal strictures, reminiscent of Foote's burlesque of Macklin, were satiric, but the satire this time was aimed at Thomas Sheridan. Sheridan had been forced out of Smock Alley by opposition from Barry and Woodward, and on coming to London he played with Garrick at Drury Lane. Their rivalry grew too great when Sheridan was preferred to Garrick by George III in a command performance of Shakespeare's *King John* on December 23, 1760, and Sheridan was forced to leave.[64] Though a popular player, Sheridan always seemed more interested in elocution than acting, and in May, 1761, he began to give three courses of lectures on oratory, the final one beginning in March, 1762 at Pewterers' Hall. These courses consisted of eight lectures given four times a week, and they began at noon.[65]

Foote's lectures also began at noon, April 28, in imitation of Sheridan, but on May 4 they moved to the more convenient hour of one o'clock, and by June 21, when the patent theatres had closed for the season, Foote began evening performances. Of course, Foote imitated Sheridan in more ways than the use of the same hour of performance. Besides mimicking his voice and mannerisms, he burlesqued Sheridan's complex and pompous theory of elocution in the long-winded and boring exordium. Foote using Swiftian-like satire, acts the part of a projector, offering with a straight face ridiculous proposals to benefit England, but it is almost impossible to follow Foote's disjointed ideas. In this act all the humor is lost without the mimicry.

The second act, which mocks the incidents surrounding the Cock-Lane ghost affair, is much more lively. The history of this affair is too complex to render in its entirety here, but by January, 1762, all of London knew that the ghost of Fanny Lynes, through the medium of an eleven-year-old girl, had accused her brother-in-law of poisoning her. This information was transmitted by mysterious, ghostly knocks, one meaning "yes," and two, "no." Since the life, or at least the reputation, of the accused was at stake, Sir Samuel Floodyer, Lord Mayor of London, arranged to appoint a committee to determine whether the ghost actually existed. Johnson, as spokesman for the committee, described the investigations and concluded: "It is therefore, the opinion of the whole assembly, that the child has some art of making or counterfeiting a particular noise, and that there is no agency of any higher cause." [66]

In Foote's play, since his students merely imitated a court of law to practice their oratorical skills, it was appropriate that an imaginary being, Fanny Phantom, be put on trial. Foote continued his satire on Methodism by having as witness for the prosecution an ex-tailor turned Methodist preacher who insisted he had been visited by the spirit. Further investigation proved this spirit to be more concerned with lustful propagation than with scratching and knocking. For rebuttal, Peter Paragraph, a witness for the defense, was called, and Foote appeared, hopping on one leg in imitation of George Faulkner, the one-legged Dublin printer:

> Paragraph: . . . Last week I went to visit a *peer,* for I know *peers,* and *peers* know me. Quoth his lordship to me, Mr. Paragraph, with respect to your Journal, I would wish that your paper was whiter, or your ink blacker. Quoth I to the peer, by way of *reply,* I hope you will own there is enough for the money; his lordship was pleased to laugh. It was such a pretty repartee, he, he, he, he—

> Justice: Pray, Mr. Paragraph, what might be your business in England?
>
> Para.: Hem—a little love affair, please your worship.
>
> Counsellor: A wife, I suppose—
>
> Para.: Something tending that way; even so long ago as January 1739-40, there past some amorous glances between us: she is the daughter of old Vamp of the Turnstile; but at that time I stifled my passion, Mrs. Paragraph being then in the land of the living.
>
> Coun.: She is now dead?
>
> Para.: Three years and three quarters, please your worship: we were exceeding happy together; she was, indeed, a little apt to be jealous.
>
> Coun.: No wonder—
>
> Para.: Yes: they can't help it, poor souls; but, notwithstanding, at her death, I gave her a prodigious good character in my Journal.[67]

Though the caricature was ludicrous, many who knew Faulkner maintained that even Foote could not do real justice to this vain and eccentric individual.

The third act originally included another exordium by Foote, a satire on stage oratory. Foote used the incident of the Gunpowder-Plot to ridicule the taste for Greek tragedy and chorus.[68] Though this lecture has never been printed, a contemporary reports the following plot of a play Foote was thinking of writing:

> His plan was as follows:—He was to introduce but one personage, who was to be a mock despotic monarch, attended by a chorus of tinkers, tailors, blacksmiths, musicians, bakers, &c. This character was to strut about the stage, boast of the unlimited extent of his Imperial power, threaten all with fire and sword, take the city of London, storm the Tower, and even threaten to dethrone the sovereign himself.
>
> The chorus, terrified at these exploits and menaces,

were then to fall upon their knees, tear their hair, beat their breasts, and supplicate his Imperial Highness to spare the effusion of so much human blood; to which, after a conflict of contending passions during the course of five acts, the hero was to agree, and the piece was then to conclude with a full hymn of thanksgiving for the deliverance of so many individuals.[69]

He then completed this act by imitating a lawyer who had been prominent in the Elizabeth Canning case.[70] By May 18, Foote incorporated a new third act into the play which was later included in the printed edition. This new act ostensibly satirizes the Robin Hood Society,[71] a famous debating club.[72] The members debate in ironic legal fashion the virtues of Irish whiskey, and the language and procedure are a burlesque of any lawmaking body, especially an English or an Irish parliament.

It was received well by most critics, but *The Monthly Review,* perhaps retaliating against Foote for his sarcastic remarks in *The Liar,* chose to ironically praise Foote's acting in the play and pedantically squash it as literature:

> The success attending Mr. Sheridan's late public lectures on Oratory has furnished this arch-droll, this eminent Professor of Mimicry, with a fine opportunity for raising a summer's contribution on the Public; no unusual expedient with Mr. Foote, who has made many a lucky campaign of this kind. . . . It may be doing Mr. Foote, therefore a friendly office, perhaps, to acquaint him that he is by no means qualified to shine in print. To accommodate wit, spirit or humor, to the model of literary composition, requires the genius and understanding of a MAN. The shining talents of the present writer resemble those of an animal of an inferior species; so that, placing his admiring audience in a rank of beings something

higher than himself, we may make a little variation in the words of The Poet, and transfer their application with propriety from a Newton to a Foote:

Superior Beings, when of late they saw
A wag *take off* the Senate and the Law,
Admir'd such antick Pow'rs in human shape
And praised a Foote as one would praise an ape.[73]

But no single reviewer, no matter how hostile, could keep Foote from the enthusiastic recognition of the public. His witticisms and embroilments were part of London's daily gossip, and his scoffing, whimsical, extravagant, and mimical self on stage confirmed to the audience everything they had heard about the man. On stage and off, as licensed jester he could do and say things that no one else would dare. But though Foote's followers would forgive him lapses that if made by others might cause riots, they would not pay to see him do mere comedy, no matter how finely written and acted. They came to see Foote; if they wanted traditional stage fare, Garrick, Barry, Quin, and others were easily available. The great financial success of *The Minor* and *The Orators* and the poor reception given *The Liar* reinforced knowledge Foote already had. He also knew, particularly since *The Minor*, that no matter how popular a play of his might be with a Garrick at Drury Lane, no matter how well presented and acted, yet he could realize far more money by putting on the piece himself at the Haymarket, even with an inexperienced company. From this time on Foote made sure that no dog act or burletta could lease the Haymarket for the summer months. During that time, the theatre was his and remained so until he retired from the stage.

NOTES

1. Boswell, *Life*, Vol. II, p. 155, n. 2.
2. *Ibid.*, Vol. II, p. 299.
3. Cooke, *Table-Talk*, p. 145.
4. *DNB;* and *Letters of Laurence Sterne*, ed. Lewis P. Curtis (Oxford, 1935), p. 260.
5. *The Whitefoord Papers*, ed. W. A. S. Hewins (Oxford, 1898), p. 229.
6. *Letters of Laurence Sterne*, p. 261, n. 4.
7. Murphy's letter to Garrick dated May 13, 1760, cited by Boaden, Vol. I, pp. 116-127.
8. Wilkinson, Vol. II, pp. 212-213.
9. *Ibid.*, p. 218; and Cooke, *Foote*, Vol. II, pp. 68-69.
10. Wilkinson, Vol. II, p. 184.
11. Foote, *The Dramatic Works*, Vol. II, p. 15.
12. She appears in three of Hogarth's prints: *Enthusiasm Delineated, Industry and Idleness* (Plate XI, "The March to Tyburn"), and The *March to Finchley*.
13. Foote, *The Dramatic Works*, Vol. II, 23-24.
14. *Ibid.*, p. 55.
15. Stone, *London Stage*, Vol. II, pp. 755 ff.
16. Wilkinson, Vol. II, p. 184.
17. Belden, p. 85.
18. Ms letter from Foote to Garrick in Murphy's extra illustrated *Life of David Garrick*, p. 360, at The Folger Shakespeare Library.
19. A "Rev. Mr. M..d..n" is given credit for this pamphlet in a footnote in Foote's *Apology for The Minor. In a letter to the Rev. Mr. Baine* (Edinburgh, 1771). See Belden, p. 86 and n. 8.
20. *A Letter from Mr. Foote, To the Reverend Author of the Remarks Critical and Christian on The Minor* (London, 1760).
21. Cited by Belden, p. 90. The author does not otherwise identify the issue.
22. Rev. Luke Tyerman, *The Life of the Rev. George Whitefield* (London, 1877), Vol. II, p. 423.
23. Umphrey Lee, *The Historical Backgrounds of Early Methodist Enthusiasm* (New York, 1931), p. 107.
24. *Ibid.*, p. 116.
25. Anon., *The Life and Times of the Countess of Huntington* (London, 1801), Vol. I, p. 209.
26. Belden, p. 92.
27. Walpole, Vol. IX, pp. 326-327.
28. Boaden, Vol. I, p. 120.
29. Belden, p. 92.
30. Joseph Byrnes, "Four Plays of Samuel Foote," unpublished Ph.D. dissertation (New York University, 1963), Vol. I, p. 156.

31. Wilkinson, Vol. III, pp. 19-20.
32. *Ibid.*, p. 24.
33. *Ibid.*, p. 26.
34. Lloyd had a disparaging portrayal of Foote in *The Actor:*

> But let the generous actor still forbear
> To copy features with a mimic's care!
> 'Tis a poor skill which ev'ry fool can reach,
> A vile stage custom honour'd in the breach.
> Worse as more close, the disingenuous art
> But shows the wanton looseness of the heart.
> When I behold a wretch of talents mean,
> Drag private foible on the public scene,
> Forsaking Nature's fair and open road
> To mark some whim, some strange peculiar mode,
> Fir'd with disgust I loath his servile plan
> Despise the mimic, and abhor the man.
> Go to the lame, to hospitals repair,
> And hunt for humour in distortions there!
> Fill up the measure of the motley whim
> With shrug, wink, snuffle, and convulsive limb,
> Then shame at once, to please a trifling age,
> Good sense, good manners, virtue, and the stage!

(*The Works of the English Poets,* ed. A. Chalmers, Vol. XV [London, 1810], p. 77.)
35. Dunbar, pp. 106-121.
36. See Murphy's satires on this incident, *An Ode to the Naiads of Fleet Ditch* (London, 1761) and *The Examiner* (London, 1761).
37. *Poetical Works of Charles Churchill,* ed. Douglas Grant (Oxford, 1956), p. 14.
38. Anon., *The Scrubs of Parnassus: or All in the Wrong* (London, 1761), p. 26.
39. The manuscript is in the Larpent Collection at the Huntington Library. See Dougald MacMillan, ed. *Catalogue of the Larpent Plays in the Huntington Library* (San Marino, California, 1939), p. 34, item 194.
40. The purpose of Foote's satire was discovered by Edward H. Weatherly, "Foote's Revenge on Churchill and Lloyd," *HLQ,* IX (1945), 49-60.
41. MS of *Modern Tragedy* (p. 1).
42. Genest, Vol. IV, p. 600.
43. Stone, *London Stage,* Vol. II, p. 854.
44. Byrnes, "Four Plays of Samuel Foote," Vol. I, p. 139.
45. Belden, pp. 185-186, demonstrates the similarity between Mother Cole and Mrs. Snarewell. Both bawds, though converted by Whitefield, still pursue their business with as much enthusiasm as they mouth the pieties of their religion. Many of their speeches are undeniably similar.
46. Murphy, Vol. I, p. 360.
47. Dunbar, p. 123.

48. Foot, pp. 173-174.
49. *Ibid.*
50. Dunbar, p. 124.
51. Murphy, Vol. I, p. 361.
52. Foot, p. 173.
53. *Biographica Dramatica*, Vol. II, p. 402.
54. Walpole, Vol. IX, pp. 372-373, 381-383.
55. Stone, *London Stage*, Vol. II, p. 902.
56. Belden, pp. 188-189; and see Genest, Vol. IV, pp. 649-650.
57. Foote's edition was *The Comic Theatre, Being a Free Translation of all the Best French Comedies. By Samuel Foote, Esq. and Others.* Foote was supposed to have translated the first play only, *The Young Hypocrite* (*CBEL*, II, 450). Though finally published in five volumes, the edition originally advertised in *The St. James Chronicle*, May 1-4, 1762, that on completion of the first volume eleven additional volumes would be published.
58. Belden, p. 188.
59. Cooke, *Foote*, Vol. I, p. 119.
60. H. B. Baker, *English Actors from Shakespeare to Macready* (New York, 1879), Vol. I, p. 244. See Belden, pp. 108-109.
61. Stone, *London Stage*, Vol. II, pp. 933 ff.
62. *Memoirs of Charles Lee Lewes* (London, 1805), Vol. I, p. 183.
63. *Public Advertiser*, April 30, 1762; also cited by Belden, p. 110, and Stone, *London Stage*, Vol. II, p. 934.
64. Davies, Vol. I, pp. 293-302.
65. Douglas Grant, pp. 489-490.
66. Boswell, *Life*, Vol. I, p. 407, n. 3.
67. Foote, *The Dramatic Works*, Vol. II, 173-174.
68. Belden, p. 114, and other commentators seem to think that the printed version of the play represents the original three-act production, except for minor changes. *Exshaw's Magazine*, May, 1762, pp. 298-299, contains a description of this production which clarifies this point.
69. Cooke, *Foote*, Vol. III, p. 47.
70. This interesting case electrified all England in 1753. Elizabeth Canning, a servant girl, returned home in disarray after having been away for four weeks. She claimed to have been abducted by a Mother Wells to a bawdy house and to have been robbed by Mary Squires, a gypsy. Though much of the girl's story was contradictory, Wells was imprisoned and branded, and Squires was sentenced to death. After the branding, but before the death penalty could be carried out, further inquiries completely discredited the girl. She was then tried for perjury in 1754, found guilty, and sentenced to seven years' transportation. The country was divided between the Canningites who believed the girl's tale and the Egyptians who believed in Squire's innocence. Foote made merry with this trial when it was news and revived it because public interest in the case renewed with the unfounded rumor that Canning had returned to England to collect a legacy of £300. A full account of

this case appears in *Villainy Detected,* ed. Lillian de la Torre (New York, 947), pp. 112-131.

71. This part was given a separate and favorable review in *The St. James's Chronicle,* June 1-3, 1762, under the heading "An Additional Act—The Robin Hood Society."

72. See Peter Pounce [pseud. of Richard Lewis], *The Robin Hood Society: A Satire with Notes Variorum* (London, 1756); and *The History of the Robin Hood Society,* Anon., (London, 1764).

73. *Monthly Review,* June, 1762, pp. 475-476. The quatrain is a parody taken from Pope's *Essay on Man:*

> Superior beings, when of late they saw
> A mortal Man unfold all Nature's law,
> Admir'd such wisdom in an earthly shape,
> And shew'd a NEWTON as we shew an Ape.

Chapter VII

DEPEDITATION, 1762-1766

When Foote's lucrative summer season ended, he did not take his usual European vacation. Instead, he left for Dublin in the fall, probably taking some of his key performers with him. It undoubtedly took more bravado than prudence to beard Faulkner so close to home, but Foote seemed confident in his charmed life. Foote's judgment might have been proved sound if Faulkner had not been moved by his friend Lord Chesterfield to take action against him. Chesterfield saw *The Orators* that summer and could not resist telling his friend how he should resent the insult:

> London, 1 July 1762
>
> . . . Would you think it? Mr. Foote, who, if I mistake not, was one of your *Symposion* while you were in London, and if so the worse man he, takes you off, as it is vulgarly called, that is, acts you in his new farce, called *The Orators*. As the government here cannot properly take notice of it, would it be amiss that you should show some spirit upon this occasion, either by way of stricture, contempt, or by bringing an action against him? I do not mean for writing the said farce, but for acting it. . . . Any orders that you shall think fit to send me in this affair, as to retaining counsel, filing a bill of Faulkner *versus* Foote, or bringing

a common action upon the case, which I should think
would be the best of all, the case itself being actionable
shall be punctually executed by
                    Your faithful friend and servant.[1]

Though the tone of the letter is bantering, Chesterfield
obviously knew his man, for Faulkner did sue Foote for libel at
the end of the year and won damages of £300. This was more
than Foote would or could pay, so he jumped bail and took the
next ship back to England.[2] Obviously delighted that his joke
took root, Chesterfield wrote Faulkner an offensively effusive
letter which no man of even the dimmest intelligence would have
taken at face value—except, perhaps, George Faulker:

                              London, 4 January 1763
        Many thanks to you for your letter, many thanks to
    you for your almanac, and more thanks to you for your
    friend Swift's works; in which last, you have outdone your
    usual outdoings—for the paper is whit-ish, and the ink
    is black-ish.[3] I only wish that the margin had been a little
    broader. However, without flattery, it beats Elzevir, Aldus,
    Vascosan; and I make no doubt but that, in seven or eight
    hundred years, the learned and the curious in those times
    will, like the learned and the curious in these, who prefer
    the impression of a book to the matter of it, collect with
    pains and expense all the books that were published ex
    Typographia Faulkneriana. But I am impatient to con-
    gratulate you upon your late triumph; you have made (if
    you will forgive a quibble upon so serious a subject) your
    enemy your Foot-stool—a victory which the divine Socrates
    had not influence enough to obtain at Athens over Aris-
    tophanes; nor the great Pompey at Rome, over the actor
    who had the insolence to abuse him . . . A man of less
    philosophy than yourself would perhaps have chastised
    Mr. Foote corporally, and made him feel that your wooden
    leg which he mimicked had an avenging arm to protect

it; but you scorned so inglorious a victory, and called justice and the laws of your country to punish the criminal, and to avenge your cause. You triumphed; and I heartily join my weak voice to the loud acclamations of the good citizens of Dublin upon this occasion.

I take it for granted that some of your many tributary wits have already presented you with gratulatory poems, odes, etc., upon this subject. I own I had some thoughts myself of inscribing a short poem to you upon your triumph, but, to tell you the truth, when I had writ not above two thousand verses to it, my Muse forsook me, my poetic vein stopped, I threw away my pen, and I burned my poem, to the irreparable loss, not only of the present age, but also of latest posterity.[4]

Later, the sarcastic peer wrote to the Bishop of Waterford about the incident, but he played another tune:

I rejoice at my friend George Faulkner's triumph, who made his enemy his Foot-stool. Perhaps he was a little too irascible, and did not agree with Lord Shaftesbury in thinking that ridicule, when groundless, only exposed the author of it, and I would rather have expected a noble contempt, than a legal process, from my philosophical friend. Socrates never prosecuted Aristophanes for having attempted to ridicule him.[5]

When Foote began his summer campaign at the Haymarket in the summer of 1763, he retaliated against Faulkner and the Irish judges who found him guilty of libel by adding an epilogue to *The Orators: The Trial of Samuel Foote, esq. for a Libel on Peter Paragraph*.[6] Foote advertised the performance for May 11:

Will be revived a Course of Lectures on English Oratory,

by Mr. Foote: On which Occasion, together with several
new Subjects, will be produced two Specimens of Bar
Oratory: First the Trial of Fanny Phantom, for Scratching
and Fluttering. The other, of Mr. Foote for Libeling
Peter Paragraph, lately imported from another Kingdom.
To begin at one o'clock.[7]

Foote not only burlesqued the court but continued to expose
Faulkner, finding him guilty of printing and selling *The Orators*
and of libeling himself.[8] Foote also added *An Address to the
Public* which described a suit for libel by one Peter Petros against
Aristophanes.[9] This historical parallel, which was used by Foote's
counsel in arguing precedence for Foote's caricatures of real
people, was widely reported and gained Foote the honor of being
known as the English Aristophanes.

Foote had difficulties in beginning the evening performances
which opened his regular season. His matinee performances,
given from May 11 to June 3, consisted of parts taken from
The Orators and were comparable to *Diversions of the Morning*
in that they both lacked a regular dramatic form and took less
time to give than the evening performances. Foote advertised
that his evening performances would start in early June by
permission of the Lord Chamberlain, but he did not begin them
until June 20.[10] Despite his earlier successes in avoiding the
consequences of the Licensing Act, in matters of regular evening
drama he was dependent upon the Lord Chamberlain, who was
responsive to complaints made by the managers of the patent
theatres in relation to their monopoly. It is likely that his evening
performances were delayed because Foote had to wait for Garrick
and Rich to finish their seasons.

Foote planned this summer campaign far more carefully
than his previous summer ventures. Though his morning oratorical lectures required only a small group of actors, for his evening
performances he more than doubled the number of actors used
during the preceding summer, raising the number to twenty-nine
and adding seven dancers.[11] He also tried to improve the quality
of the acting by sending one member of his troupe, Mr. Kennedy,

to Norwich to see Wilkinson, calm his ruffled feathers, and hire him for the summer. After all, Foote could find no other actor who was so enthusiastic a performer of his plays. In addition, "Foote said he was convinced one person perpetually before the audience, be he ever so excellent and meritorious, had not so great an advantage as by a little space ere he was seen again." [12] Foote assured Wilkinson of the best treatment, and Wilkinson gloatingly told of the terms: "He would be glad to see me not only as an actor but as his particular friend; that his house and table should always be at my service, if I would do him the favor to make it my home whenever not better engaged.—This was a change! and it was flattering, profitable, and reputable." [13] Foote wanted Wilkinson primarily for a revival of *The Minor* so that they could split the original fourfold role and have Wilkinson play Shift, a takeoff of himself, and Squintum and Foote play Mother Cole and Smirk. Foote had also written a new farce, and to accommodate Wilkinson's talent for mimicry he had written in a role for him that was not an integral part of the play. Foote also asked Wilkinson to re-engage a former actor of his, Thomas Weston, who had played a servant's role in *The Minor* and was now doing poorly as a strolling player in Norwich.[14] Foote must have seen extraordinary powers in Weston, for he destined the little actor for one of the leading roles in his new play.

Foote's new piece was a two-act farce called *The Mayor of Garratt*. Supposedly Foote got his idea for the play by watching the mock elections held in Garret,[15] a tiny town in Surrey. These elections of a mayor for the town probably were originated early in the century by the inhabitants to insure their rights to a common. Eventually the event became ritualized into parody and continued to be perpetrated by the town and surrounding hamlets because the huge throngs of attending Londoners brought in a considerable windfall each election year.[16] When the elections were held in 1761, Foote, Garrick, and Wilkes rented a room for nine guineas to watch the proceedings and to participate in the fun by writing some of the candidates' addresses.[17]

The play begins as the recently knighted Sir Jacob prepares his household for the elections. The apothecary and part-time surgeon, Lint, enters to insist on extra payment for treating the bruises and broken bones that will result from political enthusiasm. Though Lint is not essential to the plot, he gives Foote a chance to hit once more at his favorite target, quacks. Lint defends his high fees by attacking the advertised testimonials of miraculous cures that Sir Jacob reads from the papers to prove that any cheap nostrum can cure:

> Sir Jacob: Formerly, indeed, a fit of illness was very expensive; but now, physic is cheaper than food.
> Lint: Marry, heaven forbid!
> Sir Jac.: No, no; your essences, elixirs, emetics, sweats, drops, and your pastes, and your pills, have silenced your pestles and mortars. Why a fever, that would formerly have cost you a fortune, you may now cure for twelve penn'orth of powder.
> Lint: Or kill, Sir Jacob. . . .
> Sir Jac.: Here, look at the list of their cures.
> The oath of Margery Squab, of Ratcliff-Highway, spinster.
> Lint: Perjuries.
> Sir Jac.: And see here, the churchwardens have signed it.
> Lint: Fictitious, Sir Jacob.
> Sir Jac.: Sworn before the worshipful Mr. Justice Drowsy, this thirteenth day of—
> Lint: Forgery.
> Sir Jac.: Why, hark'ye, sirrah, do you think Mr. Justice Drowsy would set his hand to a forgery?
> Lint: I know, Sir Jacob, that woman; she has been cured of fifty diseases in a fortnight, and every one of 'em mortal.
> Sir Jac.: You impudent—
> Lint: Of a dropsy, by West—
> Sir Jac.: Audacious—
> Lint: A cancer, by Cleland.
> Sir Jac.: Arrogant—

> Lint: A palsy, by Walker—
> Sir Jac.: Impertinent—
> Lint: Gout and sciatica, by Rock.
> Sir Jac.: Insolent—
> Lint: Consumption, by Stevens's drops—
> Sir Jac.: Paltry—
> Lint: And squinting by the Chevalier Taylor—
> Sir Jac.: Pill-gilding puppy!
> Lint: And as to the Justice, so the affidavit brings him
> a shilling—
> Sir Jac.: Why hark'ye, rascal, how dare you abuse
> the commission?—You blood-letting, tooth-drawing, corn-
> cutting, worm-killing, blistering, glistering—[18]

Foote then enters, ridiculously over-accoutred as Major Sturgeon from the Middlesex militia.[19] Part of this portrait is personal.
According to one source, Foote was dunned and arrested for debt
by his fishmonger, one Mr. Lamb, a justice of the peace and a
major in the Middlesex militia.[20] In retaliation, Foote put him
on stage and slyly refers to his real name at one point when the
major insists on the peaceful and amiable qualities of the militia
officer:

> Sir Jacob: Quiet and peaceable.
> Major: As lambs, Sir Jacob.[21]

But Foote's satire on his fishmonger was incidental. The real
satire lay in exposing the country clods who ranked as officers
in the militia and played the game of soldier. The Seven Years'
War with France was just over, and Foote could now voice the
Londoner's view without fear of government censorship or popular reprisal.[22] The major took on the familiar pattern of many
of Foote's rogues when he described his occupational proficiency
and praised the master who had taught him the skill:

Major: . . . We have had some desperate duty, Sir Jacob.

Sir Jacob: No doubt.

Maj.: Oh! such marchings and counter-marchings, from Brentford to Eling, from Eling to Acton, from Acton to Uxbridge; the dust flying, sun scorching, men sweating Why, there was our last expedition to Hounslow, that day's work carried off Major Molossas. Bunhill-fields never saw a braver commander! He was an irreparable loss to the service. . . .

Sir Jac.: But you soon supplied the loss of Molossas?

Maj.: In part only; no, Sir Jacob, he had great experience; he was train'd up to arms from his youth: at sixteen he trailed a pike in the Artillery-ground; at eighteen got a company in the Smithfield pioneers; and by the time he was twenty, was made aid-de-camp to Sir Jeffery Grub, Knight, Alderman, and Colonel of *the Yellow*.

Sir Jac.: A Rapid rise!

Maj.: Yes, he had a genius for war.[23]

In the second act the electioneering for mayor begins, with Peter Primmer and Matthew Mug among the candidates. Primmer, played by Wilkinson, was a take-off on poor Thomas Sheridan again. He proposes to improve Garratt through elocution lessons and, to prove his proficiency, recites all the verses of a popular ballad, "Nancy Dawson." [24] (The part, as mentioned before, was not integral to the play, and, after Wilkinson's performance in it that summer, it was eliminated. The part was omitted when Foote played the farce in the fall at Drury Lane, and it does not exist in any printed edition of the play.[25]) As Matthew Mug, Foote came out on stage again, this time imitating the Duke of Newcastle. Grabbing every constituent by the hand or the head, he pretended to know the name and the family of every voter he met, promising positions as he went. Joseph Cradock met the Duke a year later and was surprised at how little he seemed to be affected by the satire: "It was unaccountable to me that as much as he had been ridiculed by Foote, on the stage, that he could not restrain himself, even in the street, from seizing your head and holding it between his hands, whilst perhaps he would ask the most unmeaning and trifling questions." [26] The other candidates for the office were also satires, in name at least, of the participants in the Garret election held in 1761.[27]

The remaining part of the second act is taken up by Jerry Sneak; his wife, the daughter of Sir Jacob; and the major. Sneak, played by Weston, is henpecked by his wife and cuckolded by the military gallantries of the major. Although Sneak's attempt at courage quickly vanishes, Sneak's brother-in-law, Bruin, momentarily infuses some spirit into the poor wretch:

> Sneak: . . . Since you provoke me, I will tell you a bit of my mind: what, I am the husband, I hope?
> Bruin: That's right: at her again.
> Sneak: Yes; and you sha'n't think to hector and domineer over me as you have done; for I'll go to the club when I please, and stay out as late as I list, and row in a boat to Putney on Sunday, and visit my friends at Vitsontide, and keep the key of the till, and help myself at table to what vittles I like, and I'll have a bit of the brown.[28]

To everybody's surprise, the unknown Weston rivaled Foote's superb performance as the major,[29] and through Jerry Sneak, Weston eventually became known as England's foremost low comedian. Despite Weston's irresponsibility,[30] Foote was astute enough to retain this popular actor (who also played at Drury Lane during the regular season) permanently at the Haymarket and took advantage of his special abilities by writing parts expressly for him.[31]

The Mayor of Garratt was presented on opening night, June 20, 1763, at the Haymarket as afterpiece to *The Minor* and was an immediate hit. It played for twenty-four consecutive performances that summer, thirty-six in all, and went on to become Foote's most popular play, performed a total of 167 times by

1776.[32] Like *The Liar,* it was performed frequently after his death, becoming a favorite in Victorian times.[33] Even today the farce retains much of its humor without the necessity of annotation. No special knowledge is needed to understand the satire leveled against the pseudo-military airs of the militia, and the mock elections held at Garret can easily represent the corrupt state of all elections held in eighteenth-century England. To this quality can be added Foote's usual mastery of low and farcical dialogue, and, uncharacteristically, the play has relatively tight construction. To this reader, at least, it is Foote's best play. It also proved to be one of Foote's most lucrative productions. He cleared enough money that summer to alter his town and country houses and to spend £1200 for a set of plate. Foote defended this last extravagance by saying that "as he knew he could never keep his *gold,* he very prudently laid out his money in *silver,* which would not only last longer, but in the end sell for nearly as much as it originally cost." [34] If, as Cooke says, "his purse was generally the barometer to his spirits," [35] Foote was a happy man as he left for Paris to take his winter vacation.[36]

Foote came back from Europe in time to play Major Sturgeon at the Drury Lane Theatre before the Christmas season. His arrangements were to take two benefits, as author and as actor. He made a profit of £24.7s.6d. as author after charges of £84 were subtracted from the gross receipts of his last performance. Though the figures are not available for December 5, when he played Gomez for his benefit as an actor, Foote probably made about £150 for little more than a week's work.[37] This was the last time Foote played at one of the patent theatres during the regular season, though he continued to perform occasionally at the patent theatres in Scotland and Ireland. Perhaps Foote felt that he would lose as summer patrons those who had seen him at Covent Garden or Drury Lane in the winter, and, of course, Foote took a higher percentage of profit from his Haymarket audience. It also seems probable that Drury Lane made a special effort to have Foote perform, even briefly, because Garrick, the main attraction, had left England for an extended tour of the continent.

Foote planned his summer season of 1764 as carefully as

he had that of the previous year. He hired approximately the same number of actors, and even though Weston was now an established favorite at the Haymarket, he again signed Wilkinson for the summer season.

Foote's new comedy, *The Patron*, was written in three acts and was based upon Marmontel's *Contes Moraux, le Connaisseur*, which Foote acknowledged in his dedication to Earl Gower, the new Lord Chamberlain. *The Patron* is very close to the French model in plot and even in some of the dialogue.[38] Sir Thomas Lofty, a would-be patron of the arts, has written a play on *Robinson Crusoe* which is going to be performed. Too vain to risk his reputation, Sir Thomas is searching for a trustworthy scapegoat to take the blame should the play fail. Richard Bever, in love with Lofty's niece, Juliet, to his bewilderment finds himself the author of the piece as Lofty takes advantage of the young man's reluctance to endanger his situation with Juliet. Juliet is engaged to Rust, an antiquarian who sees in his future bride a proper resemblance to the Cleopatras of the past. Rust's greatest treasure is a recently acquired copy of the *North Britain No. 45* which had just been snatched from the flames to which it had been condemned. The play reaches its happy conclusion with the complete failure of *Robinson Crusoe*. Bever is given his Juliet by Lofty as consolation for his new reputation as exploded poet and as assurance of his silence. Rust, who has overheard this negotiation, threatens the exposure of Lofty unless he gets his promised bride. Bever reminds Rust that since his precious *North Britain* had not suffered the full penalty of the law, it might be burnt again if silence were not kept on all sides. Rust quickly agrees, for there are many girls but only one copy of the scorched *North Britain*.

A number of personal portraits and many references to topical events appear in this play, but not all of them are identifiable. Sir Thomas Lofty was Foote's belated revenge on George Bubb Doddington, Lord Melcombe, who had died in 1762, for commanding him to perform *The Wishes* in 1761. Cumberland, in describing the event, says, "upon the hint of *The Wishes* and the entertainment at La Trappe, where Foote had been a guest, that wicked wit took the measure of his host, and founded the satirical drama of *The Patron*—in short, he feasted, flattered and lampooned." [39] This is only partly true, for Foote opportunistically found that the plot suited the situation and needed little alteration to fit his eminently suitable subject.[40] Foote's other portrait, Sir Peter Pepperpot, a volatile West Indian, though unidentified is probably a personal satire, for he is not necessary to the plot. The role of Rust, the antiquarian, was intended to ridicule the Society of Antiquarians which had recently been established.[41] The characters of Puff, the publisher, and Dactyl, the poetaster, seem to be general portraits, and their quarrel is similar to the falling out of Puff and Carmine in *Taste.*[42]

Of the topical allusions, the most obvious and amusing is the reference to the rescue of the *North Britain No. 45* from the fire by the Wilkites after it had been condemned to be burnt by the common hangman on December 3, 1762.[43] Another allusion, less obvious, seems to refer to Churchill's satires. In this passage Puff, who scorns Dactyl's panegyrics, praises the viciously satiric works that scandalize and sell:

> Panegyric and praise! and what will that do with the public? Why who the devil will give money to be told, that Mr. Such-a-one is a wiser or better man than himself? No, no; 'tis quite and clean out of nature. A good sousing satire now, well powdered with personal pepper, and seasoned with the spirit of party; that demolishes a conspicuous character, and sinks him below our own level; there, there, we are pleased; there we chuckle, and grin, and toss the half-crowns on the counter.[44]

Foote might have intended his dedication to reflect upon Lord Chesterfield's well known rebuff of Johnson. Although the famous letter in which Johnson repudiated Chesterfield as a patron had not yet been printed, Chesterfield was not hesitant to exhibit the letter, and the incident was renowned.[45] Foote, who was to make

slighting references to Chesterfield in *The Cozeners,* had probably
heard of Chesterfield's letters to Faulkner:

> In humble hopes, then, my Lord, of not being thought
> the meanest in the Muses' train, I have taken the liberty
> to prefix your name to this dedication, and publicly to
> acknowledge my obligations to your Lordship; which, let
> me boast too, I had had the happiness to receive, un-
> tainted by the insolence of domestics, the delays of office,
> or the chilling superiority of rank; mortifications which
> have been too often experienced by much greater writers
> than myself, from much less men than your Lordship.[46]

Though *The Patron* was played seventeen times that season,
it was not received with those "bursts of applause" that had been
freely given to his more popular works.[47] Despite this lack of
public favor, Foote professed to have been pleased with its
reception and thought *The Patron* his best play up to this time.[48]
He seemed greatly attracted to satire that uncovered intellectual
fraud in the arts resulting from the incredible vanity of those
pretending to talent and understanding. His preface to *Taste* is
similar to the dedication to *The Patron;* both plays have similar
speeches, scenes, and characters that express this same didactic
purpose. It is possible that *The Patron* has the most successful
mixture of the satirically didactic and the extravagant and absurd,
but the audience recognized Foote's genius in a Major Sturgeon
or a Lady Pentweazle rather than a Thomas Lofty.

Despite the relatively cool reception of the new play, the
season, in general, was a success. Wilkinson took sick and was
unable to work until July 16, but after his recovery his imitations,
which he inserted in every piece he played,[49] still drew large
audiences.[50] Foote also reworked his *Tragedy à la Mode,* using
dumb actors dressed in high tragedy style instead of pasteboard
figures. They assisted Wilkinson in his imitations, probably
through pantomime, and this time the piece was received with

great applause.[51] Perhaps the best indication of financial success
was that Foote did not find it necessary to go on tour after he
closed for the summer.

For the summer season of 1765, Foote retrenched somewhat,
reducing his company from thirty to nineteen, but increasing the
number of performances from forty-three to fifty-three.[52] As an
actor, Foote continued to dominate the Haymarket by appearing
in forty-six mainpieces and twenty-four afterpieces, as compared
to forty-one and thirty-four during the previous season.[53] He
also kept the practice of hiring a popular comedian, and since
Wilkinson was not available, he took on Edward Shuter, an actor
who had risen to considerable prominence since Foote had used
him in *The Knights*.

Foote's new piece for the season was *The Commissary*, a
three-act satirical comedy aimed at the jobbers and army con-
tractors who made immense wealth during the war with France,
and who, with the Treaty of Paris signed in 1763, were now
trying to climb into the ranks of society. Though Foote had
taken hints from Molière's *Le Bourgeois gentilhomme* and Dan-
court's *La Femme d'intrigue* for the characters Zachary Fungus,
commissary, and Mrs. Mechlin, knave of all trades, the play was
his own.[54] Mrs. Mechlin, in one of her roles as matchmaker, is
trying to foist her ruined daughter, Dolly, on Fungus by pretending that the girl's family dates back to Malcom of Scotland.
Fungus, who seeks this match to raise his status, is also taking
lessons in oratory from Mr. Gruel and in poetry from Dr. Catgut,
and lessons in dancing, riding, and fencing from other masters.
Though his honest and simple brother, Isaac, tries to dissuade
him from learning at fifty arts that take many years to master,
Zachary scorns his brother as an ignorant mechanic and continues
to make an ass of himself. But after he proposes to Dolly, he
learns truth about her. He has signed a marriage contract, however, and must marry the wench or pay a large penalty. As Fungus
fumes and squirms, Mrs. Mechlin underlines the moral for the
audience:

And why so, my good master Fungus? Is it because

I have practised that trade by retail which you have carried
on in *the gross?* What injury do I do the world? I feed
on their follies, 'tis true; and the game, the plunder is
fair; but the fangs of you and your tribe,

A whole people have felt, and for ages will feel.
To their candour and justice I make my appeal:
Though a poor humble scourge in a national cause,
As I trust I deserve, I demand your applause.[55]

As usual, Foote seasoned his play with much personal satire.
Zachary Fungus, the would-be gentleman, was a portrait of Peter
Taylor of Portsmouth, a silversmith turned jobber, and Isaac
was his son, Robert Paris Taylor.[56] Dr. Catgut was to represent
Thomas Arne, a well known composer of songs for opera, burletta,
and musical comedy. As he had done to Garrick many years
before in satirizing *Lethe,* Foote found someone who looked
exactly like Arne and dressed him for the role in the composer's
cast-off clothing. Supposedly, on opening night many people
though that Arne himself was playing the part of Catgut. Mr.
Gruel was Thomas Sheridan again, and this time the orator began
action against Foote:

The Orator we hear has already commenced three
actions, one against Mr. Foote, for writing the part; one
against Mr. Shuter, for playing it; and one against Miss
Cheney, for saying something about it in her character
of Mrs. Mechlin. Dr. Catgut shews more stoicism; we are
told, he affects to laugh at the ridicule levelled against
him; though the part is rendered additionally severe by
being placed in the hands of a performer, so excessively
like him in person and manner, that were they both together there would be scarce a possibility of distinguishing
the real Sophia from the counterfeit.[57]

Sheridan, however, apparently dropped his suit, for no more was heard of it.

The piece was very well received, playing a total of twenty-nine times that season. It continued to retain its popularity during Foote's lifetime, and was performed at Covent Garden and the Haymarket 106 times until 1776.[58] The play, striking out in a dozen different directions, was written in Foote's most effective style; if unity was lost, pace, diversity, and invention compensated for that deficiency. The moral, too, would be cheered by every right-thinking Englishman.

The five years following Foote's breakthrough with *The Minor* had been phenomenally successful and productive; his fame and profits were at their peak and were all the sweeter for being hard-earned. His social life continued to prosper as well; in February he visited his aristocratic friends, Lord and Lady Mexborough, at Cannon Park in Hampshire, twelve miles from London. The house, though small and far from elegant, still retained the notoriety of being built on the former estate of the Duke of Chandos. Most people still thought of the place as the model of "Timon's villa," the lavish example of bad taste in Pope's *Epistle to Burlington*. The Delaval brothers were also there, as was the Duke of York, the guest of honor, just back from Europe. According to Cooke, the guests began to tease Foote about his horsemanship and finally got him to boast "that although he generally preferred the luxury of a post-chaise, he could ride as well as most men he ever knew." They then urged him to try the Duke of York's spirited animal. By this time Foote undoubtedly knew he was being baited into an uneven match, but his pride would not let him back out. He no sooner mounted, than the horse threw him heavily to the ground. Foote lay writhing in pain, and it was soon obvious to the quickly sobered party that he had broken his leg.[59] His acting days seemed over.

The Duke of York's own physician and surgeon, William Bromfield, was promptly summoned to attend to the broken bone, and the doctor found that Foote had suffered a compound fracture below his knee. At that time doctors could not set with certainty even a simple fracture, and though Bromfield tried his best to save the leg, in the end he was forced to amputate.[60] Furthermore, it was necessary to make the cut above the knee so that it would be possible for the patient to use a wooden leg.[61] Modern anesthetics were unknown, so that the incredible pain of the operation could be alleviated only by opium and liquor. After the operation, a burst artery continued to endanger Foote's life, and the pain kept him from sleeping unless he took opium. The accident occurred on February 3, and for the next few weeks his friends tried to cheer him in every way, but Foote could barely respond. On the thirteenth, Garrick wrote him a letter declaring his friendship and offering to prove it: "Should you be prevented from persuing any plan for y^r Theatre, I am Wholly at y^r Service, & will labour in y^r vineyard for you, in any Capacity, till you are able to do it, so much better, for yourself." [62] But Foote, when he was allowed to write, rejected the kindly offer:

Feb. 26, 1766

Nothing can be more generous and obliging, nor, I am sure, at the same time would be more beneficial for me, than your offers of assistance for my hovel in the Haymarket; but the stage for me at present is a very distant object, for, notwithstanding all the flattery of appearances, I look upon my hold in life to depend upon a very slender tenure; and besides, admitting the best that can happen, is a mutilated man, a miserable instance of the weakness and frailty of human nature, a proper object to excite those emotions which can only be produced from vacant minds, discharged of every melancholy or pensive taint? [63]

Foote's accident, as his letter to Garrick so clearly reveals, embittered him deeply. After many years of failure or partial success, Foote had finally begun to gain the security of fame and fortune, and, at the moment of attainment, an unlucky accident brought him down. Even if he fully recovered, Foote could feel only diffident about regaining his former status without the use of a leg. Could he ever mock the natural infirmities of an ApReece, a Whitefield, a Faulkner, without having the laugh directed against himself? Even now his enemies were gloating and punning over his "depeditation," [64] with Chesterfield in full cry in his letter to Faulkner:

> I cannot help observing, and with some satisfaction, that Heaven has avenged your cause, as well and still more severely than the courts of temporal justice in Ireland did, having punished your adversary in the part offending. The vulgar saying, that mocking is catching, is verified in his case: you may in your turn mock him, without danger to your adapted leg. [65]

The papers too could not be repressed, and they were filled with various kinds of punning verse that commented on the accident with great glee:

> *On an Unlucky Poet*
> What measure shouldst though ever keep,
> Friend Sam! thy fate is such—
> A Foot too little now you are;
> Before a Foote too much. [66]

> *On a Late Accident*
> Alas for Farce's fav'rite son!
> After poor F——— no more we run,
> The public laugh commanding:
> For tho' his brain's not hurt at all,
> The wicked beast contriv'd his fall
> To spoil his *Understanding*. [67]

———

> The Ass once bold, threw out his heel,
> To make the bed-rid Lion feel;
>   Cowards are ever rash:

And so *you* think, ye scribbling crew,
Now Foote is down, that, valiant, you
Will give him *Dash* for *Dash.*

O let your desperate folly rest,
Approach not with a ribbald jest
Misfortune's sacred bed!
Still you shall live in fear of him;
For tho' the Wit has lost a limb,
He has not lost his head.[68]

This reaction to Foote's painful amputation does not reveal a depraved century, but the public's estimation of Foote. He was a man who played to the gallery and considered everything and everyone fair game. With one leg, he became fair game himself. Even in his critical situation, he was not to be taken seriously as man or actor, and for that response Foote had only himself to blame.

NOTES

1. *The Letters of Philip Dormer Stanhope, 4th Earl of Chesterfield,* ed. Bonamy Dobree (London, 1932), Vol. VI, pp. 2394-2395.
2. *The Universal Museum and Complete Magazine,* March, 1766, p. 128; and this account is also given in *The English Aristophanes,* p. 13. The actual detail of this incident is not clear. Belden, p. 113, states that Foote had his trial deferred and was released on £400 bail. Despite an injunction laid on him in the meantime to prevent any performances of *The Orators,* Foote persisted, even embellishing the satire with a poetical address (printed in *The Public Advertiser,* January 28, 1763). But fearing imprisonment and fine, he jumped bail. Miss Belden. however, also adds that he paid heavy damages to Faulkner. Foote, of course, would not pay damages and jump bail. It is more likely, considering his twenty years' absence from Ireland, that he jumped bail to avoid paying damages. And though, as Belden states, he eventually reimbursed the friends who put up his bail, Faulkner never collected his money.
3. Chesterfield is mocking him with Foote's own joke.
4. *Chesterfield,* Vol. VI, pp. 2464-2465.
5. *Ibid.,* p. 2467.

6. This skit is reprinted in Wilkinson, *The Wandering Patentee*, Vol. IV; and Cooke, *Foote*, Vol. III.

7. Stone, *London Stage*, Vol. II, p. 906.

8. Faulkner was guilty as charged. See Cooke, *Foote*, Vol. III, p. 137.

9. It first appeared in *Gentleman's Magazine*, January, 1763, p. 39.

10. Stone, *London Stage*, Vol. II, p. 998.

11. *Ibid.*, p. 950.

12. Wilkinson, *Memoirs*, Vol. III, p. 133.

13. *Ibid.*, pp. 133-134.

14. Cooke, *Foote*, Vol. I, pp. 126-129.

15. This is the spelling of the town and was so spelled in the first edition of the play. See Byrnes, "Four Plays of Samuel Foote," Vol. II, p. 385; and Belden, p. 115.

16. *The Book of Days*, ed. Robert Chambers (Edinburgh, 1863), Vol. I, pp. 659-664.

17. Forster, p. 441; and Belden, pp. 115-116.

18. Foote, *The Dramatic Works*, Vol. II, pp. 194-195. Foote had satirized Taylor and Rock in his earlier works.

19. Zoffany's painting of Foote in this role is reproduced in Stone, *London Stage*, Vol. III.

20. *The English Aristophanes*, p. 14.

21. Foote, *The Dramatic Works*, Vol. II, p. 198.

22. This was not completely true outside of London, however. In 1765 Wilkinson nearly faced a duel for acting the role in Shrewsbury (Wilkinson, *Memoirs*, Vol. III, pp. 165-170).

23. Foote, *Dramatic Works*, Vol. II, pp. 196-199.

24. Wilkinson, *Memoirs*, Vol. III, p. 153.

25. The manuscript survives, however, in the Larpent Collection, and Joseph Byrnes has included this part in "Four Plays of Samuel Foote," Vol. II, pp. 470-473.

26. Joseph Cradock, *Literary and Miscellaneous Memoirs* (London, 1826-28), Vol. IV, p. 118.

27. See Belden, pp. 117-118; and *Public Advertiser*, November 3, 1769, and May 16, 1770, for further identification of Garret villagers in Foote's play.

28. Foote, *The Dramatic Works*, Vol. II, pp. 232-233.

29. Cooke, *Foote*, Vol. I, p. 130.

30. Weston was a heavy drinker and spendthrift who was frequently in debt. Foote and Garrick would have to bail him out at the last minute so his duns would let him act. Weston's promises to reform were short lived; and on one such occasion, Foote was enraged to see Weston smuggling a bottle of gin to his room. Foote broke the bottle in his anger, but was forced to pay for it when Weston refused to play for a waiting house until he had his money. See the anonymous *Memoirs of that Celebrated and Very Singular Genius, Thomas Weston* (London, 1776), pp. 37-38, 44.

31. Cooke, *Foote*, Vol. I, p. 135.

32. Stone, *London Stage*, Vol. II, p. 1000 and *passim*.

33. Forster, p. 420.

34. Cooke, *Foote,* Vol. I, pp. 124-125.
35. *Ibid.,* p. 124.
36. *The Letters of David Garrick,* Vol. II, p. 430.
37. Stone, *London Stage,* Vol. II, p. 1025.
38. See Belden, p. 119, for a summary of Marmontel's play.
39. Cumberland, pp. 115-116.
40. He had been satirized by Pope in *Epistle to Richard Boyle; Epistle to Arbuthnot;* and *Epilogue to Satires.*
41. Belden, p. 121.
42. Belden, p. 121, thinks that Foote does intend a personal satire in Puff; but she mistakenly ascribes Dactyl's quackery to Puff, and, no doubt, this specific trait led her to think an individual was intended. Dactyl's peculiar combination of poet and quack might be a reference to Dr. John Hill; see Boswell, *Life,* Vol. II, p. 38, n. 2.
43. Belden, p. 121.
44. Foote, *The Dramatic Works,* Vol. II, pp. 255-266.
45. Boswell, *Life,* Vol. I, pp. 264-265.
46. Foote, *The Dramatic Works,* Vol. II, p. 244.
47. Cooke, *Foote,* Vol. I, p. 137. According to Stone, *London Stage,* Vol. II, p. 1063 and p*assim, The Patron* was played only ten more times after this season.
48. Foote, *The Dramatic Works,* Vol. II, pp. 243-244.
49. *The Minor, The Rehearsal, The Apprentice,* and *Tragedy à la Mode.*
50. Wilkinson, *Memoirs,* Vol. III, p. 158, stated that Churchill who had called him "that mere mere mimic's mimic" in *The Rosciad,* was so pleased by his imitations as Bayes the previous summer, that he took back his jibe and admitted the originality of the actor's work.
51. Genest, Vol. V, pp. 60-61.
52. Stone, *London Stage,* Vol. II, p. 1072.
53. The popularity of *The Mayor of Garratt* accounts for the unusual number of afterpieces in 1763.
54. Austin W. Kinne, *Revivals and Importations of French Comedies in England 1749-1800* (New York, 1939), pp. 90-92.
55. Foote, *The Dramatic Works,* Vol. II, p. 358.
56. Belden, pp. 122-123; and Cradock, Vol. IV, p. 119.
57. *Exshaw's Magazine,* June, 1765, p. 323.
58. Stone, *London Stage,* Vol. II, p. 1119 and *passim.*
59. Cooke, Foote, Vol. I, pp. 139-140.
60. *Town and Country Magazine,* November, 1777, p. 598. There are few references which tell which leg was amputated, and contemporary prints of Foote are not consistent in portraying the injury. In *The Memoirs of J. Decastro, Comedian,* ed. R. Humphreys (London, 1824), p. 8, Decastro describes an interview with Foote that took place in 1776, shortly after Weston's death. Foote quoted the newspapers that said "he had lost his right hand (meaning the death of poor Weston) as well as his right leg."
61. *The English Aristophanes,* p. 20; and *Town and Country Magazine,* November, 1777, p. 598.
62. *Letters of David Garrick,* Vol. II, p. 493.

63. Broaden, Vol. I, pp. 221-222.
64. The word was Johnson's coinage. "George [Faulkner] will rejoice at the *depeditation* of Foote," was Johnson's remark when he heard of Foote's accident. (Boswell, *Life,* Vol. V, p. 130.)
65. Chesterfield, Vol. VI, pp. 2737-2738.
66. *London Chronicle,* February 13-15, 1766.
67. *Ibid.*
68. *London Chronicle,* February 18-20, 1766. This verse was written by Garrick "Upon Some Attempts,/(Weak, as inhuman) to jest upon M[r] Foote's/late Accident." See *Letters of David Garrick,* Vol. II, pp. 500, 501, n. 4.

Mr. Foote in the character of Doctor Squintum. Courtesy of the Henry E. Huntington Library and Art Gallery.

Samuel Foote as Major Sturgeon. Haid engraving after print by Zoffany.
Courtesy of The New York Public Library.

The MINOR.

Mʳ. FOOTE *as* **Mʳˢ COLE.**

My thoughts are fix'd upon a better place.
What, I suppose Mʳ. Loader, you will be
for your old Friend the black-ey'd Girl, &c.

Act I.

Dodd delin.   W. Walker sc.

Publish'd 26 July 1777, by T. Lowndes & Partners.

Mr. Foote as Mrs. Cole, in *The Minor*. Courtesy of the Victoria and Albert Museum, London.

J.Roberts del.   Publish'd for Bells British Theatre June 4th 1776.   Thornthwaite S.

Mr FOOTE in the Character of FONDLEWIFE.

Speak I say, have you consider'd what it is

to Cuckold your Husband?

Mr. Foote as Fondlewife, in *Old Batchelor*. Courtesy of the Victoria and Albert Museum, London.

Mr. Foote and Mr. Weston in the characters of The President and Dr. Last. Engraving by Finlayson after a painting by Zoffany. Courtesy of the Henry E. Huntington Library and Art Gallery.

Mr. FOOTE in the Character of the DEVIL
upon two Sticks. Act I.
Printed for J. Smith Nº 35 Cheapside & R. Sayer Nº 53 Fleet Street Oct. 1. 1768.

Samuel Foote as the Devil *in The Devil Upon Two Sticks*. Courtesy of the Victoria Art Gallery and Municipal Libraries, Bath.

CHAPTER VIII

ROYAL ATONEMENT: A PATENT FOR
THE HAYMARKET, 1766-1769

Foote began to improve after his last letter to Garrick, and his next letter to the actor revealed that despite the pain he had regained his sense of humor:

> March 2, 1766
>
> Before I had the favour of yours I had discovered the Blunder with regard to My Letter [to Holland] it is transmitted to you by this Post. Davies' Letter was a noble present indeed, pray can you conceive what he means by the necessity he now supposes me under of growing speedily rich. If one could suspect so grave sententious and respectable a Character of the Vice of Punning I should imagine his insinuation to be that now I have but one leg it wont be so easy for me to run out, but here perhaps like Warburton on Shakespeare I have found out a meaning the Author never had. . . .
>
> I won't tell you what my Wishes are upon this Occasion nor indeed anybody here, for ever since I have been ill they have refus'd me every one thing that I have Lik'd. I thank you for your Comedy [Clandestine Marriage] Lady Stanhope has seen it and is Charmed, but I am determined not to look at a line, till I am quite out of Pain.

You will have this Letter by Capt. Millbank who is call'd to Town by an Appointment in Pye's Squadron for the West Indies. I think I am something better than when I wrote you my last tho I have not been free from Pain one minute since my Cruel Misfortune, nor slept a Wink without the Assistance of Laudanum. The People below expect to see you on Wednesday—you must allow for and indeed allmost decypher my Letters, but then consider My Dear Sir thirty days upon my Back: &c., &c., &c. I assure you it is with great difficulty, and many shifts, I am obliged to make to be able to scribble at all. Little Derrick will give the Etiquet of the Bath, and be exceedingly useful. I am quite exhausted, God Bless you Sir [1]

His condition continued to improve, and Foote soon changed his mind about the propriety of a mutilated man inducing an audience to laughter. When the Duke of York visited him two weeks later, Foote took the courage to ask for what probably had been in his mind for years: the patent right to the Haymarket Theatre. The Duke, feeling partly responsible for Foote's condition, agreed to do all that he could. Foote describes this situation in a letter to John Delaval dated March 19:

I suppose you know that the Duke of York has been here these three days, you likewise know with what singular humanity and generosity he behaved at the time of my dreadful calamity, he warmly expressed a desire of securing me from the only additional distress that now befalls me, poverty. I took the liberty to mention to his Royal Highness that a patent from the Crown for the House in the Haymarket during my life would protect me from want, that I had hitherto been permitted to exhibit there at only the time that no other playhouse would open their doors, that I had been oblig'd to write all that was spoke there, and speak almost all that was wrote. That from the uncertainty of my tenure, the Chamberlain's staff so often shifting into different hands, I could not venture to ingage proper assistants, or decorate the Theatre in a manner worthy the guests that I have very often the honor to see there. That the grant would be an injury to none from the great increase of the Capital, and that I had some reason to think the public would be rather pleased to see me possesed of this little provision. His Royal Highness had the goodness to approve of the plan and to promise me all his assistance. I find the Duke has mentioned it to my Lord Chamberlain. His Grace most readily concurr'd in the propriety of the Duke of York's Application so that I am in great hopes my little scheme will succeed.

With regard to my health about which I am sure your Friendship will make you solicitous, I am better rather from what I am told, than what I personally feel: I am weak in pain & get no sleep but from opiates, but however the Artery's bleeding is stopp'd and they flatter me that in less than a fortnight I shall be upon Crutches, and then with safety may be conducted to London. This I wish, not that changes of place can make much difference to a man in my unfortunate way, but that I may have an opportunity of returning you and Lady Delaval my personal thanks for the goodness humanity and Friendship with which you have honor'd your poor and unfortunate oblig'd & Devoted Servant [2]

Foote's next letter to Garrick in which he described his protest to Beard of Covent Garden about an unauthorized reduction of *The Commissary* to two acts, reveals that Foote had survived his ordeal with his sarcastic wit intact: "I saw by the papers that the ingenious Mr. Smith the Aesopus of Covt. Garden had advertised my piece of the Commissary for his benefit reduc'd into two acts . . . I have remonstrated to Mr. Beard and I believe with some warmth, intimating that if my poetical limbs wanted amputation the professors of his house were the very last people that I should chuse for my surgeons." Foote showed so much life at this point that Garrick tried to calm him down: "I must intreat You not to let any triffling Accidents discompose You; Your remonstrance to Beard will immediatly finish that foolish affair [3]—had not You had a Bromfield, perhaps we had all lamented it, but I defy the most Arrant dramatic Bungler to destroy y^r Commissary; they may maim him a little, but they can no more extinguish his Spirit, than they can Yours." [4]

It seems strange that after this warm exchange of letters between Garrick and Foote their friendship did not continue. According to Davies, "Foote's malevolence didn't break out with any degree of violence till after the Duke of York had obtained a patent for him of the Hay-market Theatre." [5] This statement seems to imply that Foote resented Garrick even more than before because their competition was now on a more equal basis. However, Foote's renewed virulence might be attributed not only to envy but to a reasonable objection to Garrick's behavior. Garrick avoided the consequences of his actions by manipulating from behind the scenes and denying all responsibility for the results. It was he who secretly sent Wilkinson to Dublin to compete with Barry, Woodward, and Foote. He was probably responsible for Murphy's rejection by the Middle Temple,[6] and he was certainly responsible for deliberately angering Murphy so as to force his resignation from Drury Lane in favor of George Colman in 1761.[7] His behavior toward Goldsmith's *Good Natured Man* in 1768 is another example of his meanness. Not daring to turn down the play directly, he forced Goldsmith to take it back by asking for unreasonable alterations. Then, afraid for his reputation if the play should succeed at Covent Garden, he brought out Hugh Kelly's *False Delicacy* as competition.[8] No matter what the situation, Garrick always insisted on his good intentions.

Foote might have been angered also by the terms of his patent. It was limited to his lifetime, as he requested, but it also restricted the Haymarket to summer performances. Unless Foote was given special dispensation by the Lord Chamberlain, he could open his doors only from May 15 through September 15. Since Foote had complained to the Duke of York that he had "been permitted to exhibit there [the Haymarket] at only the time that no other playhouse would open their doors," and that given his wish he would be able to compete with the patent houses, for "the grant would be an injury to none from the great increase of the Capital," [9] it is evident that he expected no time limitation on his patent. Foote undoubtedly knew that the Lord Chamberlain had consulted with the patentees of Covent Garden and Drury Lane before setting the terms of his patent and, naturally, had acted upon their recommendations.[10] Since the owners of Covent Garden were in the process of selling their patent,[11] Garrick and Lacy had probably defended their interests by protecting their monopoly. Garrick's action in insisting on or, at least, acquiescing to the limitation of the grant needs no defense, but it is consistent with his behavior that he would profess entirely different sentiments to Foote, not daring to express his real interests or feelings.

Despite Foote's disappointment with the terms of the patent,[12] he decided to make plans to act that summer of 1766 at the Haymarket. His first task, however, was to learn to walk, and for that purpose he had two wooden legs made. One was a mere stick, but the other, to be worn for the stage and formal dress occasions, was equipped with silk stocking and a polished shoe with a gold buckle. The younger Colman, who was a child at the time of Foote's accident, was intrigued by his peg-leg: "I remember following him after a shower of rain, upon a nicely rolled terrace, in which he stumped a deep round hole at every other step he took, till it appeared as if the gardener had been there with his dibble, preparing . . . to plant a long row of cabbages in a grand walk." [13] For further assistance in walking, Foote also used a crutched cane, gold for dress purposes;[14] thus accoutered he was ready to take the stage again and resume his career.

Foote played in only twenty-one mainpieces and seven afterpieces during the summer, and this reduced schedule was not entirely due to his recent amputation. Spranger Barry and Mrs. Anne (Street) Dancer, bringing with them a skeleton troupe of actors from Dublin, rented the Opera-house in the Haymarket, next to Foote's Little Theatre, for the purpose of presenting serious drama. Although it is not clear exactly what arrangements Foote made with his unwelcome neighbors,[15] he was forced to come to some agreement with them. For the most part, direct daily competition was avoided, and on their nights off Foote's company helped fill out roles for Barry. Foote himself helped Barry out on two occasions and even played *The Minor* at the Opera-house on August 20.[16] It was not a profitable arrangement, but Foote had little choice. Barry's excellence as a tragedian rivalled Garrick's in a number of roles, and because of his long absence from the London stage, Barry filled the theatre to capacity every evening he performed.[17]

Foote opened with *The Minor,* and, of course, great crowds of the curious came to see the recovered actor hobbling about on one leg. An amusing letter signed "Bipes" comments on Foote's extraordinary popularity:

> It has been said an hundred times, Mr. Printer, . . . *We English are strange creatures*—I am one of the ten thousand that was turned away from Foote's theatre this Evening, and whose principal inducement for going there was to *see* Mr. Foote's *left* Leg exhibited invisibly *under Mother Cole's Petticoats*—As I am disappointed, give me leave, in the old way, to comfort myself by reflecting on the folly of all that got in—Is it not strange that ten men would go to see Foote now he has but one leg, for one that went when he had two? . . . I am inclined to believe, if Foote was to enter as a dancer next winter, at the Opera-house, it would bring that theatre into vogue—and every animal Bipes would run after him that they think to be more than a man, for being unipes. The rogue is a witty fellow and cracks his jokes, but do the audience think the joke's in the wooden leg, as Bayes places it in the boot? If there is so much wit in one wooden leg, there must be a double portion of it in two; and if Sam was to appear in the character of Witherington on his stumps, he would be as rich as a Commissary. He is the British midas; his very limbs are gold, but the asses ears belong to the heads of the audience.
>
> I am under much pain for my countrymen on another

account: they are as fond of imitation as they are of novelty and strange sights; and I am afraid, lest the spirit of imitation should bring wooden legs into fashion. We have seen thousands lay aside their own eyes as useless, and disdain to look like the vulgar, through any but glass. And as spectacles are not generally in use; but the single glass is the ton, it is plain the beau monde even look upon one eye as much politer than two. Some historians inform us, that in the reign of Richard the third, no man appeared at court, without having one shoulder higher, and one leg shorter, than the other, as proof of his gentility. May we not therefore expect to see the company at the Bedford coffee-house, stumping about the room with their wooden legs, in hopes of being as witty as Foote? [18]

Though he offered no new comedy, Foote chose his roles with great discretion. As Mother Cole he walked with a limp because of her "rheumatism." As Peter Paragraph in *The Orators,* he indeed could take off George Faulkner to the life, as he had said he would immediately after his amputation.[19] Foote's high point in mocking his own limp came when he played Zachary Fungus astride a hobbyhorse, learning the gentle art of riding:

> Bridoun: Now, let me see you vault nimbly into your seat.—Zounds! you are got on the wrong side, Mr. Fungus.
> Fungus: I am so, indeed, but we'll soon rectify that. Now we are right: may I have leave to lay hold of the mane?
> Brid.: If you can't mount him without.
> Fun.: I will try; but this steed is so devilish tall!—Mr. Bridoun, you don't think he'll throw me?
> Brid.: Never fear.
> Fun.: Well, if he should, he can't kick; that's one comfort, however.
> Brid.: Now mind your position.
> Fun.: Stay till I recover my wind.
> Brid.: Let your head be erect.

Fun.: There.

Brid.: And your shoulders fall easily back.

Fun.: Ho—there.

Brid.: Your switch perpendicular in your right hand— your right—that is it; your left to the bridle.

Fun.: There.

Brid.: Your knees in, and your toes out.

Fun.: There.

Brid.: Are you ready?

Fun.: When you will.

Brid.: Off you go.

Fun.: Don't let him gallop at first.

Brid.: Very well: preserve your position.

Fun.: I warrant.

Brid.: Does he carry you easy?

Fun.: All the world like a cradle. But, Mr. Bridoun, I go at a wonderful rate.

Brid.: Mind your knees.

Fun.: Ay, ay, I can't think but this here horse stands still very near as fast as another can gallop.

Brid.: Mind your toes.

Fun.: Ho, Stop the horse. Zounds! I'm out of the stirrups, I can't sit him no longer; there I go—

[Falls off]

Brid.: I hope you ar'n't hurt?

Fun.: My left hip has a little contusion.

Brid.: A trifle, quite an accident; it might happen to the very best rider in England. . . . But you are vastly improved.

Fun.: Why, I am grown bolder a little; and, Mr. Bridoun, when do you think I may venture to ride a live horse?

Brid.: The very instant you are able to keep your seat on a dead one.[20]

By burlesquing his own fall, as he does in this scene, Foote's method of self-protection becomes obvious. To forestall any jeers that might be directed against the impropriety of a mutilated man acting farce, Foote took care to lead the laughter against himself.

Foote took less trouble to suit himself so exactly in the afterpieces, and, evidently, the audience accepted him as Major Sturgeon and even as Fondlewife. With great spirit and determination, Foote had been able to go on stage, and without looking for pity he made the audience enjoy him as they had in the past. But a quick glance at Foote behind the curtains by a fellow actor corrects the attitude caught by the audience—that Foote was even funnier on one leg:

> With all his high comic humour, one could not help pitying him sometimes, as he stood upon one leg, leaning against the wall, whilst his servant was putting in his stage false leg, with shoe and stocking, and fastening it to the stump: he looked sorrowful, but instantly resuming all his high comic humour and mirth, hobbled forward, entered the scene, and gave the audience what they expected—their plenty of laugh and delight.[21]

Though the short season could not have been too profitable for Foote, his increased popularity gave him needed reassurance that he could continue acting and please the crowds.

Foote began preparations early for the season of 1767. With his newly acquired patent, he now felt free to purchase the Haymarket from the executors of Potter, a carpenter who had originally built the theatre in 1720.[22] After his purchase, Foote painted, refurbished, added an upper gallery to the Haymarket, and gave it a new facade as well.[23] Foote also purchased a house on Suffolk Street directly in back of the theatre, so that it could be connected to the Haymarket. The theatre was too small to accommodate sufficient wardrobe space or a proper green room, and part of the house was converted to serve as an annex for these purposes.[24] The rest of the house served as Foote's living quarters in town and was a great convenience to a man who walked with difficulty.

Foote also had to come to terms with Barry and Dancer, who were continuing to play at the Opera-house. This time, however, he engaged them at his theatre against the advice of his friends who thought he could not make any money at the salaries he had to pay them. Foote told them, "Why to tell you the truth, I have no great occasion for them; but they were such *bad neighbors* last year that I find it cheaper to give them room and lodging for nothing, than to have them any longer opposite to me." [25] Shuter had proved irresponsible the previous season, so Foote tried to engage Wilkinson again by offering him a part in a new burlesque, *The Tailors*. Wilkinson declined, but Foote was able to strengthen his cast by hiring Charles Bannister, a mimic, and "Gentleman" John Palmer, an established comedian from Drury Lane. With these actors, in addition to Shuter and Weston, Foote had the best comedians in London. Altogether, he hired thirty-seven actors, seven more than he had before,[26] but they supported Barry and Dancer in addition to acting in Foote's comedies.

Though Foote had contributed no new pieces to the season, he did write an *Occasional Prelude* as an introduction to the rebuilt Haymarket.[27] It consisted of a *Rehearsal*-like scene wherein Laconic, a poet, and Snarl, a pamphleteer, quarrel and begin to expose each other's trade secrets. When this exposure becomes too painful, they agree to a truce and go to the Haymarket for the latest gossip. After some bantering conversation with Foote, who appears as himself, they leave to get a promising new actress for the Haymarket. As Foote waits for their return, Scaffold, the carpenter, duns Foote for three months of hard work in altering the playhouse. Part of the joke was that Scaffold actually was the carpenter, who was persuaded to play the part of himself.[28] Foote pleads poverty, and advises Scaffold that if he hopes for payment, he must beg it of the audience, for only their faithful attendance can assure payment of the debt. Foote's audience, especially the gallery, loved the scene, but its popularity proved to be disrupting. On June 22 the gallery grew bored with Barry as Romeo, and they whistled and catcalled for the *Occasional Prelude* until Foote was forced to give in to their wishes.[29]

The new piece of the season was *The Tailors*. Though Foote's name appears as author on some editions of the play, in a letter to Wilkinson he expressly denied writing it: "I have a piece of three acts, not my own, which I shall give in the month of May, called *The Tailors*." [30] The piece satirized in mock-heroic blank verse a recent quarrel between the master-tailors and their journeymen and also parodied "the best passages in the most favorite plays." [31] But exquisite as the parodies might be, the galleries hooted down the play in the third act, their patience apparently exhausted by this literary exercise, and again called for the *Occasional Prelude*. Though the literati in the boxes wanted the play to go on, their objections were drowned out by the noise of the gallery audience who were given their wish by a defeated Foote.[32] He desperately revised *The Tailors* and finally reduced it to an afterpiece on August 11. His ministrations revived the play through ten more performances, but he never used it again.[33]

The season was certainly a disappointment. Though the playhouse was open for fifty-eight performances, Foote appeared in only twenty-five mainpieces and fifteen afterpieces; the remaining performances were given by Barry and Dancer. Furthermore, he had to endure an abusive attack upon himself and his performers, Weston excepted, by George Savile Carey. Entitled *Momus—a Poem or a critical examination into the merits of the performers and comic pieces of the Theatre Royal in the Haymarket,* this poem also condemned Foote's plays because of their personal abuse but at the same time described them as "laughable and new." The only bright part of the season was the *Occasional Prelude,* and even that caused considerable difficulty. But Foote seemed as gay and unconcerned as ever. Joseph Cradock caught a glimpse of him in February at the Theatrical Club, whose meetings were then held at Wright's Coffee House near Covent Garden. To one Mr. Howard, who was considering printing a second edition of his *Thoughts and Maxims,* Foote prudently said, "Right, Sir, second thoughts are often best." And to another who mentioned a game leg in a joke, Foote turned and with affected anger snarled, "Pray, Sir, make no allusion to my weakest part; did I ever attack your head?" [34]

Perhaps by that time Foote's merriment was justified. He was in the process of completing his first play since his accident, and his unwanted summer boarders, Barry and Dancer, had been signed by Garrick and Lacy. The season of 1768 promised clear sailing. Optimistically, Foote hired thirty-seven actors, the same number he had shared with Barry and Dancer the previous year, but he took on no new comic performers. He kept Weston and wrote the part of Dr. Last for him in the new play, and he introduced Miss Edwards as a principal singer and ingenue. The Haymarket was open for fifty performances, Foote appearing in forty-two mainpieces and four afterpieces.[35] It is interesting to note that although Foote made as many appearances in a summer season as before his accident, in 1766, 1767, and 1768 he rarely appeared in both afterpiece and mainpiece on the same night. It took him three years to regain his former physical endurance, and only remarkable vitality and persistence could have allowed Foote that achievement.

The title of Foote's new piece, *The Devil upon Two Sticks,* was taken from the English translation of Le Sage's *Diable Boiteux* which was well known in England, the 1708 translation having gone through more than twelve editions before 1800.[36] The same title was also used by a 1729 burletta,[37] and a satiric novel published in 1755 proclaimed Le Sage's influence with the title, *The Devil upon Crutches, or, Night-Scenes in London.*[38] Foote's three-act farce cleverly exploited the current taste for this satirical picaresque work, and the title provided Foote with an excuse for hobbling on stage with two crutch-headed canes in the title role of a lame devil.[39]

The plot of the farce is secondary to the satire. The play opens in Madrid where Harriet, a young girl, is kept locked in her room by her father, an English consul, because she has threatened to elope with Invoice, a mere clerk. In rebellion against her father's tyranny and with the help of her aunt, a decided feminist, she does escape the locked room when Invoice appears to rescue her. When the eloping pair stop for a moment in an apothecary's shop to elude their pursuers, a voice, seemingly imprisoned in a bottle, begs to be set free. When the bottle is broken, a lame devil dressed as an ordinary English gentleman appears out of the billows of smoke and agrees to grant them a wish. Since the lovers' need to leave Spain is paramount, they ask the devil to transport them to England. Their wish is granted immediately, but the pair have been away from their native country for so many years that they ask the obliging devil to reorient them to the traditions and customs of England so that they may begin to support themselves in some likely occupation. The devil mocks all the professions, especially medicine. The doctors' cozening ways are exposed in the ludicrous parody of a current squabble between the physicians. After disposing of most of the so-called honorable professions, the devil suggests that the pair take up acting and recommends them to Foote's Haymarket. He warns them that it is "an eccentric, narrow establishment, but it may do for a *coup d'essai,* and prove no bad foundation for a future engagement." It is necessary to add that this summary does little justice to the play because it is Foote's most topical work and underwent changes daily. At the end of each performance Foote made satirical comments on the happenings of the day,[40] and these monologues were rarely printed.

The first victim of satire in the play was Mrs. Macaulay, the blue-stocking historian, in the person of Mrs. Margaret Maxwell, Harriet's republican aunt. Threatening her brother because of his autocratic attitude toward Harriet, Margaret warns him, "The same pen that has dared to scourge the arbitrary actions of some of our monarchs, shall do equal justice to the oppressive power of parents! . . . I may, perhaps, be too late to get you in the historical text; but, I promise you, you shall be soundly swinged in the marginal notes." [41] Foote's reference was good humored, and even the victim appeared flattered. Walpole wrote that Mrs. Macaulay "goes to see herself represented, and I suppose figures herself very like Socrates." [42]

The satire on doctors, which takes up most of acts two and three, was based on a current dispute between the Licentiate and the Royal College of Physicians. The college awarded licenses to doctors with continental and Scots degrees but refused to allow them to become voting fellows of the college, reserving that privilege to the graduates of Oxford and Cambridge. Sir William Browne, president of the college, lowered the requirements for Licentiate hoping to stop the outsiders' objections to being kept out of the college. They were not appeased by this peculiar measure which, after all, merely emphasized the contempt Browne and the regular physicians had for the education of the non-affiliated practitioners, and on September 24, 1767, the irregulars stormed the walls of the Royal College to gain their demands by force. The walls held, however, and later legal requests for recognition were turned down by the courts.[43] In the play, Foote dramatized the doctors' war, making both sides ridiculous. The devil had magical powers of impersonation, and in that character Foote took off Sir William Browne as Hellebore and Dr. Richard Brocklesby as Squib, a doctor more interested in politics than medicine. Browne took no public offense at the impersonation and even sent Foote a muff to complete the portrait. [44]

Not all the impersonations were accepted so amicably despite the genial aspect of Foote's satire. Dr. John Fothergill, a Quaker physician who was responsible for instigating the law suit against the Royal College, was mocked in the character of Dr. Melchisedech Broadbrim. Though ridiculed gently, he objected strongly in a letter to his colleague, Dr. William Hunter:

> Pray, dear Doctor would it be practicable for Lord H[ertford] to dismiss me with any decency from the stage? I am brought there to say nothing but what is proper, but to say it and appear in a ridiculous manner. Is not this as great an insult upon me, and even upon any character that is opposite to vice and folly as can be offered! Buffoonery should only be let loose on these; not to render their opposites contemptible. If thro' weakness or indiscretion I slide into mistakes, I bear most patiently the chastisement, whether public or private. But in this instance I am doubly hurt. I am held up for the whole town to laugh at, and the people with whom I am connected likewise. Nor does the faculty in general derive much benefit from the contempt thrown on an individual, tho' individuals may rejoice in it.[45]

The part that pleased the audience most was Hellebore's examination of Dr. Last, played by Weston. Foote was satirizing the lowered standards for the Licentiate. Last is an ignorant cobbler who has found his true vocation in the pleasures of burning, pulling, and cutting the offending parts of his poor patients:

> Hellebore: But now, Dr. Last, to proceed in due form; are you qualified to administer remedies to such diseases as belong to the head?
>
> Last: I believe I may.
>
> Hel.: Name some to the College.
>
> Last: The tooth-ache.
>
> Hel.: What do you hold the best method to treat it? . . .
>
> Last: Why, I pulls em' up by the roots.
>
> Hel.: Well replied, brothers! that, without doubt, is a radical cure. . . . Thus far as to the head: proceed we next to the middle! When, Dr. Last, you are called in to a patient with a pain in his bowels, what then is your method of practice?
>
> Last: I claps a trencher, hot, to the part.
>
> Hel.: Embrocation; very well! But if this application should fail, what is the next step that you take?
>
> Last: I gi's a vomit and a purge.
>
> Hel.: Well replied! for it is plain there is a disagreeable guest in the house; he has opened both doors; if he will go out at neither it is none of his fault. . . . We have now dispatched the middle, and head: come we finally to the other extremity, the feet! Are you equally skillful in the disorders incidental to them?
>
> Last: I believe I may.
>
> Hel.: Name some.
>
> Last: I have a great vogue all our way for curing of corns.
>
> Hel.: What are the means that you use?
>
> Last: I cuts them out.
>
> Hel.: Well replied! extirpation: no better method of curing can be practised. Well, brethren, I think we may

now, after this strict and impartial enquiry, safely certify, that Dr. Emanuel Last, from top to toe, is an able physician.[46]

But the practice of the college physicians, as exemplified by the lecture of Doctor Hellebore on the treatment of jaundice, while less brutal is far more ingeniously foolish:

> Hel.: Those two yellow drops there were drawn from a subject afflicted with the jaundice.—Well, what d'ye see?
> Last: [*Peering through a miscroscope*] Some little creatures like yellow flies, that are hopping and skipping about.
> Hel.: Right. Those yellow flies give the tinge to the skin, and undoubtedly cause the disease: and, now, for the cure! I administer to every patient the two-and-fiftieth part of a scruple of the ovaria or eggs of the spider; these are thrown by the digestive powers into the secretory, there separated from the alimentory, and then precipitated into the circulatory; where finding a proper nidus, or nest, they quit their torpid state, and vivify, and, upon vivification, discerning the flies, their natural food, they immediately fall foul of them, extirpate the race out of the blood, and restore the patient to health.
> Last: And what becomes of the spiders?
> Hel.: Oh, they die, you know, for want of nutrition.
> Then I send the patient down to Brighthelmstone; and a couple of dips in the salt-water, washes the cobwebs entirely out of the blood.[47]

Foote's profits from this play were enormous. He was supposed to have netted between three and four thousands pounds for the season of fifty performances. This sum compares favorably to Garrick's average yearly take as actor, director, occasional dramatist, and patentee of the Drury Lane.[48] This was the kind of play that always made money for Foote. With great emphasis upon topical matters, the play had so little structure that Foote could comment freely on anything by substitution or addition of new material without affecting the plot at all. His mimicry of various characters could be also altered with as little penalty.

Despite the demands of his theatre, Foote continued to be very socially active that summer. The financial gains from his new play encouraged him to buy a new country house in North End, a more convenient and fashionable location than the one in Blackheath, and to entertain frequently on a lavish scale. It might have been here that Foote, in proudly showing Murphy his new home, pointed out a bust of Garrick on his bureau. In answer to Murphy's astonished smile, Foote responded, "I don't wonder you should laugh at me for allowing him to be so near my gold; but then please to observe *he has no hands.*" [49]

The following unpublished letter, probably sent to the Mexboroughs, gives a lively account of Foote's activities at the time. The letter is dated August 11, and the year, 1768, is ascertained by the reference to the King of Denmark's visit to England:

Indeed my Dear Sir I was exceedingly unhappy in being oblig'd to give Sir George Savile an opinion so little favorable to his Comedy, but it is a most execrable composition, and I would no more flatter a poet, than he would a prince. He desir'd my judgment without Apology, and I gave it him in the following words.

"The Comedy is of the modern kind, where for singularity of Character, and usefull pointed observations on the prevailing manners, we are presented with a string of Adventures that never did, or can happen, conducted by such persons as never existed who are furnished with a language that was never spoken. The conduct too, the sole merit of these subaltern products, is most exceedingly faulty, for not to mention a total neglect of the Unitys, probability nay even possibility is entirely destroyed." His answer is sensible, with some degree of humor.

"Sir

I have always heard that Managers treat Authors very ill and keep them long in suspense. Now I have not been acquainted with Authors and Managers above a fortnight, and the whole of my experience contradicts this notion. I think myself oblig'd &c." Tho' between ourselves I can't help thinking but he has had rather a longer knowledge of Authors.

I hope it is unnecessary for me to say how much I think myself oblig'd to Lord and Lady Mexborough for their polite and friendly invitation nor how eagerly I should seize every occasion of passing my time in a family to every branch of which I have so many obligations, but I find some little return of the complaint I had in the early part of the Winter and which I am told the Salt Water will entirely remove. If necessity does not drive me there, every pleasurable motive will attract me to Methly at the close of my Season.

I have changed my usual habitation since I saw you, and now write from what I flatter myself you will think an elegant villa in the parish of Fulham about three miles from London.

Yesterday Lds Gower and Weymouth, Mrs. Rigby and Doctor Hay din'd here, and tomorrcw I have the Garricks Male and Female Mrs. Hale and Chetwynd.

The King of Denmark is come, and I am told intended to make his abode with Charlote Hays or Mrs Pelham, but I find they have persuaded him to reside at St James & I suppose I shall see him in the Haymarket, more for my emolument that his entertainment for he does not understand a word of our language.

My Lord Chamberlain has received orders to procure some bon mots with a proper parcel of shrewd observations for the use of his Majesty during his residence here.

I am my dear Sir with every wish for the happiness and Welfare of every body with you.[50]

Foote's critical comments on Savile's play recall an anecdote of of a playwright who complained to Foote that critics did not do his plays justice and added that he would get even with them by laughing at their criticism. "You do perfectly right, my friend," Foote agreed, "for by this method you will not only disappoint your enemies, but lead the *merriest life* of any man in England." [51]

Foote's relationship with Garrick was rarely more cordial than at this time. Foote even did Garrick the favor of playing *The Lying Valet* with his *Devil upon Two Sticks;* Garrick, however, made the mistake of gloating that Foote was now forced to admit that he was glad to play one of Garrick's farces. Foote quickly deflated him. "Why, yes, David, what could I do better? I must have some *ventilator* for this excessive hot weather." [52]

They saw each other frequently and exchanged various gifts from their country houses. On one occasion, Foote asked Garrick for the use of his dog, Biddy, for stud purposes: "Mr. Barrel has prevailed upon me to pimp for a four leg'd favorite of his and to send a card to one of your little gentlemen to beg me favor of his Company for a day or two. Mr. Barrel will send a chair at any appointed hour." [53] Garrick ruefully refused:

Had I a *Pompey* or *Caesar* He sh^d be much at Mr Barrel's Cleopatra's Service; but I have not been master of one for some Years. . . .

I hope you will not forget next Sunday Sen'-night perhaps Mr Fitzherbert will venture here, when he is Sure of having a pleasant Companion in a post chaise—The Bargain is, you know, that I am in return to attend You in ye Country upon demand; and I think, my dear Devil, that I have never shew'd more Skill in *Bargain-making* in all my Life, for I have *Nick'd* you both ways—

Go on & Prosper my dear Sir [54]

On one of these visits, Foote had given Garrick some geese, and Garrick, having forgotten to take the present, later sent a servant with this message:

Dear Foote, I love Your Wit, & like your Wine,
And hope, when next with You I dine,
Indeed I do not care how soon,
I hope—nay beg it as a boon,
That You will get Decanters six,
(Your various Wines that number fix:)
So may the generous grape you give,
(To give it, may You Ages live!)
From Bottle to Decanter pass,
And not a cloud to stain the glass

Your liquor then each Taste will hit,
Pure clear & sparkling as Your Wit
I took my leave in such a hurry,
With drinking too in such a flurry,
With Gibes, & Jests so cramm'd my Mind,
Again we left the Geese behind:
Which by the Bearer please to send,
To Me your very thankfull Friend.
And as they come, dear Sam, from Thee,
Well fed, & happy shall they be;

The Silver Thames Shall swim upon,
Each Goose of yours shall be a Swan!
And when the Old have Young ones bred,
These shall be taught, as well as fed:
True Classic Geese, I'll teach 'Em all,
To save their Master's *Capitol:*
Slaves of my Pleasures, & the Tools,
To cackle at th'Approach of Fools:
At Men of Wit to change their Note,
And only murmer in the throat;
But Mute, & of Obedience full,
They'll bow to You, the Great Mogul.[55]

Foote's immediate response to this gracious and deferential jingle
was probably cordial, but the following quatrain he seems to have

circulated at about this time reveals the gratuitously malicious nature of the many barbs he directed against the thin-skinned Garrick:

> Whenever Garrick dines or sleeps
> He drops a dogg'rel rhyme
> The snail thus marks the road she creeps,
> By slobb'ring sordid slime.[56]

One is continually surprised, considering the enmity and quarrels between them, at the years of reciprocal friendship.

During this active season Foote also made out his will, dated August 13, 1768. The document ultimately had little meaning for his executors, William Fitzherbert and Archibald Hamilton, or for his beneficiaries, his illegitimate sons George and Francis, his mother, his brother Edward, and his long-faithful servant and treasurer, William Jewel. Although Jewel, Hamilton, and the two sons survived Foote's death in 1777, what had worth in the will, Foote's Haymarket property and adjoining house, had been sold to George Colman the Elder in 1776, and Foote's debts took up whatever other negotiable property he held. The will is interesting, however, because it shows the great affection Foote had for his servant: in it are detailed minutely the generous benefits that Foote intended for Jewel.

It is not known when Foote first took Jewel into his service, but the earliest reference to him was made on August 8, 1765, when a benefit was announced for Jewel and David, a minor actor. It was noted that this was the first benefit for Jewel, who had replaced the former treasurer, the recently deceased Mr. Mendez.[57] Subsequent benefits for Jewel in 1766 and 1767 were not shared by other performers, and in 1767 Foote played Gomez in *The Spanish Fryar*, a role he had not played in years, to increase the worth of Jewel's benefit. But after the summer of 1768, Foote's attitude changed sharply towards Jewel. Sometime during the summer season, Jewel and Foote's new singer, Miss Edwards, secretly married and told Foote what they had done only after the season was over. Miss Edwards had originally been a house servant to Foote, and, supposedly, she caught Foote's notice by her excellent singing. He prepared her for the stage in a few months, and she first appeared in Cibber's ballad farce, *Damon and Phillida.* She continued to play minor roles for two seasons, and in 1768 she took on principal singing roles as well as the ingenue part of Harriet in Foote's new play. Jewel fell in love with her when she became a principal, and, fearing Foote's anger and disapproval, they were married secretly. Their fears were justified, for when Foote did find out, he summarily dismissed the pair, supposedly telling Jewel, "Though I *love* thee, never more be *officer* of mine." [58] Mrs. Jewel tried to earn a living and help her unemployed husband by singing for various benefits during the winter season, and undoubtedly she hoped that Foote's disapproval would soften.[59] But during the summer of 1769, Foote hired Mrs. Arthur to play the parts formerly taken by Mrs. Jewel. A magazine noticed the change and, probably aware of the incident, asked for the return of Mrs. Jewel.[60] Foote, for his part, found that he missed the ministrations of his formerly faithful servant and decided he would have him back, wife and all. The reconciliation evidently took place before June 12, 1769, the day that Mrs. Jewel replaced Mrs. Arthur as Harriet, and thereafter she appeared in her usual roles.[61]

At the end of the summer season, Foote did not accept the Mexboroughs' invitation to visit them at Methly, but took his doctor's advice to visit the resort of Bath for his health. Though told to take salt water as part of his cure, Foote obviously thought little of the efficacy of the treatment, except, perhaps, to wash the cobwebs out of the blood. During his stay at Bath Foote seems to have done little more than sit at a table surrounded by card players. He was no match for these professionals, though he did amuse them by telling jokes and stories as they raked his money in. He began to lose at such an alarming rate that his friend Richard Rigby, recently made paymaster of the forces, admonished Foote to stop playing, warning him that the players were cheating him and that if he didn't mind his cards, he would lose all his money. His pride hurt, Foote sharply told Rigby that *"he* [Foote] could always draw on his talents when a courtier could not always find the king's treasury for support." But the paymaster, greatly experienced in crooked dealings, was right, and in that evening Foote lost all his available cash, about £2000.[62]

Fortunately, Foote had made prior arrangements to play his new production in Ireland that winter, and though he had to borrow £100 for travel expenses, Foote was right about his ability to draw on his talents. *The Devil* again brought crowded houses, about £150 to £200 a night, and since the theatre had small expenses, Foote was able to recoup a good part of his gambling losses.[63] His purse replenished by the end of the year, Foote left for Paris and did not return to London until early February of 1769.[64]

Foote had prepared nothing new for the coming summer season of 1769. Certainly, the previous year had allowed him little time to write a new play, but subsequent events inspired a renewal of creativity. The May 6 to 9 issue of *The St. James's Chronicle* carried the first announcement of Garrick's proposed Jubilee in honor of Shakespeare. The event was to be held in Stratford for three days beginning September 6.[65] Foote immediately interpreted this affair as a contemptible act of self-glorification on the part of Garrick, who, as the foremost interpreter of Shakespeare, would naturally be identified with his idol. Throughout the season, as the clamor about the Jubilee grew in intensity, Foote revised a number of his plays to air his vitriolic wit on what he considered Garrick's folly. However, Foote certainly recognized the business potential of Shakespeare, now considerably increased by Garrick's activity, and he hired his old target, the Orator himself, Thomas Sheridan, to act in a series of Shakespearian plays from August to mid-September.[66] Bardolatry was so catching that even Weston, though admittedly as a joke, yearned to act *Richard III* for his benefit. Fortunately for Shakespeare, Weston grew faint-hearted at the last minute and asked Francis Gentleman to act the lead role.[67] Anticipating a good season, Foote hired his largest company, forty-three actors, the most notable addition being Sparks from Dublin. The Haymarket was open for fifty-five performances, and despite Sheridan's appearance, Foote dominated the stage as usual by acting in thirty-seven mainpieces and fourteen afterpieces. He had obviously regained his old vigor.[68]

Though Foote wrote no new pieces, he did help Isaac Bicker-staffe write a new farce, *Dr. Last in his Chariot*. This adaptation of Molière's *Malade Imaginaire* was written to profit from the immense popularity of Weston's acting in Foote's play. Foote acted Ailwould, the hypochondriac, and wrote some humorous scenes that depicted consultations of physicians. The first night of this production went off so badly that catcalls from pit and gallery prevented the conclusion of the play. Foote apologized to the audience by saying "it was not his piece, but taken from Molière by a gentleman who had often met applause as a dramatic writer—that he was, however, sorry to find the *shoemaker had gone beyond his last.*" [69] Foote tried to save the play by senti-mentalizing the conclusion, but the audience, though happy with Foote's acting and the scenes that Foote had originally written, still did not like the farce. For Bickerstaffe's sake, Foote persisted to the sixth night and told the audience after the performance: "I have got rid of my wife—I have got rid of my complaints—and, thank God, I have now got rid of this piece." [70] But Bicker-staffe, who begged for one more benefit, moved Foote to play the piece three more times; however, to avoid cumulative audience reaction, these subsequent performances were spaced two weeks apart.

Despite these distractions, it was the Jubilee that occupied Foote's attention. He made his sentiments known on opening day at the Haymarket at the conclusion of *The Devil upon Two Sticks,* when the devil queries Invoice on his choice of vocation:

> Devil: What think you then by way of laying a founda-tion of treating the public with a *Ridotto al Fesco* or a *Bal pare?*
>
> Invoice: Oh, Sir, that is impossible, for I have not money to make the necessary preparations.
>
> Dev.: There is no occasion for any, the public advance

the money, and you in return are to treat them with—
just nothing at all.

    Inv.: I can never submit to such an imposition.

    Dev.: You're very nice, but you will soon have enough
to keep you in countenance.[71]

The Author, revived because of Apreece's death, was also revised
to satirize the Jubilee.[72] In addition to voicing his attitude on
stage, Foote used the newspapers and the coffee houses to publicize
his witty and malicious invectives. It did not take long for the
"Devil," as Foote was called, to become a synonym for anti-
Jubilee and anti-Garrick sentiment.[73]

    Later, Foote announced his intention of going to the Jubilee
to collect material for a "humorous Piece" to be called *The
Drugger's Jubilee.* This threat, periodically announced but never
performed, was aimed at Garrick who was associated with the role
of Abel Drugger, the sly but moronic assistant in Jonson's *Alchem-
ist.* Foote had no need to write this farce, for his purpose was
served in the mere telling. Garrick lived in fear of Foote's ridicule
and timidly tried to soften the blows before they were delivered
by propitiating his tormentor. Among the hundreds of items
found in Garrick's memoranda on the Jubilee, this was an important reminder: "To secure Some good Lodgings for my Friends
—a good bed for Mr Foote." [74] And Foote, fully aware of Garrick's
fear, was cheekily able to ask for assistance from the Drury Lane
wardrobe to help clothe the ghost for Sheridan's performance of
Hamlet: [75]

    My Dear Sir
        You and I are a couple of Buckets, whilst you are
    raising the expectation of Shakespeare, I am endeavoring
    to sink it, and for this purpose, I shall give next Monday
    the Tragedy of Hamlet, the prince by &c. but even in
    this situation we shall want your assistance to pull our
    poet above ground; the ghost's armor, which if you will

give your housekeeper orders to deliver to North End
Thursday will be extremely kind to your affectionate
servant.[76]

It is extremely unlikely that Garrick refused this request.

With the season about over, Foote, taking Macklin with
him, joined the rest of fashionable London in the pilgrimage
to Stratford. With Garrick's influence, Foote and Macklin were
lodged at the Bear Inn in the neighboring hamlet of Bridgetown.
Their room was located directly over the cache of fireworks that
were to be set off the second evening of the Jubilee. Pretending
to fear for his life, Foote accused Garrick of planning a second
Gunpowder Plot to destroy all opposition to the Jubilee.[77] The
joke, however, proved better than the gunpowder, which failed
to ignite because of the dampness. The Jubilee, too, fizzled out.
Though there were some memorable moments, heavy rains and
greedy Stratfordians turned the event into an expensive and
muddy fiasco. Foote, who under the best of circumstances would
have damned the Jubilee for a Harlequinade, hardly needed
to exert himself to satire as the rains continued to fall heavily,
cancelling the fireworks and the actors' procession.[78] "Well, Sam,
what do you think of all this?" Garrick asked gloomily as he
watched the rain spoil his momentous project. "Think of it!"
came Foote's smug pronouncement. "Why as a Christian should
do. I think it is God's revenge against vanity." [79] With the elements and Foote ganged up against him, poor Garrick was happy
to get back to London.

But Foote was waiting for him there too. When *The Devil
upon Two Sticks* played again in the Haymarket on September
13, Foote inserted his "Devil's Definition" of the Jubilee, which
became the public's favorite comment on the whole affair:

A Jubilee as it has lately appeared is a public invitation, urged by puffing, to go post without horses, to an
obscure borough without representatives, governed by a
mayor and alderman, who are no magistrates, to celebrate

a great poet whose own works have made him immortal, by an ode without poetry, music without harmony, dinners without victuals, and lodgings without beds; a masquerade where half the people appeared bare-faced, a horserace up to the knees in water, fire-works extinguished as soon as they were lighted, and a gingerbread amphitheatre, which, like a house of cards, tumbled to pieces as soon as as it was finished.[80]

There is an amusing drawing opposite the "Devil's Definition" in *Town and Country Magazine* which shows how closely Foote was identified with anti-Jubilee sentiment. On a three-legged table, each leg labeled "al Fresco," "Bal Pare," and "Stratford Jubilee," the bottle conjurer of 1749, half out of his bottle, stood singing with open arms. Foote, who had long been suspected of being the conjurer, revived this old joke when he came out of the bottle as a lame devil in his play. The association was made unmistakable by the cloven hoofs and devilish gargoyles that decorated the legs of the table. The purpose of the drawing was to denounce the Jubilee by equating it with outdoor frolics at public gardens and to imply that such events are ridiculous frauds perpetrated on a gullible public.

Although Garrick was disheartened and considerably deflated by the failure of the Jubilee and the opposition that it raised, he kept his nerve and decided to stage the procession that the rain had cancelled. Colman at Covent Garden learned of his plans and tried to forestall him with a procession of his own called *Man and Wife: or The Stratford Jubilee*, produced on October 7. In his opening interlude, Colman tried to atone for this theft by praising Garrick's Jubilee and condemning its critics, except for Foote. "His friend Pasquin," Colman explained, "was no mere mudslinger, for his satire was like fuller's earth which cleansed and did not stain." [81] Foote would be no party to Colman's oily praise and snapped that "it put him in mind of a *Ludgate hill* Prostitute tickling Mr. Garrick with one hand, and picking his pocket with the other." [82]

Garrick, who had already lost £2000 because of the Jubilee,[83] took great care not to lose this contest to Colman. Sparing no expense in costume and carpentry, Garrick's procession completely overwhelmed Covent Garden's effort, and Colman was obliged to bow out of the competition after a week of empty seats. Disarming his detractors with a long-practiced hand, Garrick incorporated the various shafts of criticism directed at the Stratford venture into the musical pageantry of his *Jubilee,* transforming the barbs into harmless jests. Even the "Devil's Definition" became the song, "What's a Jubilee?":

> This is Sir a Jubilee
> Crowded without Company
> Riot without Jollity
> That's a Jubilee . . .
> Odes Sir without Poetry
> Music without Melody
> Singing without Harmony. . . .
> Blankets without Sheeting Sir
> Dinners without Eating Sir
> Not without much cheating Sir
> Thus 'tis night & day Sir
> I hope that you will stay Sir
>   To see our Jubilee.[84]

Despite Garrick's apprehension because of the anti-Jubilee sentiment, approval of the Drury Lane Production was almost unanimous. The *Jubilee* made theatrical history with a record run of ninety-one performances for the 1769-70 season, and the performances repaid Garrick many times for his original loss. Though serious critics still concurred with Foote's strictures, success and victory, as Foote defined it, lay with Garrick. The audience in mighty numbers voted for the musical pageant, and Foote was mortified.

    Foote continued to bait Garrick with more threats of impending ridicule, but this time his fish did not rise readily to the hook.[85] Deciding that the time had come for action, Foote let it be known that he was going to bring out a procession of his own; the actors dressed in a ragged parody of Drury Lane's magnificence. At the fore of the procession, raised to mock-eminence, the Steward of the Jubilee would appear with wand, white gloves, and mulberry tree medallion—looking remarkably like Garrick. One of the ragamuffins from the crowd was to approach him and address him in lines that Poet Laureate Whitehead had written about Garrick in 1747: "A nation's taste depends on you,/ Perhaps a nation's virtue too." The Steward was to respond by flapping his arms and crowing, "Cock-a-doodle-doo." Foote excused his malignity by accusing Garrick of making public a loan of £500 he had made to Foote.[86] Garrick's anguish at this ultimate threat of ridicule was so great that a mutual friend, the Marquis of Stafford, asked Foote to drop his project. The two met in the Marquis' house as if by accident, and after a pregnant silence, Garrick asked, "Is it war or peace?" "O! peace by all means," Foote replied, allowing Garrick to breathe easily again.[87]

Foote had promised not to ridicule Garrick on this occasion, but he did not forswear his right to criticism. On January 16, 1770,[88] Foote spoke a critical prologue at the Haymarket condemning the low use of machinery and costumes to exalt Shakespeare:

> Not small the sin t'have sunk the people's taste,
> Chill'd their fine fires, their solid sense debased;
> Turn'd useful mirth and salutary woe
> To idle pagentry and empty show;
> Wit, men, and manners, incident and plot,
> Passion and pathos totally forgot;
> Blasted the bays on ev'ry classic brow,
> Taylors are deemed the only poets now:
> Hark! what a roar at Lear's old surtout,
> Falstaff's stuffed vest, and Pistol's hat and boot!
> To solemn sounds see sordid scenemen stalk,
> And the great Shakespeare's vast creation—walk!
> Can a lean wardrobe all his pow'rs express?
> Can his fine phrenzy creep into a dress?

> E'en Roscius blushes at his own success,
> And feels some transient touches for his crime,
> To have sunk these scenes below a pantomime.[89]

Foote continued in later years to scorn the Jubilee and to make Garrick uneasy in many other ways, but, in general, this reconciliation at the Marquis of Stafford's house ended the heated warfare Foote was waging on Garrick. Garrick, except at unguarded moments, was always conciliatory, and Foote, surprisingly, kept his satire within bounds, so the two continued to remain, outwardly at least, on friendly terms until Foote's death.

NOTES

1. The MS is in the Harvard Theatre Collection and printed with minor revisions in *Some Unpublished Correspondence of David Garrick,* ed. George P. Baker (Boston. 1907), p. 26.
2. Delaval MS at Newcastle Library; and Askham, pp. 113-114.
3. *Letters of David Garrick,* Vol. II, p. 501, n. 3. Foote's letter to Beard seems to have had its effect, for Smith's benefit did not include *The Commissary* as an afterpiece.
4. *Letters to David Garrick,* Vol. II, p. 500.
5. Davies, Vol. II, p. 246.
6. Dunbar, p. 37. Garrick's judicious use of one of Murphy's intemperate letters probably kept him from being accepted as a templar in 1757.
7. *Ibid.,* pp. 106-121.
8. Knight, p. 238.
9. Delaval MS at Newcastle Library.
10. Nicholson, p. 153, quotes from Colman's acting manager's speech to the audience clarifying the terms of his patent: "When a Royal Patent was about to be granted to the late Mr. Foote, it was inquired, with that justice which characterizes the English throne, what annual extent of term might be allowed him, without injury to theatrical patents then existing in this metropolis. The proprietors of the winter theatres were interrogated on this point, and, in consequence of their documents, a patent was granted to Foote for his life, to open a theatre annually, from the 15th of May to the 15th of September, inclusive."
11. According to Garrick, Foote and a number of potential backers expressed interest in the sale of the patent but could not raise the £60,000. (*Letters of David Garrick,* Vol. II, pp. 528-529.) The patent was finally sold in 1767 to George Colman and three others: Thomas

Harris, a soap-boiler, John Rutherford, a wine seller, and William Powell, a leading actor at Drury Lane.

12. It was officially granted on July 5, 1766. See Cooke, *Foote*, Vol. III, pp. 202-208.

13. George Colman the Younger, *Random Records* (London, 1830), Vol. I, p. 114.

14. In Foote's "Will" the "best Goldheaded Crutched Cane" is left to his friend Archibald Hamilton, founder of *The Critical Review*.

15. Garrick wrote Colman that Foote "is now very uneasy that *Barry* & *Dancer* are coming to join him at ye *Opera house*—he is to give them half ye Profits;; ye Expences will be great, & he finds that all his friends think him in ye wrong to have them—*You'll* think so too, & when *Barry* comes, he'll find *Foote* very cold—they say he abuses him already." *(Letters of David Garrick,* Vol. II, pp. 528-529.)

16. In a letter to Wilkinson, Foote wrote that this extra work injured his health: "I cannot say I am quite so well as I had reason to expect: I thought myself obliged to give Barry a lift two critical nights, which injured me extremely." (Wilkinson, *Memoirs,* Vol. IV, pp. 263-264.)

17. Cooke, *Memoirs of Charles Macklin,* pp. 164-169.

18. *The Universal Museum and Complete Magazine,* June, 1776, pp. 294-295.

19. Genest, Vol. V, p. 113.

20. Foote, *The Dramatic Works,* Vol. II, pp. 344-346.

21. John O'Keefe, *Recollections of the Life of John O'Keefe* (London, 1826), Vol. I, p. 328.

22. Cooke, *Foote,* Vol. I, p. 144.

23. *The English Aristophanes,* p. 21; and Stone, *London Stage,* Vol. II, p. 1253.

24. *The English Aristophanes,* p. 21.

25. Genest, Vol. V, p. 114; and see Cooke, *Memoirs of Charles Macklin,* pp. 164-169.

26. Stone, *London Stage,* Vol. II, p. 1182.

27. The *Occasional Prelude* is printed in Cooke's biography of Foote, in Badcock's edition, and in Thomas Holcroft's *Memoirs,* ed. W. Hazlitt (London, 1816), Vol. I, pp. 288-291.

28. Stone, *London Stage,* Vol. II, p. 1253.

29. *Ibid.,* p. 1256.

30. Wilkinson, *Memoirs,* Vol. IV, pp. 263-264. The question of authorship is discussed by Belden, p. 31, n. 17. I agree with her conclusion that Foote is not the author of the piece he disclaimed; but her reason, that the lack of a dramatic prelude provides negative evidence is absurd. Most of Foote's plays do not have dramatic preludes. I think it is more relevant to point out that Foote had never written a literary burlesque in blank verse before, nor was he disposed to write such subtleties in his farces. Furthermore, his next two plays, *The Devil upon Two Sticks* and *The Lame Lover,* herald his lameness as part of the title and jokes are made on his wooden leg. In *The Tailors,* Francisco as played by Foote does refer to his gout, but the reference is so

brief and irrelevant, it is likely that Foot had it written in. There is no hint as to its true author.

31. This is Foote's own description. Wilkinson, *Memoirs*, Vol. IV, pp. 263-264.
32. Stone, *London Stage*, Vol. II, pp. 1257-1258; and *The Diary of Sylas Neville*, ed. Basil Cozens-Hardy (London, 1950), pp. 15-16.
33. Stone, *London Stage*, Vol. II, p. 1258.
34. Cradock, Vol. I, pp. 30-35.
35. Stone, *London Stage*, Vol. III, p. 1273.
36. *CBEL*, Vol. II, p. 541.
37. Belden, p. 125.
38. *CBEL*, Vol. II, p. 545.
39. *The English Aristophanes*, p. 24.
40. Benjamin Victor, *The History of the Theatres of London and Dublin* (London, 1761-71), Vol. III, p. 192.
41. Foote, *The Dramatic Works*, Vol. III, pp. 8-9.
42. *The Letters of Horace Walpole*, ed. P. Toynbee (London, 1903), Vol. VII, p. 199.
43. Betty Copping Corner, "Dr. Melchisedech Broadbrim and the Playwright," *Journal of the History of Medicine*, VII (Spring, 1952), 122-135.
44. John Nichols, *Literary Anecdotes of the Eighteenth Century* (London, 1812-16), Vol. III, p. 326.
45. R. Hingston Fox, *William Hunter: Anatomist, Physician, Obstetrician, 1718-1783* (London, 1901), pp. 67-69.
46. Foote, *The Dramatic Works*, Vol. III, pp. 47-48.
47. *Ibid.*, pp. 50-51.
48. Kalman A. Burnim, *David Garrick Director* (Pittsburgh, 1961), p. 4.
49. Cooke, *Table-Talk*, p. 99.
50. A.L.S. in Victoria and Albert Museum, Enthoven Collection.
51. Cooke, *Table-Talk*, p. 37.
52. *Ibid.*, p. 51.
53. A.L.S. in Pierpont Morgan Library, New York City.
54. *The Letters of David Garrick*, Vol. II, pp. 611-612. The italicized words at the end of the letter refer to Foote's comments in *The Devil upon Two Sticks*. At the end of the play the devil tells the lovers, who seek careers on the stage, that he cannot help them at either of the winter houses. The managers of Covent Garden are filled with discord, "and as to the other house, the manager has great merit himself, with skill to discern, and candor to allow it in others; but I can be of no use in making your bargain, for in that he would be too many for the cunningest Devil amongst us."
55. *Ibid.*, pp. 623-624.
56. Askham, p. 112.
57. Stone, *London Stage*, Vol. II, p. 1124.
58. *Theatrical Biography: or Memoirs of the Principal Performers of the Theatres Royal, Drury Lane, Covent Garden, Haymarket, together with*

Critical and Impartial Remarks on their Respective Merits (London, 1772), Vol. I, pp. 102-105.

59. Stone, *London Stage,* Vol. III, p. 1383. This time she sang under her married name.

60. *Town and Country Magazine,* May, 1769, pp. 241-243.

61. Stone, *London Stage,* Vol. III, p. 1413.

62. Cooke, *Foote,* Vol. I, p. 155. *The St. James Chronicle,* November 22-24, 1768, carried this item in its gossip column: "A certain person having lately lost in one evening all which the comedy of the *Devil upon Two Sticks* had produced had Lady——say 'What had been got over the Devil's Back had been lost under his Belly.' "

63. Cooke, *Foote,* Vol. I, p. 156.

64. *Diary of Sylas Neville,* p. 62. Mr. Neville states that on February 15, Foote, at Davies with Cleland, was ridiculing the French, indicting their foolish humor, gross indelicacy, and terrible food.

65. Christian Deelman, *The Great Shakespeare Jubilee* (New York, 1964), p. 74.

66. Stone, *London Stage,* Vol. III, pp. 1415-1418. Sheriden played *Hamlet, Richard III, Othello,* and *Julius Caesar.*

67. *Ibid.,* p. 1418.

68. *Ibid.,* p. 1407.

69. *Town and Country Magazine,* June, 1769, p. 326.

70. *Town and Country Magazine,* October, 1769, p. 525.

71. *Town and Country Magazine,* May, 1769, p. 243.

72. *Town and Country Magazine,* August, 1769, p. 434.

73. Martha Winburn England, *Garrick's Jubilee* (Ohio State University Press, 1964), pp. 12-13.

74. *The Letters of David Garrick,* Vl. III, p. 1355.

75. This performance was scheduled for August 7.

76. A.L.S. in Harvard Theatre Collection; also found in Boaden, p. 221; and Forster, p. 440.

77. Deelman, pp. 178-179.

78. The cancelling of the procession averted a clash between Garrick and Lacy. The weather was so threatening on the first day that Lacy insisted he would not endanger £5000 of wardrobe property by exposure to probable rain. Garrick hoped for better weather, but, according to Foote, Lacy told his friends that "Garrick and his mummers may parade it as much as they please, but *none of the clothes shall walk.*" (Cooke, Foote, Vol. II, p 86.) But perhaps Garrick was lucky. According to Cradock, Vol. I, p. 217, "The dresses could not have borne either daylight or any other examination. And Foote prepared for the procession."

79. Cooke, *Foote,* Vol. II, pp. 85-86.

80. *Town and Country Magazine,* September, 1769, p. 477.

81. George Colman, *Man and Wife: or The Stratford Jubilee* (London, 1770), p. iv.

82. *Town and Country Magazine,* October, 1769, p. 547.

83. *The Letters of David Garrick,* Vol. II, pp. 721-722.
84. *Three Plays by David Garrick,* ed. Elizabeth Stein (New York, 1926), p. 74.
85. England, p. 87.
86. Cooke, *Foote,* Vol. I, p. 169; also Davies, Vol. II, pp. 259-260.
87. Cooke, *Foote,* Vol. I, pp. 166-169.
88. Deelman, p. 285.
89. *Town and Country Magazine,* May, 1770, pp. 229-230; and see England, pp. 107-108, and p. 121, n. 29.

CHAPTER IX

FOOTE'S ESTABLISHMENT:
THE GOLDEN AGE, 1770-1774

Foote's theatre was becoming a summer institution, and he was even more popular than before his accident. Far from being a handicap, the false leg became the object of many of Foote's jokes, and the limp was accepted as part of the act. Tate Wilkinson, now a minor monarch of strolling players, found that he could no longer imitate his master as in the past. Once, when acting Major Sturgeon in Foote's manner, Wilkinson was hissed off the stage by the audience because he did not play the role with a limp.[1] Even the historian Gibbon valued Foote's contributions that so enlivened the traditional dullness of a London summer. Responding to his sister's request that he leave the heat of the city, Gibbon declined, saying that he found London pleasing for its solitude in the summer and "when I am tired of the Roman Empire I can laugh away the Evening at Foote's Theatre."[2] That was indeed a testimonal!

Foote planned his 1770 campaign with a new three-act piece, the first new play he had written since *The Devil upon Two Sticks* in 1768.[3] He retained Sparks and Sheridan[4] from the previous season and hired no new starring performers. Foote used thirty-two players and kept the Haymarket open for fifty-nine performances. He himself acted in forty-three mainpieces and fourteen afterpieces.[5]

Foote opened his season by reciting his occasional prologue

that mocked Jubilee sentiment and followed this with *The Devil upon Two Sticks* which also aimed some new thrusts at Garrick.[6] Though the papers carried accounts of several new pieces that were to brighten Foote's season,[7] the only new play that season was *The Lame Lover*. The plot, a thin one, is about a lawyer who is cuckolded by his daughter's suitor, and the satire is aimed at lawyers: their hair splitting, sharp practice, and abysmal ignorance of matters not directly pertaining to their profession.

In the course of events, Foote, whose role was that of the suitor, Luke Limp, was also able to get off many jokes on his wooden leg. And, as usual in Foote's plays, there was much personal satire and mimicry. Sergeant Whittaker, the lawyer who was a candidate for Middlesex with Wilkes and Luttrel in April, 1769, was mimicked by Foote, along with many lesser legal lights. The character of Luke Limp was based upon John Skrimshire Boothby, a snob who adored the lords of the land. Foote has him breaking one dinner engagement after another, as knight takes precedence over alderman, earl over knight, and finally, as his servant stands in a state of utter confusion about which dinner dates to confirm or deny, Limp hobbles out the door to take lunch with a waiting duke. Foote found that his satire on Boothby drew laughter as did his jokes on his wooden leg, but the audience did not respond to the second and third acts, which were aimed at the courts and the lawyers. Accordingly, he made several alterations for the performance on June 27 that pacified rather than pleased his critics.[8] The play went on to fifteen performances that summer, a poor showing in comparison to Foote's previous successes, and it was rarely performed afterwards.[9]

During this summer, Foote fell into a quarrel with Dr. Paul Hiffernan that narrowly escaped serious consequences. Hiffernan, a hanger-on in dramatic circles, tried to have Foote employ him as dramatist for the Haymarket. Foote refused, and when Hiffernan tried to raise money through subscriptions, he used his forceful selling techniques on Foote, who promptly lost his temper and called Hiffernan a common thief. In revenge, Hiffernan then wrote a criticism of Foote's anti-Jubliee prologue, *Foote's Prologue Detected; with a Miniature-Prose Epilogue of his Manner in Speaking It. By Philo-Technicus Miso-Mimicles*.[10] Foote, prob-

ably suspecting an attempt to win Garrick's favor, refused Hiffer-
man free use of the Haymarket, a privilege that patentees normally
extended to all practicing dramatists. Hiffernan retorted that he
would pay after-money, as the fee was called, but warned Foote
that if his appearance came after the second act of the mainpiece,
he would pay only half the price, which was the practice in the
winter houses. Hiffernan then wrote a letter to the newspapers
claiming that the Haymarket should not have privileges refused
to Drury Lane and Covent Garden. Fortunately, the publisher
showed the letter to Foote, who, fearing for the safety of his
playhouse,[11] sent a letter to Garrick asking him to use his influence
to silence Hiffernan:

July, 1770

Dear Sir,

Last night a letter written by Doctor Hiffernan was
brought me by a director of one of the newspapers, containing in express words, an invitation to the public to
come and pull my playhouse down for not taking after
money. . . . Upon the whole, it is, I think, worthy of
consideration whether there is not something immoral,
as well as impolitic, in encouraging a fellow, who without
parts, principles, property, or profession, has subsisted
these twenty years by raising contributions under false
pretenses, and finding how necessary the public good opinion is to every subject of the stage, has with all the qualities
of a footpad but the courage, extorted money from every
individual by presenting, instead of a pistol, a pen to his
breast.[12]

Garrick thanked Foote for his trust and promised his fullest coop-
eration.[13] To Foote's relief, Garrick had enough influence to
silence Hiffernan.

Shortly after this incident, in August, Foote made preparations to take most of his company with him to Edinburgh. Some
of the arrangements for this trip were probably made by Wilkin-

son, who invited Foote to visit him on his way to the north. Foote accepted the invitation in a chatty letter describing the sad decline of his one-time target, Thomas Sheridan:

> I have this summer entertained the veteran Sheridan, who is dwindled to a mere cock and bottle Chelsea pensioner:—He has enlisted some new recruits, unfit for service, and such as might be expected to issue from his discipline.
>
> I shall be glad to chop upon you in my way to Edinburgh, for which place I shall set out about the middle of Oct.
>
> Ross is with me, ill and indolent; but however, thanks to my own industry, the campaign has been lucky enough.[14]

Foote's trip was exceedingly daring, for, with the exception of his own previous trip to Edinburgh, no starring London actor traveled beyond Bath or Dublin, and to transport a full troupe to Scotland was unheard of. The Haymarket actors numbered twenty men and eight women, including Woodward, Weston, and Mrs. Jewel.[15] The inclusion of Woodward in this venture is surprising, but Foote needed another star performer to insure the success of this risky undertaking and induced Woodward to accompany him, offering him the salary of £14 per week;[16] his regular salary at Covent Garden had been £2/15s per diem.[17] The former manager of the Edinburgh Theatre, David Ross, whom Foote mentioned in his letter to Wilkinson, found meagre pickings in the northern capital; and when a *New Rosciad* appeared in January, 1770, savagely attacking his troupe, Ross became discouraged and looked for the first opportunity to lease or sell his theatre. When Foote heard of his difficulties, he made an agreement with him to lease the theatre for three years at £500 per year.[18]

It is impossible to find out exactly what performances were given that season, though Dibdin gives a skeletal account. Foote opened the season on November 17 with *The Commissary* and

The Lying Valet,[19] and, in addition, he acted Mother Cole, Shylock, and Fondlewife in succeeding productions. Woodward played Marplot in Centlivre's *Busybody* and Boabdil in Jonson's *Every Man in His Humour;* Mrs. Jewel sang Polly's role in *The Beggar's Opera*.[20] These productions delighted the theatrically starved Edinburgh audience, and Boswell, in a letter to Garrick, confirmed the success of Foote's troupe:

> Mar. 30, 1771
>
> We have been kept laughing all this winter by Foote, who has made a Very good Campaign of it here. Woodward has been exceedingly admired & has been a great support to the House; for you know Mr Foot's drollery Cannot entertain long in a Theatre where there is not a variety of audiences. I hear he is not to return but has transferred his lease of the Theatre for the two remaining years.
>
> His Favorite Mrs. Jewel has not taken here, her poorness of figure & aukward inanimate action disgust us much & we wonder how she had been praised so much in London.[21]

Garrick replied that Foote described matters differently:

> April 18, 1771
>
> Our Friend Foote has convinc'd Me that he has brought from Scotland a ballance of above one thousand pounds— but his Account of the theatrical matters there, differs widely from Yours—He tells me (this is between ourselves) that he was much follow'd & that Woodward was deserted, & that likewise Mrs. Jewel was much approv'd of—the Good People of Edinburgh will not be satisy'd with Aristophanical flashes of Merriment, & with ye Mere Sallies of Wit, & humour, they require a Substantial classical drama—*to cut & come again,* as the vulgar Saying is . . .[22]

The northern trip was adventurous and profitable, but obviously it was too arduous to bear seasonal repetition, and Foote was not anxious to return to Scotland the following year. Even though he had leased the theatre from Ross for three years, upon his return to London, Foote tried to sell the remainder of the lease, and, finally, in 1771, he was forced to sell it at a loss to the actors West Digges and Bland.[23] Digges, unfortunately, was soon arrested for debt, and Ross, retaining Arthur Murphy as his lawyer, brought siut against Foote for two years' rent. After several years of litigation, Ross finally won his suit on May 26, 1774.[24] When Ross presented Foote with the bill, Foote paid and sarcastically remarked that he presumed that Ross would be returning to Edinburgh, after the manner of his race, in the cheapest way. "Ay Ay," the Scot told him, tapping the money. "I shall travel on *foot.*" "I am heartily sorry for that," said Foote, "for I know no man who more richly deserves horsing." [25]

Foote caused another altercation in Edinburgh when he produced *The Minor* on November 24, 1770. Whitefield had died in Massachusetts on September 30 of that year, and it is possible that the news of his death had just arrived. There seemed to be no objection by the clergy or the audience to the first performance of the play, and the theatre was well filled. But on the second showing, given on the twenty-fourth, there was spare attendance, for the women boycotted the performance. The clergy then denounced Foote for not showing proper respect for the dead.[26] Under these circumstances it seems likely that the news of Whitefield's death did not reach Edinburgh until between the first and second playings of *The Minor.*

Despite the furor, Foote insisted on performing his piece, and for the next few weeks clergymen in the area thundered against its impropriety. One of these clergymen, James Baine of the Kirk of Relief, published his strictures: *The Theatre Licentious and Perverted, or a Sermon for Reformation of manners. Preached on the Lord's Day, Dec. 2, 1770. Partly occasioned by the acting of a comedy entitled, The Minor, in the licensed Theatre of Edinburgh, on Saturday the 24th of November preceding. By James Baine, A.M., Minister of the Gospel at Edinburgh. In-*

scribed to Samuel Foote, Esq. Foote decided that, since Baine merely rehashed all the old charges made against the play in 1760 and 1761, it would not be necessary to add anything new to his reply that he had not printed before. *An Apology for the Minor in a Letter to the Rev. Mr. Baine. To which is added the Original Epilogue. By Samuel Foote, Esq.*,[27] is an almost verbatim copy of the defense Foote had made earlier in his *Letter to the Reverend Author of the Christian and Critical Remarks.* Foote's original letter was witty and contemptuous; in the present situation it would confirm the prejudices of those in either camp.

Foote had disposed of his detractors, but trouble was still to come from his sincerest flatterer. Shortly after his triumphant return to London with gold still jingling in his pockets, he received an interesting letter of apology from Wilkinson for illegally performing *The Devil upon Two Sticks.* Wilkinson had got hold of a stolen copy of the play, probably from a member of Foote's company on his way south, and naturally performed it with his strollers in the northern provinces. Afraid that Foote would hear of it and bring action against him, Wilkinson foolishly tried to forestall this possibility by writing the letter and hoping that Foote would forgive the "prank." Foote did see the humor of the situation and responded quickly:

> Your favour brought me the first account of the *Devil upon Two Sticks* having been played upon your stage.— Your letter has delivered me from every difficulty, and will procure me the pleasure of soon seeing you in town, as I most certainly will move the Court of King's Bench against you the first day of next term. I have the honour to be my dear Sir,
>
> Your most oblig'd and
faithful and humble servant.[28]

This was not the response that Wilkinson had hoped for, so he appealed to Woodward to stop Foote from bringing suit. Wood-

ward agreed, and Foote, in a convivial moment, accepted the plea
to forgive and forget, with the proviso that Wilkinson would
never try the same trick again.[29]

Foote at this time was busy writing a new play, *The Maid of
Bath*. He took great enjoyment in reading his works in progress
to his friends, and on one occasion, Foote, surprised by a chance
visit of Garrick and Cumberland, was delighted to press them to
stay for dinner and hear parts of his new play. They were soon
joined by a titled friend of Foote's, Sir Robert Fletcher. In what
seemed a calculated move, Sir Robert rose to leave and hid himself behind a conveniently placed screen that blocked sight of the
door. When Foote began to ridicule him, Sir Robert suddenly
revealed himself: "I am not gone, Foote; spare me until I am out
of hearing; and now with your leave, I will stay till these gentle-
ment depart, and then you shall amuse me at their cost, as you
have amused them at mine." As Cumberland tells the story, Foote,
for once, was struck dumb:

> This event, which deprived Foote of all presence of mind,
> gave occasion to Garrick to display his genius and good
> nature in their brightest lustre; I never saw him in a more
> amiable light; the infinite address and ingenuity that he
> exhibited in softening the enraged guest, and reconciling
> him to pass over an affront, were at once the most comic
> and the most complete I ever witnessed. . . . I hope Foote
> was very grateful, but when a man has been completely
> humbled, he is not very fond in recollecting it.[30]

Foote, of course, was famous for reviling departed guests, but
rarely had he been caught so unprepared. Among the hundreds
of anecdotes about Foote, this is the only one I have found which
reveals him unable to top his antagonist. Garrick and Cumberland, though momentarily distracted, stayed to approve of the
play, for they contributed a prologue and epilogue to *The Maid
of Bath*.

For the 1771 season, Foote hired forty actors, including

Woodward and Mrs. Fearon, whom he had brought from Scotland to play Lady Catherine Coldstream in the new piece. The Haymarket gave fifty-six performances, of which Foote appeared in forty-six mainpieces and fifteen afterpieces. The addition of Woodward to the company affected the repertory of the Haymarket considerably that year. Foote did not rely on the usual ballad-operas, and in their stead Woodward acted in *Every Man in His Humour, The Busybody, Catherine and Petruchio, The Provoked Wife, The Brothers,* and *The West Indian.* These plays provided Foote with a needed change of pace, for few of them had ever been given by his troupe before.[31]

The Maid of Bath, hawked about town and filled with current scandal, was eagerly awaited by Foote's public. This interest even extended to the Literary Club; Johnson, Colman, Garrick, Goldsmith, Steevens, and Reynolds were among those who came to applaud the play's debut.[32] The inspiration for the piece was Miss Elizabeth Linley, the sixteen-year-old daughter of the composer Thomas Linley. Though young, the girl was already famous for her singing and her beauty, and when performing at the Assembly Room in Bath during 1770, she attracted many suitors. One of her favorites was Thomas Mathews, a wealthy rake who had long been a friend of the family. Mr. and Mrs. Linley, however, preferred Sir Walter Long, sixtyish and exceedingly wealthy. The will of the parents prevailed, and the marriage settlement was drawn. Suddenly, for reasons that were never made clear,[33] Long broke the match, was consequently sued for breach of contract by the heartbroken parents, and settled out of court. This is the stuff of storybooks, and it is a pity that Foote could not have foreseen Sheridan's dramatic elopement with the girl of everyone's dreams, and so provided a proper conclusion to his tale.

Foote, who supposedly was in Bath when this happened,[34] wrote *The Maid of Bath* to champion Elizabeth Linley's cause. Miss Linley becomes Kitty Linnet in the play, and her coarse, money-grubbing mother insists on marrying her to Solomon Flint (Sir Walter Long), played by Foote. Miss Linnet's crafty old friend, Major Racket (Thomas Mathews), is horrified to hear of the forthcoming nuptials from his quondam drinking crony, the aging and gout-stricken Sir Christopher Cripple. Though he has sworn to reform, Sir Christopher agrees to help Racket foil the mismatch. The two then influence Flint's companions, the tailor Billy Button, the apothecary Peter Poultice, Mynheer Sourcrouts and the port manufacturer Monsieur de Jersey, to play upon Flint's fears of losing his money and health by marrying a young and lively girl.

Flint's miserliness and disabilities are such that his friends have little trouble in cooling his ardor for marriage, but they cannot quench his lust. Flint runs to Miss Linnet's apartment and demands proof of their sexual compatibility before he will agree to marry one as insignificant as she is. Delighted by this excuse for dismissing Flint, Miss Linnet nobly points him to the door and this time is seconded by her mother. Racket, who has engineered this plot to gain Miss Linnet for himself, finds that Sir Christopher is determined to make an honest man of him. He tells Racket that he will settle an annuity on him if he agrees to marry the girl. But this time Miss Linnet has her say. She disowns Racket for his past sins and declares that she will, for the time, remain single and devote herself to pleasing her patron, the audience.

Foote brought not only the principals of the incident, Mrs. and Miss Linley, Long, and Mathews, into his play; the minor characters, though some have remained unidentified, also represented well-known people at Bath.[35] The play was a success, and the audience showed its appreciation repeatedly by bursting into applause.[36]

The hit of the performance was a reference to a newspaper squabble between Horne-Tooke and John Wilkes. In earlier times when Horne was a strong supporter of Wilkes, he had left in Paris a rich and colorful collection of suits which he asked the exiled Wilkes to hold until he returned; as a parson he could not wear such gay stuff in England. Wilkes complied until near the end of 1771, when Horne decided that Wilkes was not a patriot, but a self-serving rogue. In an exchange of letters in the *Public Advertiser,* Horne accused Wilkes of pawning the suits to pay debts.[37] This controversy was alluded to in the play when Billy Button tries to discourage Flint from marrying one so young be-

cause of the expense of buying new clothes to appear the gentleman in London:

> Button: And then the vast heap of fine clothes you
> must make—
> Flint: What occasion for that?
> Button: As you ar'n't known, there is no doing with-
> out; because why, everybody passes there for what they
> appears.
> Flint: Right, Billy; but I believe I have found out a
> way to do that pretty cheap.
> Button: Which way may be that?
> Flint: You have seen the minister that's come down
> to tack us together—
> Button: I have: Is he a fine man in the pulpit?
> Flint: He don't care too much to meddle with that;
> but he is a prodigious patriot, and a great politician to
> boot.
> Button: Indeed!
> Flint: And he has left behind him, at Paris, a choice
> collection of curious rich cloaths, which he has promised
> to sell me a penn'orth.[38]

Even Horne could not take offense at this whimsy, and in a letter
to Junius printed in the *Public Advertiser,* July 13, 1771, stated:

> Sir, Farce, Comedy, and Tragedy—Wilkes, Foote, and
> Junius united at the same time, against one poor Parson,
> are fearful odds. The former two are only laboring in their
> vocation, and may equally plead in excuse, that their aim
> is a livelihood. I admit the plea for the second; his is an
> honest calling, and my clothes were lawful game.[39]

In addition to its popular success, the play was well received

by the reviewers. They praised the acting and the farcical qualities of the play. "Throughout the piece, the audience are perpetually incited to laugh, and that man must indeed be a cynic
who can keep his muscles in form for half an hour." [40] One dis-
senting writer, however, gave his "Devil's Definition" of the play:

> The piece was very well received. The audience were
> interested without plot; surprised without incident; in-
> structed without moral; and diverted without a new char-
> acter. In short as Mr. Foote had a fine scope for displaying
> his inimitable talents for mimicry, the success of the piece
> is not to be wondered at. [41]

The carping critic was right; the play is thin and does not
read well today. Foote did give himself wide scope for mimicry,
but he failed to construct a strong plot because he followed so
closely the action of the original incident; indeed, that was the
reason for the play's popularity. But unlike some of his other
plays which were also liberally laced with mimicry and topical
references, Foote did not bring in any outrageous and exaggerated
caricatures of his own creation. His satire in this play was too
closely confined to reality. Neither Flint, Cripple, Button, nor
Coldstream have anything like the life of the more imaginative
creations of Sneak, Buck returning from Paris, Shift, or Cadwallader and Becky, since Foote was free to put the latter impersonations in any context he liked.

Foote, who sometimes showed good judgment on these matters, seemed to think that this was one of his better plays. Beginning in 1768 with *The Devil upon Two Sticks,* Foote stopped
publishing his successful plays, for he thought that theatregoers
might be deterred from coming to the performances more than
once if they were subsequently able to read a copy of the play
and thus keep the original production in mind. [42] He sold the
others, *The Lame Lover* and *The Bankrupt,* immediately after
their production to profit while there was still an interest in
them. He did not sell *The Maid of Bath* and was partially vin-

dicated by the eleven performances given the following year. Subsequently, however, it averaged only three performances per year from 1773 through 1776.[43]

Foote's joy at the success of his new play was dimmed on August 8 when his best friend, Sir Francis Delaval, died. Cooke writes that Foote "burst into a flood of tears, retired to his room, and saw no company for three days." On the fourth day Jewel came in, and when Foote asked him about the burial, Jewel replied that the surgeons were going to dissect the head. Foote was incredulous. "And what will they get there? I'm sure I have known poor Frank for these five and twenty years, and I could never find anything in it." [44] Foote could not resist the joke. But he did take his responsibilities to his dead friend's son seriously. Francis' brother, John, would not support the illegitimate son of Francis and Miss Roach. The boy had been left penniless, for his improvident father had been forced to sell his estate to John in return for an annual income. Young Delaval evidently had inherited some of his father's qualities for high living, and he fell heavily in debt. To keep the boy out of prison, Foote sold his interest in the Haymarket and paid the debts.[45] When his season was over, Foote took his usual trip to the continent.

In the spring, Boswell returned to frolic in London, and he writes the best account of Foote's merry and costly hospitality. Boswell called upon Foote shortly after his arrival in the capital and noted he was the "same man." [46] Foote maligned Lord Mansfield's voice and mimicked Garrick's stammer. "Sir, a man born never to finish a sentence," Foote told him. Thus greeting his visitor, Foote invited Boswell for dinner at his North End estate later in the week. Boswell arrived to find just one other guest, George Gray, an old schoolfellow who had accumulated a disruptable fortune in India. Foote entertained them by taking off George Faulkner and by telling a humorous story about Johnson. Boswell, of course, checked the story later and ascertained its falsehood. He even recounted with glee that when Foote proudly showed them his pedigree, Boswell recalled poor Cadwallader whom Foote had traduced for similar vanities in *The Author*. Boswell strongly disapproved of Foote though he sought his company and laughed at his jokes. Perhaps it was because Foote, unlike the people Boswell idolized, mocked the moral pieties that Boswell felt were so necessary to reinforce his own weak integrity. Throughout his *Life of Johnson,* Boswell frequently brought Foote into a conversation for Johnson's disapprobation; although Johnson also disapproved of Foote, he relished his wit with greater appreciation than Boswell ever dared give. But Boswell was not so unfavorably biased about food and drink:

> He gave us a very elegant dinner, all served upon plate; and he did not say, "Gentlemen, there's Madeira and port and claret." But, "Gentlemen, there's *all* sorts of wine. You'll call for what you choose." He gave us noble old hock, of which he had purchased ninety dozen—"the stock of an ambassador lately deceased," as I said. It was indeed brought from an ambassador. He gave us sparkling champagne, Constantia, and Tokay. When the latter was served round, he said, "Now you're going to drink the best wine in England"; and it was indeed exquisite. His claret flowed of course.[47]

After such expense for what must have been a casual dinner, it is no wonder that Foote's finances were only as good as his last season at the Haymarket.

Foote also spent more money than was usual in preparing for the new season in 1772. About the time he returned from Edinburgh, notices in the papers spread the rumor that he was widening the stage of the Haymarket to include some of the dressing room and green room space in order to stage pantomimes by Woodward.[48] However, since Woodward did not appear again in the Haymarket and, in fact, no pantomimes were ever staged during Foote's tenure, the rumors were probably false. When Foote returned from Edinburgh, he bought the house adjacent to his own on Suffolk Street, and it is likely that the construction the Haymarket underwent during the spring was to incorporate the new property, conveniently located behind the theatre, into an easy means of entrance and exit behind the scenes. Prior to this time the servants and performers had to enter at the box door and maneuver behind the side boxes to reach the stage, and the same awkward procedure was necessary in departing.[49] Perhaps Foote made the arduous trip to Edinburgh to raise money for this additional expense.

Foote also went to the extra expense of hiring eleven more actors than the previous year, bringing the number to fifty-one, though he did not hire any starring performers.[50] Fifty-six performances were given that season at the Haymarket, Foote appearing in fifty-two mainpieces and twelve afterpieces.[51]

Foote's new play, *The Nabob,* was a timely thrust at those who made immense fortunes in India through violent and corrupt means and upon returning home to England used the same criminal tactics to advance themselves socially and politically. Public interest in the East India Company and the nabobs reached a peak in April, 1771, when Lord Clive was formally investigated by Parliament to determine the legality of his practices in India. At this time Clive defended himself before the House of Commons by claiming that among the nabobs not one had been found "sufficiently flagitious for Mr. Foote to exhibit on the theatre in the Haymarket." [52] He spoke just in time, though his faith in Foote as the public defender of morality must have amused many.

In the play, Sir Matthew Mite, a recently returned nabob from India, places the Oldham family in debt to him through underhanded tactics in order to foreclose on their estate and force their daughter, Sophy, to marry him. If she refuses, he threatens to bring her family into financial ruin. Sophy, though in love with her paternal cousin, Young Oldham, is prepared to sacrifice her happiness to save her parents. At the last moment she is saved by her uncle, Mr. Thomas Oldham, who appears with the necessary cash. Lady Oldham, who had sneered at her brother-in-law because he was a merchant, is then forced to admit that kind hearts are more than coronets and allows her daughter to marry his son, Young Oldham.

Though the plot seems, like *The Minor,* to be sentimental beyond measure, the story takes up only a few pages at the beginning and at the end of the play. The larger part of the play deals with the various swindles, machinations, and social climbing efforts of Sir Matthew Mite, and it is in these scenes that we find the farcical humor and topical satire that were celebrated by Foote's audience. Matthew Mite, played by Foote, was primarily a takeoff of General Richard Smith, the son of a cheesemonger, though the title role probably incorporates traits of Lord Clive and Nabob Gray, Boswell's schoolmate, as well.[53] Foote did not heap all of his opprobium upon the nabobs alone; he also satirized the cooperative friends of the nabobs who were eager to corrupt themselves for money. In one scene the Christian Club from the parish of Bribe'em enter into negotiations with Mite to sell their votes, "humorously and satirically exposing the late proceedings of the Christian Club of Shoreham." [54] They are called the Christian Club because, as one member, Touchit, explains, "When the bargain is struck, and the deposit is made, as a proof that we love our neighbors as well as ourselves, we submit to an equal partition." Mite applauds these noble sentiments but wishes to withhold payment until after election. Touchit objects:

> Touchit: . . . Our club has always found, that those who don't pay before are sure never to pay.
> Mite: How! impossible! the man who breaks his word with such faithful and honest adherents, richly deserves a halter. Gentlemen, in my opinion, he deserves to be hanged.
> Touchit: Hush! . . . You see the fat man that is behind; he will be the returning officer at the election.
> Mite: What then?
> Touchit: On a gibbet, at the end of our town, there hangs a smuggler, for robbing the custom-house.
> Mite: Well?
> Touchit: The mayor's own brother, your honour: now, perhaps he may be jealous that you meant to throw some reflection on him or his family.
> Mite: Not unlikely. I say, gentlemen, whoever violates

his promise to such faithful friends as you are, in my opinion, deserves to be damned!

Touchit: That's right! stick to that! for though the Christian Club may have some fears of the gallows, they don't value damnation of a farthing.[55]

In another scene, Foote dramatized an incident that was supposed to have happened to Sir Thomas Robinson of Yorkshire who made it a habit to break in unannounced on the Duke of Burlington:

Conserve: Who is it?

Janus: That eternal teaser, Sir Timothy Tallboy. When once he gets a footing, there is no such thing as keeping him out. . . . He had like to have lost me the best place I ever had in my life.

Cons: How so?

Janus: Lord Lofty had given orders on no account to admit him. The first time, he got by me under a pretense of stroking Keeper, the housedog; the next, he nick'd me by desiring only just leave to scratch the poll of the parrot," Poll, Poll, Poll!" I thought the devil was in him if he deceived me a third; but he did, notwithstanding.

Con: Prithee, Janus, how?

Janus: By begging to set his watch by Tompion's clock in the hall; I smoked his design, and laid hold of him here [*taking hold of his coat*]: As sure as you are alive, he made but one leap from the stairs to the study, and left the skirt of his coat in my hand.

Cons: You got rid of him then?

Janus: He made one attempt more; and for fear he should slip by me, (for you know he is as thin as a slice of beef at Marybone-Gardens), I slapped the door in his face, and told him, the dog was mad, the parrot dead, and the clock stood; and, thank Heaven, I have never set eyes on him since.[56]

Foote also amused himself and his audience at the expense of The Society of Antiquaries by revealing their mania for explaining historical trivia and collecting odd pieces of junk. Mite, in a parody of what actually happened at the society, gave a paper before that learned body on the significance of Dick Whittington and his cat. The conclusion of Mite's dazzling research into the field of folklore was that no ordinary cat could give Whittington his wealth. "He constructed a vessel, which, from its agility and lightness, he aptly christened a cat. . . . it was not the whiskered, four-footed, mouse-killing cat, that was the source of the magistrate's wealth, but the coasting, sailing, coal-carrying cat; that, gentlemen, was Whittington's cat." [57] It is possible that Foote was given this inside information by Walpole, who wanted revenge for the society's cavalier treatment of his paper on Richard III:

> I had long left off going to the Antiquarian Society. This summer I learned that they intended printing some more foolish notes against my *Richard III*, and though I had taken no notice of their first publication, I thought they might at last provoke me to expose them. I determined to be at liberty by breaking with them first; and Foote having brought them on stage for sitting in council as they had done, on Whittington and his cat, I was not sorry to find them so ridiculous, or to make their being so, and upon that nonsense and the laughter that accompanied it, I struck my name out of their book.[58]

With such topical seasoning the play could not fail. It was popular with everyone, except the nabobs, of course. One general, perhaps Smith himself, grumbled loudly enough to be put into the gossip columns:

> A certain Nabob General has taken to himself a Cap held out by the facetious Aristophanes; and thinking it fits him has thought proper to wear it, though many of

his Friends have taken much pains to dissuade him from putting it on, insisting it was never made for him, and might be the means of concealing his Laurels which distinguish his Brows. The General, however, ungratefully raves at Aristophanes the Maker, and cry'd lately to a Friend. "The first time I meet the Rascal, if I don't tread on his toes, I am a Cheesemonger." "You had better take Care," replies his Friend; "for it is possible you may not make him feel; and should he return the compliment, he might make your Feet as great Sufferers as he has your Head." [59]

Cooke reports a story that Foote was waylaid in his Suffolk Street house by two cudgel-bearing nabobs who had come to revenge their honor. Foote disarmed them by saying as a "wholesale popularmonger" he meant no harm to individuals, and, in any case, he meant to expose not honorable gentlemen like themselves, but the others. Charmed by his stories and jokes, they stayed for dinner and supported The Nabob through its run.[60] The story cannot be verified, but it was certainly within Foote's powers to win over the very people he had mocked.

Though his new play ran well, Foote was angry at Garrick throughout the season because he provided too many summer distractions. Garrick's protege, Torré, had directed fireworks at Mary-le-Bone Gardens and had proved no mean competitor. In addition, Drury Lane extended its season well into June so that Foote found it impossible to play regularly at the start of his season. Half in earnest, Foote tacked up this notice at the close of the Haymarket on September 15, 1772:

As it is uncertain to what lengths the Manager of Drury-Lane Theatre may protract his ensuing season, or what foreign artists besides his friend Torré he may import next summer into this country, for *correcting its morals* and *improving its taste*, Mr. Foote dares not risk entering into any future engagement with its present performers.[61]

Though Foote was joking about opening the next season, he
was dead serious about the summer encroachments of the Drury
Lane Theatre.[62] Giving vent to something that had been on his
mind ever since he had been disappointed with the terms of his
own patent in 1766, Foote, petitioned George III on September
21 for permission to keep his theatre open all year:

> To The King's Most Excellent Majesty
> The Humble Petition of Samuel Foote one of his
> Majesty's Servants most humbly sheweth.
> That your majesty was most graciously pleas'd at the
> intercession of his late Royal Highness the Duke of York:
> and in compassion to a misfortune occasioned by your
> Petitioner's attendance on his Royal Highness, to grant
> him a Patent, for the opening a Theatre from the middle
> of May, to the middle of September, being a Season, when
> from the thinness of the Town, and the Warmth of the
> Weather, no other Theatre would venture to open:
> That from your Petitioner's productions, and Personal
> Labour he has been able to erect a Theatre, and hitherto
> support with credit, not only your Majesty's Servant under
> his direction, but to furnish the other Theatres with
> Dramatic Materials, of which they have not been spareing.
> But the Public Diversions during his Season are so
> multiply'd, and the exhibitions of the other Theatres
> particularly that of Drury Lane protracted to so unusual
> a Length: that, your Petitioner from his advanced time of
> life is afraid to engage any performers, as if, from illness,
> or any other accident: he should be disabled from acting
> himself, he must be inevitably ruined.
> Your Petitioner therefore Humbly hopes especially
> too as after Christmas the other Theatres constantly over-
> flow that your Majesty out of your great goodness would
> be most graciously pleased to extend the time limited by
> the Patent already granted by your Majesty. To Your

Majesty's most Dutiful and Most Devoted Subject and Servant.[63]

Some years later, Foote recalled the incident to Lord Mansfield, who asked, "Well, and what answer did he give you, Mr. Foote?" "My Lord," Foote told him, "he paid no more attention to it than if all the people of England had petitioned him." [64]

In June, however, at the start of his season, Foote had less perspective on the problem and planned to avenge himself on the winter theatres by playing the Haymarket during their season. William Kenrick recorded in his infamous *Love in the Suds*, which appeared in July, that "Roscius having received a formal challenge from Mr. Punch and his merry family, a pitched battle, for which great preparations are now making, will be fought between them next winter." [65] Foote, of course, could not hope to gain permission from the Lord Chamberlain to put on plays in competition with the winter houses, but he needed no special permission to put on his puppet shows.

In the meantime Foote engaged in a war of nerves against Garrick similar to the one he had waged after the Stratford Jubilee. Nor was he alone in deviling Garrick. In addition to Kenrick's vile encomium, Murphy joined the fray with a parody of Garrick's alteration of *Hamlet*, though this was a personal retaliation:

O that that too, too solid house, which Foote
Has in the Haymarket, would melt at once,
Thaw and resolve itself into a dew!
Or that the Royal Pleasure had not fix'd
A patent for the summer in his hands!
Fie on't! O fie!—Foote's an unweeded garden,
That grows to seed; things rank, and gross in nature
Possess him merely. That it should come to this!
But nine months giv'n to me! nay, not so much—
Not nine!—So excellent an actor! and to him
Hyperion to a Satyr. Heav'n and earth!

Must I remember? why, the town hangs on me
As if increase of appetite did grow
By what it fed on—Yet eight little months!
But thirty weeks—a play'r no more like me
Than I to Hercules!—Most wicked speed,
To post with such dexterity from me
To him, and on this mountain leave to feed,
To batten on that moor! to quit with scorn
My *Neck or Nothing* for his *Major Sturgeon!*
It is not, nor it cannot come to good,
But break, my heart: for I must hold my tongue! [66]

Under this battering it is no wonder that Garrick finally showed the strain, and in a letter to Elizabeth Montague dated December 4, 1772, he revealed his feelings about Foote as well as his acute sensitivity to petty gossip about himself as he heatedly commented on a tale a "friend" brought him: "In the course of conversation, my name was mentioned; you must know, (to my Credit be spoken), that Foote hates me: Mr. L[yttleton] had a mind to flatter his Host [Foote], & was pleased to say—*Garrick is so mean. . . .*" [67]

Finally, on February 15, after considerable publicity, much of it at Garrick's expense, Foote unveiled his Primitive Puppet Show called *The Handsome Housemaid; or, Piety in Pattens.* Foote had been able to arouse such curiosity through his publicity that great crowds came to see the first performance:

The Novelty of it, brought such a crowd to see it, that the Haymarket was impassable for above a hour; the doors of the theatre were broke open, and great numbers entered the house without paying anything for their admission. Several hats, swords, canes, cloaks, & etc. were lost among the mob; three ladies fainted away, and a girl had her arm broke in endeavoring to get into the pit. It did not however fully answer the expectations of the audience. At the conclusion of the Entertainment a general scene of disorder ensued; which however, soon quelled and the performance was suffered to go on.[68]

The show began at seven with a long and witty exordium by Foote. He explained that he called his entertainment a "primitive puppet show" because he intended to restore this ancient form of theatre to the honor and influence it had during the days of the Roman Empire. This was a dig at the Methodists who claimed for themselves the principles of early Christianity. In praising the Roman Empire, Foote also condemned the church which so debased the art "that it escaped the jealous and prying eyes of that minister,[69] who, under the pretence of reformation, had laid every other theatrical representation under severest restraint." [70] Foote then assured his audience that his puppets, made of native English wood, were best suited to portray the characters of that country:

> We have modern patriots made from the box, it is a wood that carries an imposing gloss, and may be easily turned; for constant lovers, we have the circling ivy, crabstocks for old maids, and weeping willows for Methodist preachers: for modish wives, we have the brittle poplar; their husbands we shall give you in hornbeam: for the serenity of philosophic unimpassioned tragedy, we have frigid actors hewn out of petrified blocks; and a Theatrical manager upon stilts made out of the mulberry tree; for incorrigible poets, we have plenty of birch; and thorns for fraudulent bankrupts, directors, and nabobs; for conjugal virtue, we have the fruitful, the unfading olive; and for public spirit, that lord of the forest, the majestic oak. Of such materials, gentlemen, are our performers composed.[71]

Foote, however, did not forget his original motive of revenging himself upon the winter houses. His real aim, as he made clear in concluding the exordium, was to mock the present mode of sentimentalism which had so sunk English drama that the plots were no better than those in puppet shows, and the acting was so stiff that wooden puppets could be used to better advantage than the real actors who merely imitated them.

The curtain then rose, and a puppet, declaring himself to be a sapling, gave a prologue recounting his varied history as a piece of wood and concluded that in his present state, he stood as a cudgel for the follies of the age.[72] The puppet show, a parody of Richardson's *Pamela,* then began. Squire Booby has designs on his servant girl, Polly, and has persuaded her to accompany him to London. Thomas, the butler, loves Polly and warns her of the squire's real intentions. The squire at first is angered at Thomas' interference, but upon reflection, and shamed by Polly's chaste refusal, he offers marriage to the girl instead. Though she loves the squire, Polly gives her hand to Thomas out of gratitude. Ennobled by such an example, the squire offers to settle a ten pound legacy on them. Polly then comes to the conclusion that she can't marry one without making the other miserable so she resolves, finally, to remain a spinster.[73] Foote then concluded his show with a skit that was very like his *Trial of Samuel Foote.* He and his puppets are arrested for vagrancy, but they are eventually released because the learned court is unable to classify Foote as man or puppet. The judges finally decide that they must wait until they can catch his body without his leg or his leg without the body.[74]

At the end of the skit the audience seated in the upper gallery refused to march out to the music. Angered by the short two-hour presentation, the delicate use of puppets when they hoped for a rough and tumble Punch and Judy show, and by the fact that the upper gallery did not allow them a full view of the stage, they began to riot. Foote, to save his theatre, tried to pacify the audience by apologizing for his poor fare and by assuring them that he would make changes that would satisfy them. Those in the boxes left quietly, but some people in the gallery tore up a few benches and a few in the pit broke down the orchestra before they were satisfied they had gotten their money's worth.[75]

Foote was but little daunted at this near catastrophe. Cradock, whose *Zobeide* had been mocked by Foote for being sentimental, gleefully told him after the performance, "I hear you have burnt your fingers." Singed them a little," admitted Foote, "but if we do not take liberties with our friends, with whom can we take liberties?" [76] Apparently still undiscouraged, Foote began to give morning "rehearsals" of his altered production. After three mornings of alterations before a paying audience, Foote decided to chance an evening production once more on March 6.[77] This time, two songs by Mrs. Jewel were added, and, to propitiate the galleries, Punch was introduced in a tête-à-tête with Foote. After mocking the state of the theatre, Punch, played by Hutton, asked Foote for a job and mimicked many of the well-known actors to prove his abilities. When Foote agreed to hire him, Punch insisted that his wife, Joan, be hired as well. Foote's refusal, couched in Garrick's familiar circuitous manner, ended the performance successfully.

Foote gave the performance seventeen times and closed his theatre on April 16.[78] He had only moderate financial success, especially in comparison to his earlier entertainments, but to succeed at all after his opening performance had required great persistence and some courage. Most of the newspapers and magazines praised it as a worthy antidote to the crying comedies of Cumberland and Kelly:

> The leading business of this Puppet Drama is to ridicule those dull sentimental Comedies which now set our Audiences fast asleep at both the theatres. Here is a fine Field and excellent Game; and in Truth Mr. Foote gave it the Chace with good Success; for the dialogue of the Puppets teemed with those hackneyed and disjointed Sentiments which are become so fashionable of late, and the Scene exhibited those unnatural Transitions of Passion which Mr. Cumberland had the Honour of bringing into

vogue. . . . It teemed with keen Humour and pointed
Satire, but the classic Dress which covered some Part of it,
concealed it from the gross Eyes of the numerous Mob.[79]

Even Garrick, once he found out that Foote merely meant to
direct a few jests at him, supported the piece generously in writing
to a friend who intended to see it: "I hope you will be Entertain'd to Night with Aristophanes—He is a Genius, & ought to
be Encourag'd, He means Me no harm I am sure; & I hope &
trust y^t you and your friends go to Support the cause, the Cause
of Wit, humor, & Genius,—You can't have a better—I wish him
Success from my Soul." [80] Though the piece put Foote in the
forefront of those who fought the sentimental mode (it predated
Goldsmith's *She Stoops to Conquer* by a month), he knew he
had written no masterpiece. The exordium was clever, but the
rest of the piece was too thin to bear print. Foote salvaged
what he could by reducing it to an interlude for the Haymarket,[81]
but he never bothered to publish it.

For the 1773 season, Foote hired forty-six actors, gave fifty-
eight performances at the Haymarket, and acted in forty-seven
mainpieces and ten afterpieces.[82] He also approved highly of
Goldsmith's new play, *She Stoops to Conquer,* for he put it on
for five performances (though he did not act in it)—an unusual
honor that Foote had accorded to no other mainpiece but his
own. Undoubtedly, its antisentimental bias was particularly ap-
pealing to him.

Foote's new piece, *The Bankrupt,* was written in response
to a wave of business failures at the time, some of them suspected
to be fraudulent. One bankruptcy in particular, that of Alexander Fordyce, was given the most publicity. Even though it was
felt that Fordyce was a man of integrity, his speculations caused
the failure of the banking firm of Neal, James, Fordyce, and
Downs.[83] According to one account, Foote was fascinated by the
banker's failure and attended almost every day the sale of Fordyce's
personal belongings at Roehampton. Empathizing closely with the
ruined man, Foote finally decided to buy one of his pillows. He
needed it, he said, as a narcotic. "For if the original proprietor

could sleep so soundly on it, at the time of owing so much as he did, it may be of singular service to me on many occasions." [84]

Foote's original intention in writing the play was to satirize those who use bankruptcy for self-enrichment, but he changed the character of the hero at the request of his friends so that there would be no association with Fordyce. Probably seeing banckruptcy as an all too likely fate of his own, Foote complied by making his hero, Robert Riscounter, a man of such integrity that the play was accused by critics of being overly sentimental. Actually the play is as much about the vicious rumor-mongering of the press as it is about bankruptcy. Robert Riscounter, who has just heard that he has lost his credit on the continent, has arranged a marriage between his daughter Lydia and Sir James Biddulph. Lydia's stepmother, however, wishes to marry her own daughter, Lucy, to the same man. To discredit Lydia, Mrs. Riscounter gets James, a clerk in love with Lydia, to plant a paragraph in the newspapers that hints at an affair between them. The conniving parties hope that the ruined Lydia will marry James to save her reputation and that Sir James Biddulph will marry Lucy. But true love wins out; Sir James stands firm in his affections, uncovers the plot, and exposes the culprits. And to add more joy to the oncoming marriage, Sir Robert is told that his credit was actually honored and that his estate is saved.

Though there are two humorous and satiric scenes in the play, one satirizing two thieving attorneys who wish Sir Robert to declare bankruptcy and one that mocks newspapers that deal in scandal and innuendo, much of the dialogue is sentimental. In his new-found mellowness, Foote took off only one person, Lord Clive, as a postscript to *The Nabob*. The prologue to *The Bankrupt,* ostensibly a comment on the play and its author, is really a clever parody of Clive's defending speech before the House of Commons on May 17.[85] The play was only a moderate financial success, and the reviews were less favorable than usual.[86] One of them stated that the play suffered because Foote's genius "rather inclines him to deviate into the extravagant and burlesque, than to trespass on the serious and sentimental." [87] The review went on to approve of the consultation between Sir Robert and his attorneys and of the scene which mocked the newspapers.

In November Foote left London for an appearance on the
Dublin stage. He had previously made arrangements with Thomas
Ryder to present some of his plays with the Dublin company.
He took only two actresses with him, Mrs. Williams and Mrs.
Jewel as performers, and, of course, he also took with him his
old friend and factotum, Jewel.[88] Foote opened with *The Maid
of Bath* and on November 19 gave *The Nabob* with a prologue
written especially for the event. He congratulated the Irish citi-
zenry for their peculiar gift of humor and gave them credit for
discovering the same gift in himself. He wryly concluded by
saying that though age had weakened his abilities, there were
some advantages to be had in lameness and old age:

> If age contracts my muscles, shrills my tone,
> No man will claim these foibles as his own;
> Nor, if I halt or hobble through the scene,
> Malice point out what citizen I mean.[89]

Unfortunately, though Foote came to praise the Dubliners, few
came to applaud him and he did not do nearly as well as he had
hoped.[90]

Nor was he through with his woes. In a lively letter sent to
Garrick on December 31, 1773, he vividly describes his narrow
escape from death:

> My Dear Sir, Had it not been for the coolness and
> resolution of my old friend, and your great admirer,
> Jewel, your humble servant would last night have been
> reduced to ashes by reading in bed, that cursed custom!
> The candles set fire to the curtains, and the bed was
> instantly set in a blaze. He rushed in, hauled me out
> of the room, tore down and trampled the paper and cur-
> tains, and so extinguished the flames. The bed was burnt,
> and poor Jewel's hands most miserably scorched. So you
> see, my dear Sir, no man can forsee the great ends for

which he was born. Macklin, though a blockhead in his manhood and youth, turns out a wit and writer on the brink of the grave; and Foote, never very remarkable for his personal graces, in the decline of his life was very near becoming a toast. . . .[91]

Foote left for London shortly after this incident. He remained only briefly in the city and then, despite the winter season and his wooden leg, took the long trip to Edinburgh to perform for three weeks. No mention is made of this trip in any of the accounts of Foote's life, nor does Boswell, who was in Edinburgh at the time, refer in his journal to Foote's presence.[92] However, James Dibdin claimed that Foote appeared in Edinburgh on February 11, 1774, to play in *The Bankrupt* and gave his last performance there on March 4,[93] and Henry Mackenzie, the novelist, noted in his journal that Foote "bragged of the names of his comic characters, Pepper and Plaster, the most appropriate to the characters, he said to me, that ever were invented." [94] Though the entry is undated, this reference to the rascally attorneys in *The Bankrupt* supports Dibdin's information and sets the date of Foote's visit as after the summer of 1773.

As might be expected, Foote's trip to Scotland during the winter months was far from smooth. He wrote to Wilkinson of the heavy snows that stopped his coach at the "dirty, dismal and desolate" village of Moffat, a watering place twenty-seven miles southwest of Edinburgh.[95] After a week at Moffat, he was so sick of primitive outposts and the stringence of travel that he told Wilkinson he would not stay at Edinburgh for more than three weeks, nor would he act for Wilkinson at York. "All my campaigns shall end with this place, and my future operations shall be confined to my own principality." [96]

Back in London, Foote turned his attention once more to the Haymarket to make arrangements for the summer season and to prepare a new play. Forty actors were hired, and Foote put on fifty-four performances, appearing in fifty mainpieces and ten afterpieces.[97]

Foote's new piece, despite the rigors of the year, was in his best manner. The plot of *The Cozeners* was thin, but it was comic, unlike the sentimental framework found in *The Minor, The Nabob, The Lame Lover,* and to a greater extent in *The Bankrupt.* The play most closely resembled *The Commissary* in its continual parade of rogues and pigeons. The two rogues, Flaw, a lawyer, and Mrs. Fleece'em, a thief who has illegally returned from American exile, have set themselves in London "to procure posts, places, preferments of all conditions and sizes; to raise cash for the indigent, and procure good securities for such as are wealthy; suitable matches for people who want husbands and wives, and divorces for those who want to get rid of them." [98] Their pigeons are an Irishman, who is offered the sinecure of exciseman in the American colonies; a Jew, who is assured that he will be admitted to those exclusive clubs that formerly black-balled him; Mrs. Simony, who has come seeking preferment for her preacher husband; and the Aircastle family from the country, who want a suitable heiress for their lout of a son, Toby. Fleece'em is finally exposed when Toby finds his future bride to be a Negro slave that Fleece'em had taken with her when she left the colonies.

As might be expected, there are topical references in almost every scene. Mrs. Simony, who has come with a hundred pound note in a hymn book to advance her husband, is a reference to Dr. William Dodd's wife. In the winter of 1773, Mrs. Dodd sent a letter to Lady Apsley promising £3000 down and an annuity of £500 for the living of St. George's at Hanover Square. Lady Apsley and her husband, the Chancellor, traced the anonymous note back to Dodd, a chaplain of the Magdalen Hospital in London, and informed the King, who promptly struck Dodd's name off the list. Though Dodd insisted that he did not know what his wife had done, the news of the incident had spread through town, so he moved to the continent in the hope that the tongues would stop wagging. It was during this period of vol-untary exile that Foote brought out his play and defeated Dodd's purpose by reviving the incident nightly at the Haymarket.[99]

In another scene Mrs. Fleece'em buys silks from a mercer and, pretending to be without money, asks the suspicious shop-keeper to come with her to her attorney's for payment. Instead, she takes him to Dr. Hellebore, who has previously been told that Fleece'em's merchant is a wealthy relative who imagines that he is a silk mercer. Of course the poor man is locked up when he begins to scream for his money. This incident was supposed to have been engineered by Mrs. Caroline Rudd, an adventuress who was in jail awaiting trial for forgery. She was acquitted on December 7, 1775, though her cohorts, the Perreaus, were hanged on January 17, 1776.[100]

Lord Chesterfield, whose letters had come out posthumously earlier in the year, was also subject to Foote's satire, probably in retaliation for Chesterfield's encouragement of George Faulkner's libel suit when *The Orators* was first played in Dublin. With pious smugness Foote said that Chesterfield's letters

> compriz'd a fine system of duplicity, deception, and adultery. That his Lordship, who seems to have studied the graces with great attention, has entirely forgot that they never appear so beautiful as when accompanied by virtue; that if the graces should be found in a brothel they would lose all their attractions, and that in the hot-bed of adultery they would be scorched to deformity.[101]

Foote is less didactic in this play, though his characters are lodged in a brothel, albeit mistakenly, and Mrs. Aircastle is in a fair way of committing adultery with an old flame. She is also most concerned about teaching her son Toby the value of Chesterfieldian grace:

> Mrs. Aircastle: . . . Toby, hold up your head.
> Toby: I does, mother, I does. . . .
> Mrs. Air.: Shoulders back, Toby; and chest a little more out!
> Mr. Air.: Now, child, look at his elbows! you have pinioned him down like a pickpocket.
> Mrs. Air.: Grace, Mr. Aircastle, grace.

Mr. Air.: Grace! he has neither grace, nor grease; his breast-bone sticks out like a turkey's.

Mrs. Air.: Nothing but grace! I wish you would read some late Posthumous Letters; you would then know the true value of grace: Do you know that the only way for a young man to thrive in the world, is to get a large dish of hypocrisy, well garnished with grace, an agreeable person, and a clear patrimonial estate? . . . Toby, be mindful of grace! and, d'ye hear? don't laugh! you may grin, indeed, to show your teeth and your manners.[102]

The scene with the most promise of scandal occurs when Toby woos the heiress that Fleece'em has procured for him. Being of a pale complexion, poor Toby is blackened with cork so that he might be more alluring to a girl who has just come from India and is used to darker faces. All goes well until Toby lifts the blinds to show the girl his presents and is horrified to find his heiress is black. This was a hit at Charles James Fox, who, to replace the fortune he had gambled away, arranged with a marriage broker, Mrs. Grieve, to provide the heiress. Walpole tells the story best:

She [Mrs. Grieve] promised him a Miss Phipps, a West Indian fortune of £150,000. Sometimes she was not landed, sometimes had the small-pox. In the meantime, Miss Phipps did not like a black man; Celadon must powder his eyebrows. He did, and cleaned himself. A thousand Jews thought he was gone to Kingsgate to settle the payment of his debts—Oh! no, he was to meet Celia at Margate.[103]

It must be admitted that some of the characters and situations in *The Cozeners* are derivative of those in Foote's previous plays, as Miss Belden points out.[104] Mrs. Fleece'em is similar to Mrs. Match'em of *The Nabob* and Mrs. Mechlin of *The Commissary*, and Foote's own role of Mr. Aircastle, a gentleman with a penchant for meandering conversations, reminds one strongly of Sir Penurius Trifle of *The Knights*.[105] The dialogue, however, was filled with humorous and satirical references to topical matters, especially incidents in the rebellious colonies in America. Fleece'em insists that her activities in Boston brought her the love of the people: "Did not my burning the first pound of souchong, and my speeches at Faneuil-hall and the Liberty-tree, against *the colonies* contributing to discharge a debt to which they owed their existence, procure me the love and esteem of the people?" [106] When the Irishman, O'Flannigan, is given his job of exciseman in the colonies, he is told by Flaw, "If you discharge well your duties, you will be found in tar and feathers for nothing."

> O'Flan.: Tar and feathers! and what the devil will I wid them, my dear?
>
> Flaw: When properly mixed, they make a genteel kind of dress, which is sometimes wore in that climate. . . . It is very light, keeps out the rain, and sticks extremely close to the skin.[107]

These timely remarks on the colonies in addition to the thrusts at Grieve, Dood, Rudd, Fox, Chesterfield, and others reduced considerably the chance that an audience in 1774 would judge the play as derivative or familar. In fact, the satire remained current enough to be played nine times in 1775 and twelve times in 1776.[108]

The years 1770 to 1774 were Foote's most productive. He wrote five plays and a puppet show in that span, and except for the latter all of his plays met with financial success, especially *The Maid of Bath, The Nabob,* and *The Cozeners.* Foote's theatre may have been an "eccentric, narrow establishment," but it was a phenomenal achievement. One man broke the monopoly of the winter houses to gain a summer patent and then produced, directed, acted, and wrote his own plays to sustain a flourishing concern that employed forty to fifty actors and gave fifty to sixty performances from May 15 to September 15. This was a unique accomplishment in the history of the English theatre and done on one leg. But even at the height of his fame Foote could not take on fewer duties, as Garrick had done. He spent his money lavishly, living from season to season, and despite his years was forced to make tours to Dublin and Edinburgh to support his household and to have enough cash to start the new season.

The work during 1774 wearied him completely; after leaving London for Paris when the last play was done, Foote wrote to Garrick to inquire if he knew someone who might want to buy a theatre:

> I am sorry I could not see you before my quitting this Country, and am more concern'd at the Cause, but as I find your gouty fit was in form, I flatter myself there will be a long parenthesis betwixt this and the next: consider:
>> You have no leisure to be sick
>> In such a Justling time.
>
> Your opponents are numerous, and Solomon says in a multitude of Counsellors there is safety, but I should suppose his Counsellors were of a different stamp from the Congregation at Covent Garden.
>
> There is more of prudence than pleasure in my Trip to the Continent. To tell you the truth I am tir'd with racking my brains toiling like a horse and Crossing Seas and Mountains in the most Dreary Seasons merely to pay Servants' wages and Tradesmen's Bills. I have therefore directed my friend Jewel to discharge the Lazy Vermin of my Hall, and let my Hall too if he can meet with a proper Tennant, help me to one if you can.
>
> You need not doubt but I shall be happy to hear from you. My Epistolary Debts it will be always in my power to pay, the others I pay when I can: is it in Man to do more. With anything that France produces I shall be proud to supply you, their Diseases always excepted, tho'

as to their Capital one you and I are I think at present
pretty secure. Your commands will reach me by being
directed to Panchaud.

    I kiss Mrs. Garrick's Hands and am

Most Truly and Sincerely
Yours Saml Foote [109]

Another letter sent to Garrick by one of his friends, Mrs. Henrietta Pye, confirms Foote's general unhappiness at the time, though perhaps she misinterprets its cause:

> I saw Foote one evening. . . . very much tired of Paris & all
> therein contained, that is to say he did not find himself
> at all known or taken notice of for which reason in a very
> few days he left it and went to seek homage at Bruxelles
> where I think he stands yet a worse chance than at Paris.[110]

Despite his low spirits, Foote could still rise to the occasion. When Foote was in Paris that year, he was invited to dinner at the house of the English ambassador. The host showed his guests a small bottle of Tokay and poured it into tiny glasses. He explained that the wine was of the most exquisite growth and very old. Foote stared disappointedly at his diminutive glass and sighed, "It is very little of its age." [111] The travel helped his recuperation for he returned to London December 12 in "high spirits," [112] stayed about two weeks, and then went with George Colman to continue his vacation at Bath.[113]

NOTES

1. *The Wandering Patentee,* Vol. I, pp. 280-281.
2. *The Letters of Edward Gibbon,* ed. J. E. Norton (London, 1956), Vol. II, pp. 78-79.
3. Belden, pp. 132-136, describes a mock oratorio celebrating Wilkes' birthday, October 28, 1769, whose authorship is ascribed to Foote in

the title: "*Wilkes: An Oratorio. As Performed at The Great Room in Bishopsgate-Street. Written by Mr. Foote. The Music by Signor Carlos Francesco Baritini,* London. As Miss Belden states, it is impossible to prove or disprove. Foote's authorship, though the author meant the piece to be taken as Foote's work. In my opinion, this skit, which is in the Harvard Theatre Collection, was not written by Foote. Its tone is familiar and its intent is friendly, but Foote was not a close friend of Wilkes. In the past, Foote even had reason to be wary of him because of his close friendship and collaboration with Charles Churchill. Furthermore, Foote did not like to take sides in political controversy. When Foote was in Edinburgh, Cooke relates that some people in the audience asked Foote to imitate Wilkes. The request was refused because, as the comic explained, "as he intended to *take himself off* for London, in a few days, he did not choose to *sup on brickbats and rotten eggs* the first night of his arrival in the Metropolis." Cooke *Table-Talk,* p. 30.

4. Thomas Sheridan was not a regular player in Foote's company. He played the lead in a number of plays, mostly Shakespearean, and received a percentage of the profits.

5. Stone, *London Stage,* Vol. III, pp. 1478 ff.

6. *Town and Country Magazine,* May, 1770, pp. 229-230.

7. *Ibid. The Drugger's Jubilee* and *The Gallant Sharper,* supposedly a new piece by Foote, were to have been shown that summer. Though neither play was performed, *The Gallant Sharper* might have been a tentative title for *The Lame Lover.* Macklin's *Man of the World* was also projected for the Haymarket that summer, but the author could not win the Lord Chamberlain's approval for the farce until 1781.

8. *Town and Country Magazine,* June, 1770, pp. 294-296.

9. According to Stone, *London Stage,* Vol. III, pp. 1551, 1904, the play was put on again only once in 1771 and twice in 1775.

10. *Town and Country Magazine,* July, 1770, p. 230.

11. The account of Hiffernan's quarrel with Foote is found in Boaden, I, 390-391. Foote had good reason to fear Hiffernan's threats. On January 25, 1763, Drury Lane was almost destroyed by rioters when Garrick would not take after-money. On the next day, another riot forced Garrick to yield. A month later, February 24, a similar occurrence at Covent Garden forced Beard to follow Garrick's retraction. (*Letters of David Garrick,* Vol. I, p. 373, nn. 1, 2.)

12. Boaden, Vol. I, pp. 391-392.

13. *Letters of David Garrick,* Vol. II, p. 703.

14. Wilkinson, *Memoirs,* Vol. III, p. 245.

15. John Jackson, *The History of the Scottish Stage* (Edinburgh, 1793), p. 78.

16. *English Aristophanes,* p. 26.

17. Stone, *London Stage,* Vol. III, p. 1269.

18. James C. Dibdin, *Annals of the Edinburgh Stage* (Edinburgh, 1888), pp. 152-153.

19. *English Aristophanes,* p. 26.

20. Dibdin, pp. 155-157.
21. *The Letters of David Garrick*, Vol. II, p. 733, n. 2.
22. *Ibid.*, p. 733.
23. *English Aristophanes*, p. 27.
24. *The Letters of David Garrick*, Vol. III, pp. 935-936.
25. Cooke, *Foote*, Vol. II, pp. 214-215.
26. Luke Tyerman, *Methodists* (New York, 1872), Vol. II, p. 439; and *Town and Country Magazine*, December, 1770, p. 480.
27. Edinburgh, 1771.
28. Wilkinson, *Memoirs*, Vol. III, pp. 242-243
29. *Ibid.*
30. Richard Cumberland, *The Memoirs of Richard Cumberland* (London, 1807), Vol. I, 171-173.
31. Stone, *London Stage*, Vol. III, pp. 1549 ff. Foote appeared in a record thirteen different productions this year, eleven of them his own plays.
32. *Ibid.*, p. 1556.
33. In Thomas Moore's *Memoirs of the Rt. Honourable Richard Brinsley Sheridan* (London, 1827), Vol. I, pp. 23 ff., it is stated that Long probably dropped the suit at the request of the unhappy girl and took all the blame upon himself. Moore rationalizes this implausible story by claiming that Long kept the friendship of Miss Linley and Richard Sheridan for many years after the two were married. In Walter Sichel's *Sheridan*, Vol. I (New York, 1909), p. 189 ff., it is pointed out that Long allowed the Linleys to keep his courting gifts (these were ridiculed by Foote in the play), and, further, settled on a payment of £3000 to Miss Linley to refrain from bringing a breach of promise suit. Though the reasons for the break are unknown, it is unlikely that Long was as altruistic as Moore claims. Both biographers feel that Long was not the villain that Foote made him out to be, but it is clear that Foote, who was at Bath during part of this time and was friendly with some of the principals involved, knew considerably more of the situation and perhaps was closer to the truth in his redition of the story than Sheridan's biographers will allow.
34. Sichel, Vol. I, p. 189.
35. A review of the play in *Town and Country Magazine*, July, 1771, pp. 310-311, praises Weston's performance as Billy Button, "a smart, little, self-sufficient taylor (well known at Bath)" and mentions Peter Poultice as a celebrated Bath apothecary."
36. *Lloyd's Evening Post*, June 26-28, 1771.
37. A. Sherrard, *A Life of John Wilkes* (New York, 1930), pp. 246-249; and Belden, pp. 142-143.
38. Foote, *The Dramatic Works*, Vol. III, pp. 165-166.
39. *The Letters of Junius*, ed. C. W. Everett (London, 1927), p. 106.
40. *Town and Country Magazine*, July, 1771, pp. 310-311; and see *Lloyd's Evening Post*, June 26-28, 1771, p. 612, and *Exshaw's Magazine*, July, 1771, pp. 414-415.
41. Walley C. Oulton, *The History of the Theatres of London* (London, 1796), Vol. I, p. i.

42. *English Aristophanes*, p. 26.
43. Stone, *London Stage*, Vol. III, pp. 1637 ff.
44. Cooke, *Foote*, Vol. II, pp. 75-76.
45. Askham, p. 170.
46. James Boswell, *Boswell for the Defense, 1769-1774*, eds. W. K. Wimsatt and E. A. Pottle (New York, 1959), p. 80.
47. *Ibid.*, pp. 90-91.
48. Stone, *London Stage*, Vol. III, p. 1569.
49. *English Aristophanes*, p. 27.
50. Shuter played Hartop for Weston's benefit on August 10, but he did not perform again at the Haymarket that season (Stone, *London Stage*, Vol. III, p. 1649.)
51. *Ibid.*, pp. 1569 ff.
52. *Boswell for the Defense*, p. 90.
53. W. K. Wimsatt, "Foote and a Friend of Boswell's: A Note on *The Nabob*," *MLN*, LVII (May, 1942), 325-335.
54. *Town and Country Magazine*, July 1772, p. 374.
55. Foote, *The Dramatic Works*, Vol. III, pp. 217-218.
56. *Ibid.*, p. 200. The tall knight was a remarkable figure. *Town and Country Magazine*, April, 1774, p. 179; describes him as "being about six feet four inches in height, with a longish hook nose, cheeks that have fallen in, his body somewhat resembling a waggoner's whip, and his legs so extremely taper, that it is astonishing how they support the superstructure." Fielding also satirized him as a ludicrous carving on Joseph's cudgel in *Joseph Andrews*, ed. Martin C. Battestin (Boston, 1961), pp. 202, 311.
57. *Ibid.*, pp. 225-226.
58. Walpole, Vol. XIV, p. 47; and see Vol. I, p. 265.
59. *St. James Chronicle*, July 9-11, 1772.
60. Cooke, *Foote*, Vol. I, pp. 176-182. Boaden, Vol. II, p. 41, prints a letter from George Garrick, perhaps alluding to the same incident, saying that Foote was to dine with General Smith and others, and that "Foote is afraid that they will put him in the coalhole."
61. Oulton, Vol. I, p. 6.
62. Instead of closing at the end of May or the first day or two in June, the Drury Lane remained open until June 10 in 1772 (Stone, *London Stage*, Vol. III, p. 1645.)
63. *The Correspondence of King George The Tihrd from 1760 to December 1783*, ed. Sir John Fortescue (London, 1927), Vol. II, pp. 395-396.
64. *English Aristophanes*, p. 29.
65. In July, William Kenrick, a venenuous libeler and sometime dramatist, penned a vicious poem against Garrick, *Love in the Suds; a Town Eclogue, Being the Lamentation of Roscius for the loss of his Nyky* (London, 1772). Nyky was Isaac Bickerstaffe, the prolific balladeer and dramatist, who had been accused of homosexuality in May of that year and consequently had fled to France. Kenrick, who was later forced to make public apology under threat of a lawsuit, implied that Roscius was a lover of Nyky, and in one humorous section (p. 19), Roscious

declaims against Foote in words that Garrick must have thought silently to himself on many occasions:

> Curse on that Foote; who in an ill-fated hour
> Turn'd on the heels of my theatric-power
> Who, ever ready with some biting joke,
> My peace hath long and would my heart have broke.
> Curse on his horse—one leg! but ONE to break!
> "A kingdom for a horse"—to break his neck!

66. Foote, pp. 263-264.
67. *The Letters of David Garrick*, Vol. II, pp. 835-836.
68. *Gentleman's Magazine*, February, 1773, p. 101.
69. This is a reference to John Wesley, who, like Whitefield, strongly denounced theatrical presentations.
70. Oulton, Vol. II, p. 15.
71. *Ibid.*, p. 20.
72. Baker, D. E., *Biographica Dramatica*, Vol. III, p. 154.
73. The piece has never been printed, but an MS of this skit is in the Huntington Library. The exordium and other parts of the show are never given in their complete state in the contemporary accounts.
74. Baker, D. E., *Biographica Dramatica*, Vol. III, p. 154.
75. *Ibid.*, p. 155.
76. Cradock, Vol. I, pp. 34-35.
77. Stone, *London Stage*, Vol. III, p. 1700. Maria Macklin wrote her father that "Foote's Rary Shew has been rehears'd three mornings—but he has got no money, so he shows off again at night instead—but it does not fill violently."
78. Genest, Vol. IV, p. 374.
79. *St. James's Chronicle*, February 13-16, 1773; also see the two issues of *Town and Country Magazine*, February and March, 1773.
80. *The Letters of David Garrick*, Vol. II, p. 855. Fanny Burney reports in *The Early Diary of Francis Burney, 1768-1778*, ed. Annie R. Ellis (London, 1913), Vol. II, pp. 279-280, that Charlotte Burney went to the Haymarket in June 1777, where *Piety in Pattens* was given as an afterpiece and saw Garick in the audience laughing "as much as he could have done at the most excellent piece in the world."
81. It was given twenty-one performances at the Haymarket from 1773-1776 (Stone, *London Stage*, Vol. III, pp. 1737 ff.).
82. *Ibid.*, pp. 1735 ffi.
83. Belden, p. 157.
84. Cooke, *Table-Talk*, p. 23.
85. Belden, pp. 158-159, compares the two speeches.
86. *Westminster Magazine*, July, 1773, wrote that the satire on the venality of the press was not as successful as the rest of the play; but perhaps that comment exposes the magazine more than it does Foote's play.
87. *Monthly Review*, July, 1776, p. 67.
88. Hitchcock, Vol. II, pp. 238-239.
89. Foote, *The Dramatic Works*, Vol. III, p. 184.

90. *Exshaw's Magazine,* February, 1774, p. 76, claimed that Foote met with great success and was held over by the managers. As will be discussed below, there is good reason to believe that Foote was not held over, and that the magazine exaggerated Foote's success. In Hitchcock, Vol. II, pp. 238-239, and Thomas Snagg, *Recollections of Occurrences, The Memoirs of Thomas Snagg,* ed. Harold Harrison (London, 1951), p. 93, it is stated that Foote's tour was not the success that Foote expected.

91. Forster, pp. 446-447. Foote also wrote in this letter that "at this season the winds are so variable, that I may possibly see you before you can acquaint me with this reaching your hands."

92. *Boswell for the Defense, 1769-1774,* p. 198. In an entry dated December 3, 1774, p. 42, Boswell wrote that he "dined at Fortune's with the *Stoic Club,* a society begun by Foote." Foote may have founded the club during his last visit in February, 1774.

93. Dibdin, *Annals of the Edinburgh Stage,* p. 163. Dibdin also states that Foote received £250 for seven nights' work, though Foote probably acted more than seven times during his stay.

94. *The Anecdotes and Egotisms of Henry Mackenzie,* ed. Harold W. Thompson (Oxford, 1927), p. 197.

95. David M'Culloch of Ardwall wrote a short account of Foote's enforced stay that was reprinted in the *Gallovidian,* XVII (1919), 159-161. According to him, Foote kept in good humor despite the circumstances.

96. Wilkinson, *Memoirs,* Vol. IV, pp. 246-247. This letter is dated February 16, but it does not have the year. It is evident that the year could not be 1771, the only other possibility besides 1774, because in 1770 Foote set out in October when traveling weather was still good, and he stayed in Edinburgh for three months, not the three weeks he actually did stay in 1774. Furthermore, M'Culloch (see above note), though he did not give the year or exact time of Foote's mishap, gives the month as early January. This was an impossibility in 1771, for at that time Foote had been performing in Edinburgh since November, 1770.

97. Stone, *London Stage,* Vol. III, pp. 1822 ff.

98. Foote, *The Dramatic Works,* Vol. III, p. 309.

99. Belden, pp. 163-165; and *Town and Country Magazine,* July, 1777, pp. 372-377. Dodd was later hanged on June 27, 1777, for forgery despite Johnson's generous efforts to get him a remission. *(Life,* Vol. III, pp. 139, 144, 145, 147.)

100. James Boswell, *The Ominous Years, 1774-1776,* edd. Charles Ryskamp and Frederick A. Pottle (New York, 1963), pp. 352-361. Also see Belden, pp. 162-163.

101. *Town and Country Magazine,* November, 1777, p. 600.

102. Foote, *The Dramatic Works,* Vol. III, pp. 334-336.

103. Walpole, Vol. XXXII, pp. 162-163.

104. Belden, pp. 159-160.

105. Belden, p. 160, states that Mr. Aircastle was a takeoff of a Mr. Gahagan, a man who wrote a well organized and stringently critical account of

Foote which was printed in Boaden's *Memoirs of Mrs. Siddons* (Philadelphia, 1827), pp. 31 ff.

106. Foote, *The Dramatic Works,* Vol. III, p. 308.
107. *Ibid.,* pp. 315-316.
108. Stone, *London Stage,* Vol. III, pp. 1895 ff.
109. A.L.S. in Victoria and Albert Museum. This letter is partially quoted by Boaden, *Private Correspondence,* Vol. II, pp. 5-6.
110. A.L.S. in *Garrick Correspondence,* IV, no. 34, Folger Shakespeare Library. The letter is dated November 21, 1774.
111. Cooke, *Table-Talk,* p. 3.
112. *Letters of David Garrick,* Vol. III, p. 971.
113. Gibbon, Vol. II, p. 49.

CHAPTER X

FOOTE'S LAST YEARS, 1775-1777

When Foote finally returned from his vacation, he probably started to write his new play. This time he made an unfortunate choice for the object of his satire: Elizabeth Chudleigh, Countess of Bristol and at one time Duchess of Kingston. This confusion of title came about from an early secret marriage to Captain Augustus John Hervey, brother and heir to the Earl of Bristol. Since she was maid of honor to Augusta, Princess of Wales at that time, Elizabeth chose to keep her marriage a secret in order to retain her employment. She met her husband clandestinely in London for a time, and they soon parted; but after she had become pregnant, the secret of their marriage became common knowledge in court circles. In September, 1747, Elizabeth gave birth to a son and then came back to court determined to outbrave the rumors. "Do you know, my Lord," she said to Lord Chesterfield, "that the world says I have had twins?" "Does it?" he replied. "For my part, I make it a point of believing only half of what it says." [1]

In March 1749, she made her reputation at a masquerade that lived long in the memory of those who attended. Copying her costume from a painting of Iphigenia, she wore a short petticoat drawn up on one side to show her legs and a thin gauze coverlet for her shoulders. Making her grand entrance midst a group of stunned courtiers, she was reported as saying that she was "ready for the sacrifice." [2] After this escapade, rumors of her private life were more scandalous than ever; her amours were reported to have included even the aged King George II. By 1751 she found the man she wanted, the Duke of Kingston, elderly, docile, and immensely rich. She remained his mistress until 1769, by which time she had embarked on a plan that would nullify her previous marriage to Hervey and clear the way for her ascendency to the title of duchess and all the accompanying emoluments. Because her marriage to Hervey had never been officially announced, Elizabeth decided that a suit of Jactitation of Marriage would be more convenient and certain than divorce. This meant that Hervey was called upon to give legal proof of their marriage, and if this proof were found insufficient, their marriage would be nullified. Though Hervey resented her high-handed tactics, there are credible reports that he helped her erase all evidence of their marriage for a £10,000 bribe from the Duke of Kingston. This legal maneuver proved temporarily successful, and the Duke and Elizabeth were married a month after the suit.[3]

Their marriage, which seemed to be a happy one, lasted until the Duke's death in 1773. Elizabeth inherited his entire fortune, which after her death was to pass on to the Meadowses, his sister's family. For some unexplained reason, the Duke cut off Evelyn Meadows, the eldest nephew, with £500.[4] This disinheriting of the one man who expected to succeed to the Duke's fortune was a mistake. Having little to lose and everything to gain, he tried to discredit the Duchess by any means possible. With surprisingly little trouble or money, he soon found witnesses who were able to testify to the validity of the Duchess' first marriage. This was possible because the greedy woman, while mistress to the Duke in 1759, could not resist getting proof of her marriage to Hervey when his brother was near death to insure herself of becoming at least a countess.[5] Though Meadows found that the will could not be broken even if he could prove bigamy, he had found enough evidence to have her indicted for the crime on December 10, 1774. The Duchess, who had been in Rome visiting the Pope, rushed to Calais on hearing the news and remained there for eight weeks to plan her legal campaign. In May she finally presented herself before the Court of King's

Bench, determined to postpone her trial indefinitely. After two postponements, however, the date of the trial was fixed for April 15, 1776.[6]

Foote, along with everyone in London, had been following her legal maneuverings with great interest, and he had referred to her oncoming trial in *The Cozeners*. The choice of the Duchess as a topic of ridicule was a natural one for Foote; besides her notoriety, an additional incentive to humiliate her probably arose from Foote's friendship with one of the Meadows family, Evelyn or his younger brother Charles. It seems likely that one or the other persuaded Foote to attack the Duchess in his new play.[7] When Foote opened his theatre on May 15, his play was probably near completion, and because of his habit of puffing his new pieces to all friends and acquaintances, everyone in town was in on the secret.[8] He hired forty-four actors for sixty performances at the Haymarket. Foote dominated the proceedings as usual by playing in fifty-two mainpieces and fifteen afterpieces.[9]

Foote opened his season with a command performance of *The Devil upon Two Sticks*. Foote delighted his audience by adding some new jokes to the play, and by publicly announcing his plans to produce his new piece on the Duchess of Kingston. The newspapers reported that "the groundwork of the piece is said to be the denouement of a certain *Double Marriage,* that has lately made so much noise in the polite world, and among the lawyers. We are told this piece is to be entitled the *Siege of Calais.*" [10] Foote later changed the title to *The Trip to Calais.*

The first part of the play satirizes English tradesmen who put on extravagant airs in France as well as the French who bill them as if they were the lords they pretend to be. The play opens in Calais as two young fugitives from London, Jenny Minnikin and Dick Drugget, an apprentice to Jenny's father, look for a priest who will marry them without parental consent. With Jenny's parents, aunt, and intended suitor in hot pursuit, the eloping couple find they have no time to perform the ceremony, so Jenny enters a convent as a refuge against the demands of her parents. This incident is very similar to the elopement of Richard Sheridan and Elizabeth Linley, but Jenny's character is different from Miss Linnet's of *The Maid of Bath*. Jenny is a lustful,

headstrong, spoiled brat who will have her own way, and poor
Dick has little to say about anything. She is gratuitously unpleas-
ant, and though there are no corroborating sources, it is quite
possible that Foote based the character of Jenny on Mrs. Sheridan.

In the second part of the play, the Duchess of Kingston makes
her appearance as Lady Kitty Crocodile. After the Minnikins find
the hiding place of their daughter, they appeal to Father O'Donnavan, a Capuchin, to suggest some way they might force her out
of the convent. He tells them that Lady Kity has the influence
to force her release. The scene then shifts to Lady Kitty's quarters
where she is shown hypocritically mourning the death of her
husband while pursuing every likely man under a public veil
of tears. Her cruelty is exposed by her sadistic treatment of Miss
Lydell, a poor relation whom she had taken on as a companion
when her father died. Jealous of her beauty, Lady Kitty tries to
make her leave of her own accord so that her ladyship will not
be accused of throwing poor relatives to the wolves. Colonel
Crosby, a frequent visitor at Lady Kitty's residence, has fallen
in love with Miss Lydell and is going to take her with him to
England as his wife. Furious at this loss, Lady Kitty tries to stop
the marriage by slandering the girl, but her efforts are in vain.
At this point she agrees to interview Jenny and return the girl
to her parents. Lady Kitty finds out that Jenny is no convert, but
merely wants her own way. Her ladyship then provides a solution
by suggesting that Jenny marry both her suitors, but Jenny
modestly demurs, claiming she does not have the style to carry
it off. Pleased by the girl's deportment, Lady Kitty offers her Miss
Lydell's place as a temporary haven for her difficulties. Of course
Jenny agrees, and, as it is said to Miss Lydell at the closing of
the play,

> They are very properly matched, and will prove a mutual
> plague to each other. But should it be otherwise, there
> seems to be a kind of dramatic justice in the change of
> your two situations: you, miss, are rewarded for your
> patient sufferings, by the protection of a man of honor
> and virtue; whilst she, rebellious to the mild dictates of

parental sway, is subjected to the galling yoke of a capricious and whimsical tyrant! [11]

Most of the strokes against the Duchess were familiar to a a knowing audience: her excessive mourning, her many amours, and her great ability to swoon, weep, and rave hysterically with little or no provocation. The relationship between Miss Lydell and Lady Kitty, however, is less clear. The character of the girl seems to be taken from a Miss Penrose who had been attached to the Duchess but quit her service because of her cruelty.[12] Belden suggests, and it seems likely, that Foote learned many of these details from her.[13] The one reference that even the Duchess might have smiled at occurs when Lady Kitty interviews Jenny to ascertain her true intentions:

> L. Kitty: You have no hopes that your parents will yield?
>
> Jenny: Mother, perhaps, might comply; but no mule is so headstrong as father.
>
> L. Kitty: And you, I suppose, are as determined as he?
>
> Jenny: Never once gave up a point in my life.
>
> L. Kitty: I dare say. But, if they were to desire you to marry the 'prentice—
>
> Jenny: They would find me a dutiful daughter.
>
> L. Kitty: Then you have no objection to obey their commands when they happen to contain the very things that you wish?
>
> Jenny: Not in the least.
>
> L. Kitty: And after having produced, and at their own expense trained and sustained you, you would still suffer them, I dare say, to support and protect you?
>
> Jenny: As in duty they are bound.
>
> L. Kitty: And they might direct you, provided you governed them?
>
> Jenny: In every respect.
>
> L. Kitty: Well said, my little American! [14]

In July Foote sent his play to the Lord Chamberlain, the Earl of Hertford, for approval and found to his great surprise that the newspapers predicted its rejection. On confirmation of this rumor, Foote realized that the Duchess had seen the play and asked the willing official to censor it. Foote grew furious at this display of privilege and threatened to publish the play with a dedication to her Grace. Desperately frightened at the threat of this new humiliation which was not in her power to stop, the Duchess called Foote for a private confrontation to settle the matter. Not surprisingly, she offered to buy her way clear, but, though he offered to remove passages which displeased her, Foote proudly refused the bribe:

> "Are those ear-rings composed of diamonds, are those necklaces pearl? if they are, and those candle-sticks silver, pray put them away, least I should lay my hands on them. No, Madam, when my necessities reduce me to make use of dishonourable means of requiring supplies, I will sooner go upon the Highway, than accept of an offer so much to my dishonour."—To this her Grace said, she could not see the thing in that light, nor conceive what ill consequences could arise from his taking it, especially as the transaction would not be known, as there were only my Lord Mountstuart and herself present: "Yes," replied Foote, "there is a third person present, and with whom I ever wish to remain upon the best of terms, *viz.* myself." [15]

Despite his threat of publication, Foote still hoped that he could "bully" the Lord Chamberlain into a license.[16] He wrote a long public letter to that official on August 4, hoping that public opinion would force a change in his decision:

> *To the Printer of the Morning Chronicle*
> The prophetic effusions of the collectors or makers of

paragraphs, have for once proved true, Mr. Woodfall: the
Trip to Calais has been rejected by the Lord Chamberlain;
to guess from whence these gentlemen obtained their
intelligence (as their advices preceded by many days the
delivery of the piece to the Lord Chamberlain) would be
a very difficult task; however, you find what was only
prophecy is now become history. Till I can have an opportunity of laying before the public, those scenes which
produced his Lordship's interdiction, you will print the
following letter, sent to Lord Hertford, in hopes of soft-
ening his censure.

  To Lord Hertford
  My Lord,
I did intend trouble your Lordship with an earlier address,
but the day after I received your prohibitory mandate, I
had the honour of a visit from Lord Mountstuart, to whose
interposition I find I am indebted for your first commands,
relative to the *Trip to Calais,* by Mr. Chetwynd, and your
final rejection of it by Col. Keen.

  Lord Mountstuart has, I presume, told your Lordship,
that he read with me those scenes to which your Lordship
objected, that he found them collected from general nature,
and applicable to none but those, who, through conscious-
ness, were compelled to a self-application. To such minds,
my Lord, the Whole Duty of Man, next to the Sacred
Writings, is the severest satire that ever was wrote; and
to the same mark, if Comedy directs not her aim, her
arrows are shot in the air; for by what touches no man,
no man will be mended. Lord Mountstuart desired that
I would suffer him to take the play with him, and let him
leave it with the Duchess of Kingston: he had my consent,
my Lord, and at the same time an assurance, that I was
willing to make any alteration that her Grace would suggest. Her Grace saw the play, and in consequence, I saw
her Grace; with the result of that interview, I shall not,
at this time, trouble your Lordship. It may perhaps be
necessary to observe, that her Grace could not discern,

which your Lordship, I dare say, will readily believe, a single trait in the character of Lady Kitty Crocodile, that resembled herself.

After this representation, your Lordship will, I doubt not, permit me to enjoy the fruits of my labour; nor will you think it reasonable, because a capricious individual has taken it into her head, that I have pinned her ruffles awry, that I should be punished by a poniard struck deep in my heart: your Lordship has too much candour and justice to be the instrument of so violent and ill directed a blow.

Your Lordship's determination is not only of the greatest importance to me now, but must inevitably decide my fate for the future, as, after this defeat, it will be impossible for me to muster up courage enough to face folly again; between the muse and the magistrate there is a natural confederacy; what the last cannot punish the first often corrects; but when she finds herself not only deserted by her ancient ally, but sees him armed in the defence of her foe, she has nothing left but a speedy retreat: adieu, then my Lord, to the stage. *Veleat res ludicra,* to which, I hope I may with justice add *plaudite,* as during my continuance in the service of the public, I never profited by flattering their passions, or falling in with their humours, as upon all occasions, I have exerted my little powers (as indeed, I thought it my duty) in exposing follies, how much soever the favourites of the day; and the pernicious prejudices, however protected and popular. This, my Lord, has been done, if those may be believed, who have the best right to know, sometimes with success; let me add too, that in doing this I never lost my credit with the public, because they knew that I proceeded upon principle, that I disdained being either the echo or the instrument of any man, however exalted his station, and that I never received reward or protection from any other hands than their own.

I have the honour to be, &c.

Samuel Foote.

N.B. In a few days will pe published, the Scenes objected
to by the Lord Chamberlain. With a dedication to the
Duchess of Kingston.[17]

The Lord Chamberlain was not moved by Foote's eloquence,
and in retaliation, Foote threatened not only to print his play,
but to take off the Duchess as Lady Brumpton in Steele's *The
Funeral, or, Grief à-la-Mode*. Walpole gleefully recounted the
story to Mason on August 7:

He has already printed his letter to Lord Hertford, and
not content with that, being asked why it was not licensed,
replied "Why my Lord Hertford desired me to make his
youngest son [George Seymour-Conway] a box-keeper, and
because I would not, he stopped my play." Upon my
word, if the stage and the press are not checked, we shall
have the army, on its return from Boston, besieged in the
Haymarket itself: what are we to do, if maids of honour
cannot marry two husbands in quiet.[18]

But Foote's threats and all his wit were in vain. By this time
it was too late in the season to begin a new play, and, furthermore,
Foote found himself attacked viciously in the newspapers, especially in *The Public Ledger*. There were implications of homosexuality and more outright charges of blackmail, all very painful
to a man who had to face the public almost every night during
the summer. The Rev. John Forster, the Duchess's chaplain, had
sent a note to Foote soon after his interview with her ladyship
to the effect that the Duchess wished to buy his play for £150,
the printer's price. Foote retorted angrily that the loss of his play
that season cost him £3000, and the newspapers stated that Foote
demanded that sum to stop publication.[19] One writer laughed at
Foote's threat to quit the stage if his play were not licensed and
ridiculed his claim that he was a reformer:

The facetious Manager of this House has greatly been disturbed of late by the Dead as well as the Living: Lady Betty Bigamy has stirred up the Ghosts of Mrs. Cole, Dr. Squintum, Mr. Cadwallader, and his sensible Wife Becky, Sir Penurious Trifle, and Smirk the Auctioneer; they haunt him every Night and accuse him of being the Cause of their quitting the Stage. . . . Mr. Smirk puts his Piece up to Auction and the Author hears nothing for two Hours together at Midnight, . . . but a-going for Two Thousand; and it is at last knocked down to Lady Betty Bigamy.[20]

Foote found himself vulnerable to the ridicule and the smears, and suspecting that his detractors were paid hirelings of the Duchess, he wrote a letter proposing a truce. If the scandal being printed about him were stopped, he would not print the play:

To her Grace the Duchess of Kingston
    Madam:
A *member* [John Forster] of the privy council, and a friend of your Grace's (he has begged me not to mention his name, but I suppose your Grace will easily guess him), has just left me. He has explained to me (what I did not conceive), that the publication of the scenes in *The Trip to Calais* at this juncture, with the dedication and preface, might be of infinite ill consequence to your affairs.

    I really, Madam, wish you no ill, and should be sorry to do you an injury. I therefore give up that consideration, which neither *your Grace's offers,* nor the threats of your agents, could obtain. The scenes shall not be published; nor shall anything appear at my Theatre, or from me, that can hurt you, *provided* the attacks made on me in the newspapers do not make it necessary for me to act in defence of myself. Your Grace will therefore see the necessity of giving proper directions.

I have the honour to be, &c.
North-end   *Sam. Foote*
Sunday, August 13, 1775.[21]

Stung by Foote's irony and air of independence, the Duchess scornfully refused the offer. She too sent a copy of her letter to the newspapers, so that all of England could follow the controversy between them:

Sir,

I *was* at dinner when I received your ill-judged letter. As there is little consideration required, I shall sacrifice a few moments to answer it.

A member of *your* privy council can never hope to be of a Lady's cabinet. I know too well what is due to my own dignity, to enter into a compromise with an extortionable assassin of private reputation. If I before abhorred you for your slander, I now despise you for your concessions. It is a proof of the illiberality of your satire, when you can publish, or suppress it as best suits the needy convenience of your purse. You first had the cowardly baseness to draw the sword; and if I sheathe it until I make you crouch like the subservient vassal you are, then there is not spirit in an injured woman, nor meanness in a slanderous buffoon.

To a man, my sex alone would have screened me from attack; but I am writing to the descendant of a Merry Andrew, and prostitute the term of manhood by applying it to Mr. Foote.

Clothed in my innocence as in a coat of mail, I am proof against a host of foes; and conscious of never having intentionally offended a single individual, I doubt not that a brave and generous public will protect me from the malevolence of a theatrical assassin. You shall have cause to remember, that though I would have given liberally for the relief of your necessities, I scorn to be bullied into a purchase of your silence.

There is something however in your *pity* at which my nature revolts. To make an offer of pity, at once betrays your insolence and your vanity. I will keep the *pity* you send, until the morning before you are turned off: when I will return it by a Cupid with a box of lip-salve; and a choir of choristers shall chaunt a stave to your *requiem*.

E. Kingston

Kingston House
Sunday, 13th August.
P.S. You would have received this sooner, but the servant has been a long time writing it.[22]

It was foolish of the Duchess to enter into a contest of wit with a professional, and Foote took his advantage in answering her with a brilliant letter of delicate invective. Walpole remarked on the letter that "Foote, with all the delicacy she ought to have used, replied only with wit, irony, and confounded satire. . . . Foote has given her the *coup de grace*." [23] The answer, however, is marred somewhat because Foote chose to misunderstand "prostitute" as the Duchess had used it:

Madam,
Though I have neither time nor inclination to answer the illiberal attacks of your agents, yet a public correspondence with your Grace is too great an honour for me to decline.

I cannot help thinking that it would have been prudent in your Grace to have answered my letter *before dinner* or at least postponed it to the cool hour of the morning: you would have then found that I had voluntarily granted the request which you had endeavoured by so many different ways to obtain.

Lord Mountstuart (for whose amiable qualities I have the highest respect, and whose name your agents very uncessarily produced to the public) must recollect that when I had the honour to meet him at Kingston-house by your Grace's appointment, instead of begging relief from your charity, *I rejected your splendid offers* to suppress *The Trip to Calais,* with the contempt they deserved. Indeed, Madam, the humanity of my royal and benevolent master, and the public protection, have placed me much above the reach of your bounty.

But why, Madam, put on your *coat of mail* against me? I have no hostile intentions. Folly, not vice, is the game I pursue. In those scenes which you so unaccountably apply to yourself, you must observe there is not the slightest hint at the little incidents of your life which have excited the *curiosity* of the grand inquest for the county of Middlesex. I am happy however, Madam, to hear that your robe of innocence is in such perfect repair: I was afraid it might be a little the worse for the wearing. May it hold out to keep your Grace warm the next winter.

The progenitors your Grace has done me the honour to give me, are, I presume, merely metaphorical persons; and to be considered as the authors of my muse, and not of my manhood. A Merry Andrew and a prostitute are no bad poetical parents, especially for a writer of plays: the first to give the humour and mirth; the last to furnish the graces and powers of attraction. Prostitutes, and players too, must live by pleasing the public; not but your Grace may have heard of ladies who by *private practice* have accumulated great fortunes.

If you mean that I really owe my birth to that pleasant connection, your Grace is grossly deceived. My father was, in truth, a very useful magistrate, and respectable country gentleman, as the whole county of Cornwall will tell you: my mother, the daughter of Sir Edward Goodere, baronet, who represented the county of Hereford. Her fortune was large, and her morals irreproachable till your Grace con-

descended to stain them. She was upwards of fourscore
years old when she died; and what will surprise your
Grace, *was never married but once* in her life.

Pray, Madam, is not J[ackso]n [24] the name of your
female confidential secretary: And is not *she* generally
clothed in black petticoats made of your weeds?

'So mourned the dame of Ephesus her love!'
I fancy your Grace took the hint when you last resided
at Rome. You heard then, I suppose of a certain pope;
and in humble imitation, have converted a *pious parson*
into a *chamber-maid*. The scheme is new in this country;
and has, doubtless, its particular pleasures. That you may
never want the benefit of clergy in every emergence, is
the sincere wish to

Your Grace's most devoted,
Most obliged humble servant,
Sam. Foote.[25]

At the same time that Foote's answer appeared in the papers,
Forster printed an affidavit swearing that Foote had attempted
to blackmail the Duchess:

Middlesex and Westminster to wit

The Rev. Mr. John Forster, A.M., Chaplain to her
Grace the Duchess of Kingston, maketh oath, that in the
month of July last, he waited on Mr. Samuel Foote, at his
house at North-End—by the direction of her Grace the
Duchess of Kingston, to return to the said Mr. Foote, a
manuscript Comedy entitled, a *'Trip to Calais,'* which he,
the said Mr. Foote, had left with her Grace for her perusal,
which he did accordingly deliver to him. That at this time
he took an opportunity to dissuade Mr. Foote from publishing the said Comedy, which he was informed it was
his intention to do, as it might very much disoblige the
Duchess of Kingston, and make in her a powerful enemy,
who was capable of being a very valuable friend; and that

on these considerations he advised the said Mr. Foote to make a compliment of the copy of this piece to her Grace the Duchess of Kingston, especially as the public perform- ance of it had been prohibited by the Lord Chamberlain; that the said Mr. Foote replied, that unless the Duchess of Kingston would give him Two Thousand Pounds, he would publish the 'Trip to Calais,' with a preface and dedication to her Grace; and that the said Mr. Foote commissioned him to communicate these his intentions to her Grace the Duchess of Kingston.

John Forster.

Sworn before me, this eighteenth day of August, 1775. J. Fielding.[26]

Forster may well have believed his charge to be valid. Foote, after all, did not want to print the play for the paltry profit of £150; he wanted to retaliate against the Duchess for stopping the play. And undoubtedly he felt humiliated by his failure to force the Lord Chamberlain to reverse his decision. Foote was not one to take loss of face gracefully, and when this hanger-on came to him with the Duchess' threatening request not to publish the play, Foote was probably too insulted and angry merely to refuse the haughty demand. The Duchess' action in suppressing the play cost him thousands in profit and a public defeat. Foote's reply to Forster must have been intemperate enough for a biased go- between to accuse attempted blackmail with a clear conscience.[27] Garrick, who knew how Foote operated, did not believe him guilty of the charge and in a letter to Colman wrote approvingly of Foote's letter: "Notwithstanding Foster's Oath, Foote has thrown the Duchess upon her back, & there has left her, as You and I would do—She is Sick & has given up the Cause, & has made herself very ridiculous, & hurt herself in ye struggle—Foote's letter is one of his best things, in his best manner." [28]

Still smarting from his defeat and the unceasing attacks on him in the newspapers, for which he held the Duchess accountable,

Foote wanted to retaliate in kind. He made plans to print hand-bills giving the history of the Duchess' life in the form of a Newgate narrative,

> Setting forth the birth, parentage, education, and exaltation of Lady Kitty Crocodile: who from a private station, first became an attendant upon a great lady at court, afterwards married an admiral in the British fleet, was a favorite sultana of several crowned heads abroad; and lastly, married a most noble and illustrious duke, by whom she became possessed of a large fortune, great rank, high connections, &c. &c.[29]

He also wanted the handbills bawled in front of Kingston House, but friends advised him to give up this undignified idea and to aim his wrath at William Jackson, the man responsible for the abuse spewed at Foote.

Foote took their advice but had to postpone his revenge on Jackson until the next season. The time for vacationing had come, and, as usual, Foote left for the continent shortly after September 15. As he told Boswell later, he had dinner with Johnson in Paris on October 28 and the sage had not improved his dress nor his opinion of actors:[30]

> He told me that the French were quite astonished at his figure and manner, and at his dress, which he obsti-nately continued exactly as in London;—his brown clothes, black stockings, and plain shirt. He mentioned that an Irish gentleman said to Johnson, "Sir, you have not seen the best French players." Johnson. "Players, Sir! I look upon them as no better than creatures set upon tables and jointstools to make faces and produce laughter, like dancing dogs."—"But Sir, you will allow that some players are better than others?" Johnson, "Yes, Sir, as some dogs dance better than others." [31]

He did not remain long in France, for, despite his vow never to tour again, he left for the Dublin stage in December. Perhaps he wished to make up the deficit of the last season. He arrived just after Christmas and was contracted to play at the Smock Alley Theatre. Despite the competition of a series of operas conducted by Dr. Arne and some plays starring Miss Cately at the Crow Street Theatre, Foote did very well.[32] Though the manager of Smock Alley appreciated the large audiences Foote attracted, the supporting actors resented his fly-by-night appearances. One of the Irish actors, Thomas Snagg, spoke sourly of Foote's success: "Mr. Foote again visited us, played his own pieces, took away a great deal of money and spoiled our other nights." [33]

Foote returned to London to find that Thomas Weston, his comic mainstay, had died on January 18, 1776. Having spent all his money on drink, Weston had little to leave to posterity —but all his nonworldly goods he left to Foote:

> As from Mr. Foote I derived all my consequence in life, and as it is the best thing I am in possession of, I would, in gratitude, at my decease leave it to the said Mr. Foote, but I know he neither stands in need of it as an author, actor, or as a man; the public have fully proved it in the two first, and his good nature and humanity have secured it to him in the last.

Weston added that he would have left his money, had he had any, to Garrick, "as there is nothing on earth he is so very fond of." [34] Foote sincerely mourned his loss, if not as a friend then certainly as an actor. Foote had recognized Weston's talent in his portrayal of Dick, an obscure character in *The Minor,* and after his success as Jerry Sneak, his popularity at Drury Lane and the Haymarket made him one of the best paid comedians in London.[35]

On April 15, all interest was turned to the long-awaited trial of the Duchess of Kingston before the House of Lords. Hervey's brother, the Earl of Bristol, had finally died so that the Duchess had little to lose by the trial, except her already tattered reputation. For even if the court found her guilty of bigamy and stripped her of her duchesshood, as a countess she would be protected from punishment, and her inheritance could not be confiscated. The Duke's will could not be broken whether Elizabeth was his wife or not. Though the outcome of the trial could not have affected the Duchess materially, the event drove all other gossip from the newspapers. It became a threatrical happening. A huge gallery was set up in Westminster Hall, and the great floor was completely covered with crimson carpeting. For those not belonging to the nobility, tickets were almost impossible to come by and were sold for outrageous prices. Hannah More, who saw the trial with Garrick's ticket, said that the panoply equalled a coronation:

> The prisoner was dressed in deep mourning: a black hood on her head, her hair modestly dressed and powdered; a black silk sack with crape trimmings; black gauze, deep ruffles, and black gloves. . . . The fair victim had four virgins in white behind the bar. She imitated her great predecessor, Mrs. Rudd, and affected to write very often, though I plainly perceived she only wrote as they do their love epistles on the stage, without forming a letter. . . . The Duchess has but small remains of that beauty of which kings and princes were once so enamoured. . . . She is large and ill-shaped; there was nothing white but her face, and had it not been for that she would have looked like a bale of bombasin[e].[36]

Foote's caricature of the lady was completely understated. But as the trial dragged on and lost its novelty, one could not deny the tediousness of the affair. At the end of five days the Duchess was finally found guilty of bigamy and stripped of her proud rank, but her new title of Countess of Bristol saved her from being branded on the hand. She may have been humiliated, but she left the court unpunished.[37]

Though the Duchess' star had lost its ascendency, Foote was

not yet free of its malign influence. The vicious attacks on Foote continued even more fiercely than before, with William Jackson of *The Public Ledger* leading the pack. Many people assumed at the time that the Duchess had hired this character assassin to revenge herself on Foote, but it is more probable that Jackson seized an opportunity to put the Duchess in his debt. Without even knowing her, he became her ardent defender, predicting correctly that in time he would be handsomely rewarded. Peter Stuart, who had been Jackson's printer, wrote an account of Jackson's life in the *Oracle*, May 6, 1795, which stated that Jackson did not know the Duchess at the time he attacked Foote.[38] The charge that could destroy Foote as a public figure was homosexuality. Jackson continually hammered at this issue, expecting that the brutish galleries, once Foote's supporters, would turn on the actor and drive him from the stage with jeers and hoots.[39]

Though he had hired sixty actors and planned the coming season of 1776, Foote was discouraged enough by Jackson's smears to hesitate opening his theatre until his innocence had been proved through a libel suit he had instituted against the *Public Ledger*. However, his friends encouraged him to go on, and Foote began a long and active season. Sixty performances were given, and Foote appeared in forty-nine mainpieces and twenty-six afterpieces.[40] He had not been so active on stage since the loss of his leg.

Foote's choice of opening the season with *The Bankrupt* was prompted by its satire on the scandalmongers of the press. Before the play began, Foote was in a state of terror, not knowing how the audience would receive him. Agitated almost beyond control, he stepped on stage to make an address. He was received with a tremendous ovation that took many minutes to subside. Undoubtedly relieved, but still wrestling with emotional tensions that vacillated between overwhelming gratitude and fright, Foote began to speak:

> *Gentlemen,*
> It was not my intention, after the charge that has been

made against me, to appear before the public till I had
an opportunity of proving my innocence; but as this charge
was made at the critical point of time when I usually
opened my Theatre, and having engaged as good a set of
performers for your amusement as I could procure, it was
the unanimous advice of my friends, that I should open
my house, in confidence that the public were too noble,
and too just, to discard an old servant for a mere accusation.

I am ready to answer every charge which can be
brought against me; and have pursued such legal steps to
clear my reputation from the virulent attacks of a public
paper as will speedily bring the writer to an issue in the
court of King's Bench, which has this day made the rule
absolute against the publisher.

I beg leave to return my thanks for the marks you
have now given me of your humanity and justice: permit
me to promise you, that I will never disgrace your protection.[41]

Foote did not misplace his confidence in his audience at this
critical moment. They applauded every sentence, and Foote,
whose emotions could stand no more, burst into tears at the
conclusion and went offstage to loud shouts of approval.[42] The
audience continued to show their favor by applauding throughout
the course of the play.[43]

The season thus began hopefully for Foote, though he gave
few performances during May because Drury Lane again continued to give performances until June 10. This time, however,
Foote had no objection, because Garrick had announced his
retirement and was giving a series of farewell appearances. Foote
accommodated the great actor by closing the Haymarket when
Garrick played at Drury Lane.[44] During the rest of the season,
the King, who had signally recognized Foote the previous season,
attended four command performances. Foote related that on one
such occasion, as he was lighting George III to his chair for a
performance of *The Contract* by the Rev. Thomas Francklin, the
King asked the name of the author. "It was written by one of

your Majesty's Chaplains," he was told, "but it is dull enough to have been written by a Bishop." [45] Not having his new piece ready, Foote revised some old ones to brighten his season. During a command performance of *Taste*, Foote came out as Lady Pentweazle wearing a tremendous headdress composed of large, loose feathers that fell completely off at the close of his scene. He was mocking the high fashion of the day, and he is given credit for starting the reform of this extreme dress.[46] Foote also successfully revised *The Cozeners* by adding the new scene with Mrs. Rudd that has already been described, and the play was given twelve performances.

Foote's theatrical efforts gained him the applause of his public, but his season soon proved bitter. On July 8 a discharged servant of Foote's, John Sangster, with Jackson's direction and money, charged Foote with attempted homosexual assault. It is not known whether Jackson suborned the servant to testify against Foote or was merely lucky enough to find a weapon he could finally use against him. Since Cooke makes it clear that Jackson went with Sangster to prefer charges, and that money was freely used to harass Foote with two charges of the same nature, it seems more than likely that Jackson at least knew Sangster before he went to court.[47] Stuart, in his account of Jackson's life, is ignorant of Jackson's part in Foote's indictment and the later trial, but his description of the editor's printed attacks on Foote are vivid:

It has been Foote's misfortune to incur the displeasure of the Duchess of *Kingston;* and it occurred to *Mr. Jackson,* that to attack and harass him, now that he was caught in the trammels of the law, would be a retaliation highly gratifying to her Grace. He accordingly fastened upon him, with all the ferocity of a tyger, made fierce and savage by the want of food; and scarce a day passed for weeks, and months, even pending the trial, without his being made to undergo some new torture. His whole life was reviewed with a microscopic eye; every little anecdote of him was ransacked with a most unchristianlike avidity;

his condemnation cruelly anticipated, and language itself put to the rack to mangle and destroy him.[48]

According to Cooke, Sangster and Jackson moved for a warrant to arrest Foote. Fortunately, Foote was warned in time to post bail, and their attempt to arrest him after his performance at the theatre was unsuccessful. Obviously intent upon incarcerating Foote, the malicious pair got another warrant by swearing that Foote attempted a second assault on Sangster at another time. Again forewarned, Foote's lawyers countered this move by a writ consolidating both charges, and thus moved the case to the Court of King's Bench. Foote's friends came strongly to his support; the Duke of Roxburgh, the Marquis of Townshend, Lord Ashburton, Edmund Burke, Joshua Renyolds gave him needed assistance.[49] The case was then put off until the next sessions, held in December.

It was under these circumstances that Foote began to revise his suppressed *Trip to Calais*. He changed the title to *The Capuchin* and completely rewrote the second half of the play, removing Lady Kitty Crocodile and substituting Dr. Viper, a treasonous paragrapher who will not stop at rape. The role, of course, is aimed at Jackson, and Foote as O'Donnovan got personal satisfaction by exposing Viper's character. At their meeting, O'Donnovan admits that he turned Capuchin when he was turned out of the *Scandalous Chronicle* for mistakenly reporting too many deaths and that his real name is Phelim O'Flam (a character who had been engaged in the same practice in *The Bankrupt*):

Viper: I told you, O'Flam, what would happen; why, you became a perfect Drawcansir; put more people to death than any three physicians in London.

O'Don.: What then, Doctor Viper? Sure, your poisonous pen did more mischief than me: my dead men walked about afterswards, and did their business as if nothing had happened; whilst the stabs made on people's good names,

by your rancour and malice, will admit of no consolation.
. . . In short, my dear Doctor, the only difference between
us is this; my dead men are all alive, and your live men
had much better be dead.

Viper: Do you know, sirrah, to whom you are speaking? . . .

O'Don.: A priest? What, because you was parish-clerk
to the Moravian meeting-house in the Old Jewry, and
used to snuffle out their bawdy hymns to the tune of beastly
ballads and jiggs? from thence you got expell'd for robbing
the poor's box—

Viper: Me!

O'Don.: Then you became advertisement-sticker to
lottery-offices, auctioneers, stage-coaches, and mountebank-
doctors; but being detected in selling the bills for waste-
paper to grocers, you got your dismissal, you know—

Viper: Rascal! I know!

O'Don.: After that you turned swindler, and got out
of gaol by an act for the relief of insolvent debtors.

Viper: Many honest men have been in the same
situation.

O'Don.: Lave honesty out, if you please. Then you
became doer of the *Scandalous Chronicle;* mowed down
reputations like muck; push'd yourself into the pay of
Lady Deborah Dripping, produced anonymous paragraphs
against her of your own composition, and got paid by
her for not putting them into your paper. . . . So, you
see, Doctor Viper, you are pretty well known; and all
your friends and acquaintance shall soon know you as well
as me in this town.[50]

Foote's revenge was too personal for the play to be satisfactory
to the public. One newspaper complained that Viper is "ineffec-
tive because it is a Portrait of a Man too low for Public Notice."
A more telling complaint by the same paper revealed that Foote's
history of Viper was in the same words Foote used to abuse
Jackson in public print.[51] Foote altered the play when it did

not meet with approval on the first night, but he could not rescue
it completely and continued to show it only eight more nights.[52]
Understandably, *The Capuchin* met with less success than any of
his other pieces. His hasty revision and personal involvement
fragmented the play and made the humor too self-conscious.

The season over, Foote did not take his customary vacation,
but began to look seriously for a buyer to lease his patent; he
could not sell it because it was good only for his lifetime. Though
he had thought of leaving the theatre two years before, he found
that he could not bear to relinquish the owner's crown when he
was actually approached by lessors. This time Jackson's attacks
probably diluted much of his joy in acting, and, perhaps more to
the point, Foote's age and disability had robbed him of much of
his vigor; it was noted that his acting seemed "spiritless and
tired." [53] Had Foote been in his prime, Jackson could not have
driven him from the stage.

The person most interested in leasing the Haymarket patent
was George Colman. He had found it difficult to run Covent
Garden with a group of non-theatrical partners and decided to
retire from theatrical management. Though he had been offered
a share of Drury Lane when Garrick thought of selling his
portion in December, 1775, Colman replied, with a knowledge
born of painful experience, that he would not have a partnership
in any theatre unless it were with Garrick.[54] He had wanted
earlier to lease the Haymarket only to find that Foote had with-
drawn the offer. Still eager to run his own house, he sent an
agent, John Colborne, to determine if Foote really meant to
dispose of his patent this time.

Colborne, finding Foote in earnest, had a series of meetings
with him to negotiate the terms, for Colman did not want to
make himself known to Foote as the principal until after the
terms had been agreed upon. Colman, however, did meet socially
with Foote during this period, and, on one occasion, when the
subject of leasing the patent was introduced, Foote turned to
Colman, saying:

> "Now here's Colman,—an experienced manager,—he
> will tell you that nobody can conduct so peculiar a thea-

trical concern as mine, but myself; but there's a fat-headed
fellow of an agent, who has been boring me every morning
at breakfast, with terms from some blockhead who knows
nothing about the Stage, but whose money burns in his
pocket."—

"Playhouse mad, I presume," said [Colman].

"Right," replied Foote, "and if bleeding *will bring
him to his senses, he'll find me a devilish good doctor.*" [55]

Colman soon found Foote's basic terms outlined to him by
Colborne. As Foote had promised, they were extremely expensive:

8th October, 1776

Sir,

It is now near ten o'clock, and I am but just come from
Mr. Foote, with whom I think we shall soon settle this
business, should the proceedings of the day meet your
approbation. I was obliged to advance one hundred, before
he would say anything, and soon after he felt the same
sum, I strove hard to split the other hundred, but he
declared he would never take less than sixteen hundred
pounds, in which is to be included the unpublished plays
during his life, after which they are to be his boy's, but
should the renters of the patent be desirous of purchasing
them, he will take five hundred pounds now, though he
cannot, he says, estimate them at less than one thousand
pounds, if to be sold to the trade.[56]

By October 18 all terms were agreed upon, and on the same
day Colman revealed himself as the buyer and tactfully apologized
to Foote for his silence:

My Dear Foote,

When I quitted Covent Garden, I never thought of attending to a theatre any more, and accordingly declined the
refusal of Garrick's share of Drury Lane; but a report

having prevailed some time ago of your intention to part
with your property, I was at length persuaded by my
friends, that such a theatrical situation different in many
essential respects from any other, would not be ineligible.
At my insistence, therefore, one of our common friends
then applied to you, to know your resolution, at which
time you declared the report to be ill founded, and I
dropped all thoughts of the business. But having been told
by several of our acquaintance that you had lately signified
your wish to find a purchaser, and even gone so far as to
name your price, I gain thought I might, without indelicacy or impertinence, inquire if you were serious. For this
purpose I sent Mr. Colborne to you; and though I am
not so playhouse mad as not to feel that largeness of the
sum he has agreed to on my behalf, nor so vain as to be
unconscious of the many superior advantages you possessed,
yet I shall, without much fear and trembling, put the last
hand to the bargain; only begging that you would not
ascribe my reserve, hitherto, on this occasion, to a wrong
motive, as it proceeded from my unwillingness to give you
unnecessary trouble, mixed with some little reluctance to
appear in any theatrical negociation, which was not likely
to be concluded. My proposals, however, having met with
your approbation, it is necessary for me to come forward
to complete them. I think I have property enough, independent of that which is to be contracted for, to make
you quite easy about the payment of your annuity. I shall
not be pleased if that, and every other object of the contract, is not settled to your entire satisfaction; for I not
only wish your solid interests to be consulted, but am
very desirous that we may appear to act like two friends,
rather than a couple of mere dealers. I understood, you
were yourself of opinion, that this matter should remain
in silence for the present, and indeed, I have some reasons
for wishing that my name may not be made public immediately; yet they are not so important, as not to give way
to your convenience or inclination.

    I am, Dear Foote, very faithfully yours,

                                  G. Colman [57]

Foote's answer was brief and to the point: "I should certainly prefer you, both as a successor and a paymaster." [58]

Colman agreed to pay Foote £800 semi-annually and, in addition, to pay him £500 for his unpublished plays: *The Trip to Calais, The Nabob, The Capuchin, The Maid of Bath, The Devil upon Two Sticks,* and *The Cozeners.* In return, Foote agreed to restrict his acting to the Haymarket and to give Colman first choice at any of his plays that might be written in the future.[59] Foote's promised help notwithstanding, the patent was no bargain at that rate. Colman's son, who later inherited the enterprise, spoke from considerable experience when he said, "The stipulated Rent was excessive, considering the average profits at that time, of this limited theatre, and the great risk to be run of losing even these, by unavoidably entering upon a new and enlarged plan of action,—when Foote's plays, and his performance in them, could no longer be almost the sole support of the establishment." [60] The younger Colman also berated Foote because of the moth-eaten wardrobe of the Haymarket that came with the terms of purchase. Foote, he said, jobbed what properties he needed by the night and even rented his music sheets so that he eventually paid ten times their worth and in the end owned nothing.[61]

Garrick, who was privy to the transaction, congratulated Colman on his purchase and hoped he did not make a "bad bargain." [62] On November 4 Garrick wrote to Colman again and begged him to reveal the news publicly so that he could begin planning the next season at the Haymarket. But Garrick admitted that he knew the real reason for secrecy: "Our facetious friend [Foote], I hear, damns himself, that there is no such thing & Jewel only owns to a treaty, but no bargain yet struck—I suppose He w^d not proclaim his Abdication, till the tryal is Over—that will soon be & then you will come forth." [63] It is not clear why Foote wanted the transaction kept secret until his hoped-for acquittal. Foote made public his search for a buyer long before the trial, and once the newspapers were alerted they soon nosed out the truth. They correctly named Colman as the new manager before the end of October.[64]

Though the prospect of the trial was painful, the ordeal of waiting for his name to be cleared was probably unbearable.

Jackson did not stop his attacks, and at about this time a vicious satire was pseudonymously published which is generally attributed to Foote's persecutor.[65] The title, *Sodom and Onan*, proclaims the bent of the attack. Though pretending to Vergilian parody ("Crimes and the man I sing"), the true inspirer was Charles Churchill, a former antagonist of Foote's who also wrote a poem against sexual perversity:

> Oh! that offended Genius would inspire
> Me, with one Note from Churchill's well-strung Lyre,
> To satirize those Fiends, who unconfined,
> Will stop the propagation of Mankind.[66]

The silly and tasteless jingle, ludicrous in its pious pretensions, attacked not only Foote and his friends ("An handsome Boy's a Jewel in his Eyes"), but half the nobility in England. Until his name was cleared, Foote was vulnerable even to this.

On December 9, 1776, at 9:15 a.m., Foote's trial finally began at the Court of King's Bench, Westminster, before Earl Mansfield, a judge who had been highly solicitous of the Duchess of Kingston the previous year. John Sangster, chief witness for the prosecution, gave two hours of testimony bolstered by such a wealth of plausible circumstantial detail that it seemed impossible to doubt the general truth of his story. The gist of his charges was that on May 1, John Williams, then Foote's coachman, drove Foote from North End to Foote's town house on Suffolk Street. Foote's purpose was to talk over the new season with his actors, as was his yearly custom on that date. After Foote met with his actors, he went back to his apartment, called for Sangster and made a violent assault on him. Sangster escaped by pushing Foote down and rushing out the door. The next day at North End, Foote again attempted indecencies with him, and this time Sangster gave him a severe blow. Sangster also added, though this was not part of the court charge, that Foote had made advances to him on his last tour to Dublin.

Foote's lawyers, Murphy among them, discredited the corroborating testimony of Williams the coachman, who had been dismissed by Foote with no reference. Williams was made to admit that he asked Jewel for a reference in return for which he would not testify against Foote. Jewel would not accommodate him. With Sangster's man support out of the way, his carefully detailed story began to crumple as Foote's servants denied every allegation to which he called them as witnesses. His story was completely destroyed when Foote was able to prove conclusively that he did not leave North End to visit his performers on May 1, though that had been his custom. The lawyers produced a newspaper that carried Foote's notice informing his actors that the meeting was postponed to May 6. And all of Foote's actors were in court prepared to swear that Foote did not meet with them that week.

This concluded the case for the defense, and after almost seven hours of testimony, Lord Mansfield summed up the case for the jury, plainly indicating Foote's innocence and the probability that he was framed by people not in the courtroom:

> And here is a man takes up the prosecution [Jackson], who is a stranger to the prosecutor [Sangster], does not know him, and never meddled with the affair till the 23rd of May. Who is that man? Is he a friend to justice or an enemy to Mr. Foote? I expected to have heard of the real person who acts behind the curtains. It must here be observed too, that there are two indictments, two special juries, in order to aggravate the cost, and prepossess the minds of the people with the guilt of the defendant, when the circumstances were all connected in one fact. It was expensive, it was cruel. The indictments appear founded on conspiracy, and a prosecution supported by perjury.[67]

After this address the jury did not leave their box but conferred among themselves for a brief two minutes before rendering their verdict of "Not Guilty." [68] At these words Murphy ran over to

Suffolk Street where an anxious Foote had been awaiting the verdict. Murphy furiously waved his hat in token of victory and rushed up the stairs to congratulate him. But the tension had been too much for Foote, who collapsed hysterically at the news. His mind would not function, and it took him an hour before he could understand that he had been acquitted.[69]

Murphy continued to cheer his downcast friend after the trial. By coincidence, one of Murphy's plays which had been completed for the 1761-62 season at Drury Lane and had not been performed because of differences with Garrick was finally given its production on February 22, 1777, at Covent Garden. Foote's low spirits must have been raised by *Know Your Own Mind,* Murphy's last comedy; a witty and winning character in the play, Dashwould, is a studied model of Foote:

> Bygrove: And that fellow Dashwould; he is the ruin of your son, and of poor Sir Harry into the bargain. He is the merry-andrew of the town: honour has no restraint upon him; truth he sets at naught, and friendship he is ever ready to sacrifice to a joke.
>
> Sir John: Po! Mere innocent pleasantry. Dashwould has no harm in him.
>
> Bygrove: No harm in him? I grant you the fellow has a quick sense of the ridiculous, and draws a character with a lucky hit. But everything is distorted by him. He has wit to ridicule you; invention to frame a story of you; humour to help it about; and when he has set the town a laughing, he puts on a familiar air, and shakes you by the hand.[70]

The portrait is realistic, and even Dashwould's detractor, Bygrove, is won over to him by the end of the play. Though Dashwould is shown to have many of Foote's foibles, he is the wittiest character in the play—indeed, Murphy gives him many of Foote's well-known witticisms. In addition, Dashwould's quick mind

sees through others' hypocrisies, and his kindness and good humor
sets everything right at the end. And, despite his acceptance by
the respectable characters at the end, he remains incorrigible:

> Bygrove: . . . But take my advice, and don't lose your
> friend for your joke.
> Dashwould: By no means, Mr. Bygrove;—except now
> and then, when the friend is the worst of the two.[71]

The original introduction to the play by George Daniel states
with truth that "Dashwould does Foote full justice for broadfaced
mirth, biting satire, and basic goodness of disposition." [72]

May came once more, but for the first time in many years,
Foote did not have to round up his actors, plan a summer's
program, write a new piece, and be prepared to take the acting
lead in almost every dramatic production. Out of curiosity and
habit, Foote probably went to Colman's grand opening on the
fifteenth. The theatre was repainted blue and white, and the
mainpiece offered, *The English Merchant* by Colman himself,
bespoke a new respectability. Foote was not completely forgotten
in the festivities. The introductory prologue closed by compli-
menting him as the "old favorite haymaker of the Public, . . . who
was declared to be ready to assist at the harvest-home, and help
the new farmer get in his hay." [73] But Foote missed his old place
and was not satisfied with the prospect of an occasional acting
stint. Henry Bate, a curate and editor of the early *Morning Post*
before he became a baronet, wrote harshly of Foote's wishes to
the recently retired Garrick:

> Poor Foote sighs his soul out for the loss of his *dramatic
> diadem:*—is the man mad? Or does he think that mankind
> will be apt to make no distinction between the two thea-
> trical abdications of 1776, and view one monarch retiring
> by his own choice, crowned with never fading laurels, and

the other drawn to it by the reproaches of his own conscience, no reckoning made 'with all his imperfections
on his head.' [74]

Foote never succeeded in becoming more actively engaged
in the theatre; he was even unable to complete his acting agreement with Colman. The great strain of his trial and the unceasing
harassment by the press evidently had weakened his spirits and
his health. Cooke describes his sad appearance in *The Nabob*
on May 30, his first performance at the new Haymarket:

> His cheeks were lank and withered, his eyes had lost all
> their wonted intelligence, and his whole person appeared
> sunk and emaciated.
>
> His friends and the impartial part of the audience,
> cheered him with their unbounded applause; while a few
> of another description, who still pursued him, interspersed
> their hisses. He rallied, however, a little in the course
> of the play; but the public seemed to accept his services
> rather in remembrance of what he had been than for what
> he then was.[75]

Foote next appeared in *The Devil upon Two Sticks* on June 6.[76]
About the time of this performance, Foote was seized with con-
vulsions that temporarily stopped him from acting, though apparently he continued to assist Colman with managerial duties. On
June 9, while Colman's company was acting *She Stoops to Conquer*, Foote suffered a relapse of his shaking fit, but this time
the seizure was accompanied by repeated fainting.[77] Frightened
for his life, at least for the moment, he pressed Colman to apply
for a renewal of the patent so that the Haymarket would not
be forced to close in the event of his death.[78] However, Foote
waited little more than a month to resume acting. He played
The Minor on July 7 and 25, *The Nabob* on the eleventh, and

on the thirtieth appeared in *The Maid of Bath*.[79] On August 6, Foote was to have appeared as the Devil but while rehearsing on stage was stricken with a third recurrence of his malady.[80]

After his recuperation, his doctor ordered him to bathe in the salt water at Brighthelmstone. Upon his arrival at the resort, he found two boon companions, Wilkes and Lord Lyttleton, whose gay company restored his spirits.[81] By late September Foote returned to London in high fettle and continued to give lordly dinners for his friends.[82] His doctor, however, did not think he should spend the winter in England and recommended that he travel to the south of France. Pleased with this advice, Foote promptly packed his bags and left for Dover. On October 20, he bedded down at the Ship Inn to wait for favorable winds. The next day he ate a hearty breakfast and in characteristic good humor set all the servants laughing uproariously at his jokes and stories. But by eleven o'clock he felt chills, and, fearing a return of his illness, he went to bed. His fears soon proved justified as his limbs began to tremble violently, particularly his amputated thigh. Doctors were hurriedly called to his bedside and insisted on letting his blood. Foote, who retained his senses to the end, refused. By two o'clock the trembling ceased; Foote was dead.[83]

His body was soon removed to his house on Suffolk Street, and Jewel announced his funeral for Monday night, October 27. His corpse, followed by three coaches of mourners, was taken to Westminster Abbey and buried by torchlight.[84] His implacable enemy, Jackson, left England as soon as he heard of Foote's death and rushed to the Duchess of Kingston's side at St. Petersburgh. He came back a wealthy man.[85] Garrick too breathed easier; for the first time he could vent his true feelings about Foote: "Mr. Foote dy'd a few days ago upon his landing at Calais. He had much wit, no feeling, sacrific'd friends & foes to a joke, & so has dy'd very little regretted even by his nearest acquaintance." [86] But Foote's death was regretted by the public; every newspaper and magazine in London carried an account of his life and praised the man in many ways. At least two close friends, Jewel and Murphy, mourned him to their dying days. Even his old acquaintance, Johnson, who knew his frailties well, mourned his passing in a letter to Mrs. Thrale:

Did you see Foote at Brighthelmstone?—Did you
think he would so soon be gone?—Life, says Falstaff, is a
shuttle. He was a fine fellow in his way; and the world
is really impoverished by his sinking glories. Murphy
ought to write his life, at least to give the world a Footeana.
Now will any of his contemporaries bewail him? Will
Genius change *his sex* to weep? I would really have his
life written with diligence.[87]

Johnson's view of biography was essentially moralistic; perhaps he felt that a history of Foote's life would not only preserve
knowledge of him, but that Foote's spectacular rise, his igno-
minious, retirement, and his sudden death would teach a sober
lesson of misused talent, prodigality, and religious and ethical
immorality. This was a reasonable view, for Foote attained his
enormous popularity primarily through his audacious and at
times libelous wit and his farcical acting. Although his talent
for mimicry brought him his initial notoriety and fame, through
the years he depended less and less upon this ability. Foote, of
course, hired mimics such as Wilkinson and Bannister, but his
plays, especially after *The Orators*, depended more on allusion
than mimicry. The audiences came to see well-known people
satirized who previously had been immune to theatrical attack;
mimicry was merely one of Foote's methods. Foote, after all, began
his career by defying the monopoly of Drury Lane and Covent
Garden. Though others before him had done the same, no one
so challenged the powers that could control him as Foote did
with his irreverent mimicry. Foote found out early that his battles
with theatre people—Murphy, Woodward, Macklin, Wilkinson,
T. Sheridan, and Garrick—puffed by free newspaper publicity
would bring in great audiences eager to see a bout of mudslinging.
Though Foote came to broaden his aim as he hit at Methodism, oratory, the militia, nabobs, the practice of medicine and
law, newspapers, and political corruption, he almost always had
some public figure in mind who was closely connected with the
practice that was being condemned. Whitefield, T. Sheridan,
Lamb, Clive, Browne, Whittaker, *The Monthly Review,* and the

Duke of Newcastle, were exposed to ridicule, and any objections by these subjects merely gave Foote's play added publicity and lengthened its run. Foote thrived on controversy, but it was a two-edged sword. Sheridan threatened a libel suit; Faulkner won £300 damages; Aprice stopped the showing of *The Author;* Garrick and Rich would not hire him unless they were desperate. Finally, the Duchess of Kingston not only kept him from caricaturing her in *The Trip to Calais,* but her vicious henchman, Jackson, brought Foote to trial and almost destroyed his reputation through slanderous newspaper articles. Lacking the spirit and health to continue fighting his enemies, Foote sold his theatre. His own methods, controversy, publicity, and influence, had been turned against him.

NOTES

1. Elizabeth Mavor, *The Virgin Mistress, A Study in Survival: The Life of the Duchess of Kingston* (London, 1964), pp. 48-49.
2. Mavor, p. 54; and *Town and Country Magazine,* January, 1775, p. 10.
3. Mavor, p. 62 ff.
4. *Ibid.,* p. 108.
5. *Ibid.,* pp. 68-69.
6. *Ibid.,* pp. 120-133.
7. *English Aristophanes,* p. 12.
8. He had been experimenting with the name of his heroine, calling her Betty Bigamy (*Letters and Pomes by the Late Mr. John Henderson* [London, 1786], p. 105) and Barbara Blubber (*The Case of the Duchess of Kingston* [London, 1775], pp. 13-14) before deciding on Kitty Crocodile.
9. Stone, *London Stage,* Vol. III, pp. 1893 ff. Foote was especially honored this season by an unprecedented six command performances. The dates are May 17, June 14, July 19, August 2, 30, and September 13.
10. *Town and Country Magazine,* May, 1775, pp. 258-259.
11. Foote, *The Dramatic Works of Samuel Foote,* Vol. III, p. 449.
12. C. E. Pearce, *The Amazing Duchess, Being the Romantic History of Elizabeth Chudleigh, Maid of Honour, The Honourable Mrs. Hervey, Duchess of Kingston, and Countess of Bristol* (London, 1911), II, 261.
13. Belden, p. 39.
14. Foote, *The Dramatic Works,* Vol. III, p. 444.
15. *The Case of the Duchess of Kingston,* pp. 18-19.
16. *The Letters of David Garrick,* Vol. III, p. 1020.
17. Besides being carried in *The Morning Chronicle,* this letter was re-

printed in many papers and magazines. It can be found in *The Public Advertiser*, August 4, 1776. It is also in *The Case of the Duchess of Kingston*, pp. 14-17.

18. Walpole, Vol. XXVII, pp. 218-219.

19. *The Case of the Duchess of Kingston*, pp. 20-21, 32.

20. *St. James's Chronicle*, August 10-12, 1775.

21. Foote's correspondence with the Duchess of Kingston was originally printed in the *Evening Post* (Belden, p. 43) and later included almost all publications that gave an account of the dispute. See *Exshaw's Magazine*, September, 1775, pp. 554-558; *Public Advertiser*, August 16 and 18, 1775; *Town and Country Magazine*, August, 1775, pp. 412-415. For additional references see Belden, p. 43.

22. *Ibid.*

23. Walpole, Vol. XXVIII, p. 222. Walpole's praise was heartily endorsed by his correspondent, William Mason: "Foote's answer is one of the very best things in the English language; Mr. Pope's letter to Lord Hervey is nothing to it" (Walpole, XXVIII, 224-225).

24. William Jackson, a former parson, was the editor of *The Public Ledger* and was responsible for spreading scandal about Foote.

25. See note 21.

26. *St. James Chronicle*, August 17-19, 1775.

27. *The English Aristophanes*, p. 32.

28. *The Letters of David Garrick*, Vol. III, pp. 1031-1032.

29. Cooke, *Foote*, Vol. I, p. 211.

30. *Boswell Papers*, Vol. XI, p. 141. Foote spoke to Boswell on April 19, 1776. Also see Samuel Johnson, *Diaries, Prayers, and Annals*. ed. E. L. McAdam with Donald and Mary Hyde (New Haven, 1958), p. 250.

31. *Life*, Vol. II, pp. 403-404.

32. MS letter dated January 4, 1776, by [J]ohn Walker to Mrs. Garrick in *Garrick Correspondence*, Vol. VI, Folger Shakespeare Library. Walker also mentioned that Foote played Sir Paul Plyant and Cadwallader.

33. Snagg, p. 97.

34. *Memoirs of that Celebrated Comedian and Very Singular Genius, Thomas Weston* (London, 1776), p. 54.

35. *Ibid.*, p. 60.

36. William Roberts, *Memoirs of the Life and Correspondence of Mrs. Hannah More* (New York, 1835), Vol. I, p. 55. The complete proceedings of the trial were covered by *Town and Country Magazine*, April, 1776, pp. 171-179.

37. Mavor, p. 149.

38. Cited by Lucyle Werkmeister, "Notes for a Revised Life of William Jackson, "*N&Q*, CCVI (February, 1961), 44.

39. In a May 10, 1776 entry in the *Boswell Papers*, Vol. X, p. 275, Boswell noted, "I mentioned Jackson's shocking story of Foote, [George] Stevens [sic. Steevens] said he would rather have the character of a Sodomite than of an infidel. I said I would not. Samuel Johnson. 'Yes. An infidel would be it if he inclined.' "

40. Stone, *London Stage*, Vol. III, pp. 1980 ff.
41. *St. James's Chronicle*, May 18-21, 1776; Cooke, *Foote,* Vol. I, pp. 221-222.
42. *St. James's Chronicle*, May 18-21, 1776.
43. Cooke, *Foote,* Vol. 1, p. 122.
44. *St. James's Chronicle*, June 10-13, 1776.
45. Stone, *London Stage*, Vol. III, p. 1987. Command performances were given on June 12, 26; July 10; and September 6.
46. James J. Lynch, *Box, Pit, and Gallery: Stage and Society in Johnson's London* (Berkeley and Los Angeles, 1953), p. 224.
47. Cooke, *Foote,* Vol. I, p. 223.
48. Quoted by Werkmeister, p. 44.
49. Cooke, *Foote,* Vol. I, p. 222-228. Notice of the legal proceedings against Foote first appeared in *The St. James's Chronicle*, July 9-11, 1776.
50. Foote, *The Dramatic Works,* Vol. III, pp. 469-470.
51. *St. James's Chronicle*, August 17-20, 1776.
52. *Town and Country Magazine,* August, 1776, p. 407; and Oulton, I, 49.
53. *St. James's Chronicle*, August 17-19, 1776.
54. *The Letters of David Garrick,* Vol. III, pp. 1060-1061.
55. George Colman, The Younger, *Random Records* (London, 1930), Vol. I, pp. 232-233.
56. Richard B. Peake, *Memoirs of the Colman Family* (London, 1841), Vol. I, p. 413.
57. *Ibid.,* pp. 414-415.
58. *Ibid.*
59. Cooke, *Foote,* Vol. I, p. 233; and *The London Chronicle,* May 15-17, p. 468.
60. *Random Records,* Vol. I, p. 234. Although Colman had made only one payment of £800 when Foote died, and although the King granted a yearly renewal of the patent, Colman made only marginal profit from the theatre because of encroachments into the summer season from Drury Lane and Covent Garden. As early as 1779 Colman was forced to defer opening his theatre until May 31 because his actors, upon whom he was more dependent than Foote, were engaged at the winter houses. In 1802, when the son was manager, the Haymarket was unable to open until June 26. Though the younger Colman fought the rival patentees spiritedly, he gave up the unequal battle in 1804 when he sold his directorship, though he still remained a shareholder. (*The Struggle for a Free Stage,* pp. 96, 152, 158). It is impossible that the theatre could have been run profitably with the required rent of £1600 a year. Perhaps Foote knew this, and hoped that it would return to him after a year or two when the scandal would be forgotten and he would be physically rested.
61. Colman, *Random Records,* Vol. I, p. 232.
62. *The Letters of David Garrick,* Vol. III, pp. 1136-1137.
63. *Ibid.,* pp. 1137-1138.
64. As early as October 25, *The St. James's Chronicle* named a number of

possible buyers and guessed that Colman had the advantage over the others. And despite Foote's later denials, *The London Chronicle,* October 29-31, 1776, claimed that Colman brought the lease to the patent.

65. Belden, p. 48.
66. *Sodom and Onan. A Satire inscribed to* [portrait of Foote and a picture of a human foot] *esq., alias the devil upon two sticks. by Humphrey Nettle.* (London, 1776).
67. *Town and Country Magazine,* Supplement, 1776, p. 696.
68. The information relating to Foote's trial was collated from these sources: *The Gazeteer and Daily Advertiser,* December 10, 1776, p. 2; *The London Chronicle,* December 7-10, 1776, p. 558; *Town and Country Magazine,* Supplement, 1776, pp. 693-696; and *St. James's Chronicle,* December 7-10, 1776.
69. Cooke, *Foote,* Vol. I, pp. 231-232.
70. Arthur Murphy, *Know Your Own Mind, The Way to Keep Him and Five Other Plays by Arthur Murphy,* ed. John Pike Emery (New York, 1956), p. 345.
71. *Ibid.,* p. 432.
72. "Remarks" prefaced to *Know Your Own Mind* (London, n.d.), pp. 5-6, cited by Dunbar, pp. 278-279.
73. *London Chronicle,* May 15-17, 1777, p. 468.
74. Broaden, *Correspondence,* Vol. II, pp. 265-266. An A.L.S. in the Berg Collection of the New York Public Library from Foote to Garrick is undated but relates to this period in Foote's life. Foote seems to have quarreled with Bate over scurrilous items that appeared in his newspaper: "I have directed Jewel to advertise all my performances in the *Morning Post* and if the gentleman who is supposed to be the Editor should again turn his thoughts to the Drama, me and my Stage he may ever command. I have been most cruelly used but I have thank God got to the bottom of this infernal contrivance. God for ever bless you my Dear Sir."
75. Cooke, *Foote,* Vol. I, pp. 234-235.
76. Genest, Vol. V, pp. 582-585.
77. *St. James's Chronicle,* June 10-12, 1777.
78. *London Chronicle,* October 23-25, 1777, p. 407. The lease, as has been mentioned, was renewed for the year, and Colman's yearly application for the terms of the original patent was always granted.
79. Genest, Vol. V, p. 583.
80. Cooke, *Foote,* Vol. I, p. 236; *The London Stage, Part 5,* ed. Charles B. Hogan, Vol. I, pp. 86 ff.
81. *English Aristophanes,* p. xxxi;; and *Exshaw's Magazine,* February, 1777, pp. 534-537.
82. Foote's last extant letter is dated October 10, 1777, and is an invitation to one of his friends for dinner on the twelfth. (Add MS 36, 595, f. 339 in the British Museum)
83. This account of Foote's last day was taken from Cooke, Foote, Vol. I,

pp. 237-239; *London Chronicle,* October 28-30, 1777, p. 419; and *Gazetteer and Daily Advertiser,* October 29, 1777.

84. Cooke, *Foote,* Vol. I, p. 239.

85. Werkmeister, pp. 44-45. Jackson was tried for high treason on April 23, 1795, and was found guilty. Before he was executed, guards discovered his poisoned corpse. It was never decided whether he committed suicide or was poisoned by his confederates who feared discovery.

86. *Letters of David Garrick and Georgiana Countess Spencer, 1759-1779,* edd. Earl Spencer and Christopher Dobson (Cambridge for Roxburgh Club, 1960), p. 39.

87. *The Letters of Samuel Johnson,* Vol. II, p. 561.

RECORD OF FOOTE'S
PERFORMANCES ON THE LONDON STAGE

Drury Lane, 1745-1746

Sir Harry Wildair (*Constant Couple*-Farquhar): Nov. 1, 2, 27; Dec. 7, 28; Mar. 3.
Lord Foppington (*Relapse*-Vanbrugh): Nov. 14, 15.
Tinsel (*Drummer*-Addison): Nov. 25, 27.
Sir Novelty Fashion (*Love's Last Shift*-Cibber): Dec. 11.
Bayes (*Rehearsal*-Villiers): Dec. 13; Jan. 24.
Dick (*Confederacy*-Vanbrugh): Feb. 24, 27; Apr. 3.
Younger Loveless (*The Scornful Lady*-Beaumont and Fletcher): Mar. 17, 20.
Sir Courtly Nice (*Sir Courtly Nice*-Crowne): Apr. 14.

Performances of *Tea* at the Haymarket, April-June, 1747

April 22, 25, 28, 29, 30
May 2, 4, 5, 6, 7, 8, 9, 11 (new afterpiece), 12, 13 (new character), 14, 15,16, 18, 19, 20, 21, 23, 25, 26, 27, 28, 29, 30
June (6:30 performances) 1, 2, 3, 4, 5, 6.

Covent Garden, November, 1747-February, 1748

Tea: Nov. 11, 13, 18, 19, 20, 21; Dec. 15, 22, 30; Jan. 21, 26, 28;
   Feb. 2.
Bayes (*Rehearsal*-Villiers): Nov. 23, 24.
Fondlewife (*Old Bachelor*-Congreve): Dec. 15, 22, 30.
Sir Novelty Fashion (*Love's Last Shift*-C. Cibber): Feb. 2.

Auction of Pictures at the Haymarket, April-June, 1748

April 18, 19, 20, 21, 22, 23, 25, 26, 27, 29, 30.
May 2, 3, 4, 5, 6, 7, 9, 12, 14, 16, 17, 19, 20, 21, 24, 26, 28, 30 (6:30
   performances), 31.
June 3, 6, 9, 11; 14 and 16 Foote gives *Tea.*

Auction of Pictures at the Haymarket, December, 1748-February, 1749

December 1, 5, 7, 12, 14, 16, 19, 22, 24, 28.
January 2, 7, 9, 14, 25, 27
February 4, 18.

The Haymarket, April 3-June 1, 1749

Hartop (*Knights*): April 3, 4, 5, 8, 11, 12 15, 18, 20, 22, 25, 28;
   May 1, 6, 10, 15, 19, 26; June 1.
Auction of Pictures: April 18, 20, 22, 25, 28; May 1, 6, 10, 15, 19,
   26; June 1.
Tea: April 7 at Covent Garden for Mr. Bencraft's and Mrs. Hale's
   benefit.

Drury Lane, 1753-1754

Buck (*Englishman in Paris*): Oct. 20, 22, 24, 27, 30; Nov. 2,
   12, 30; Dec. 14, 15, 20; Jan. 18, 21, 25, 29; Feb. 5, 22.
Tea: Nov. 19, 20.
Hartop (*Knights*): Feb. 9, 12, 13, 15, 22.

Fondlewife (*Old Bachelor*-Congreve): Oct. 24, 27, 30; Nov. 2, 12, 30; Dec. 15; Jan. 29; Feb. 22.
Sir Courtly Nice (*Sir Courtly Nice*-Crowne): Nov. 6; Dec. 14.
Ben (*Love for Love*-Congreve): Jan. 16, 18, 21, 25; Feb. 15.
Brazen (*Recruiting Officer*-Farquhar): Feb. 5, 13.

Covent Garden, 1754-1755

Fondlewife (*Old Bachelor*-Congreve): Oct. 14; Nov. 12.
Hartop (*Knights*): Oct. 14; Jan. 14.
Buck (*Englishman in Paris*): Nov. 12.
Lady Pentweazle (*Taste*): Mar. 18; Apr. 10.

Covent Garden, 1755-1756

Buck (*Englishman Returned from Paris*): Feb. 3, 5, 9, 11, 12, 13, 14, 16, 18, 20, 23, 25, 27; Mar. 1, 4, 8, 15, 29; April 1.
Fondlewife (*Old Bachelor*-Congreve): Feb. 9.
Myrtle (*Conscious Lovers*-Steele): Feb. 16.
Brazen (*Recruiting Officer*-Farquhar): Feb. 23.
Sir Paul Plyant (*Double Dealer*-Congreve): Mar. 1, 4.
Hartop (*Knights*): Mar. 22; May 10.
Buck (*Englishman in Paris*): Mar. 27; May 7.
Lady Pentweazle (*Taste*): Mar. 30.

Drury Lane, 1756-1757

Fondlewife (*Old Bachelor*-Congreve): Oct. 14.
Sir Paul Plyant (*Double Dealer*-Congreve): Oct. 29; Nov. 1.
Gomez (*Spanish Frier*-Dryden): Feb. 22, 26.
Buck (*Englishman in Paris*): Oct. 14; Nov. 1; Mar. 31.
Buck (*Englishman Returned from Paris*): Oct. 29.
Cadwallader (*The Author*): Feb. 5, 7, 9, 12, 15, 17, 19, 22, 26; Mar. 4, 10, 15, 28; Apr. 14, 29; May 10, 12, 20.
Hartop (*Knights*): Apr. 2.

Drury Lane, 1757-1758

Cadwallader (*Author*): Oct. 15, 18, 21, 22, 24; Jan. 26; Feb. 1.
Sir Paul Plyant (*Double Dealer*-Congreve): Oct. 18.
Gomez (*Spanish Fryar*-Dryden): Feb. 1.
Buck (*Englishman Returned from Paris*): Mar. 9 at Covent Garden for Bellamy's benefit.

Drury Lane, 1758-1759

Puzzle (*Diversions of the Morning*): Oct. 17, 27, 30; Nov. 1, 6, 9, 14, 17, 28; Dec. 18.
Fondlewife (*Old Bachelor*-Congreve): Oct. 27.
Lord Foppington (*Relapse*-Vanbrugh): Nov. 1.
Gomez (*Spanish Fryar*-Dryden): Nov. 14.
Sir Paul Plyant (*Double Dealer*-Congreve): Nov. 17.
Sir Courtly Nice (*Sir Courtly Nice*-Crowne): Nov. 24.
Buck (*Englishman in Paris*): Nov. 24.
Shylock (*Merchant of Venice*-Shakespeare): Dec. 18.

The Haymarket, Summer 1760

Mother Cole, Shift, Smirk (*Minor*): June 28; July 1, 3, 5, 8, 10, 12, 15, 17, 21, 23, 25, 28, 30; Aug. 1, 4, 6, 7, 9, 11, 13, 15, 18, 19, 20, 21, 22, 23, 25, 26, 27, 28, 29, 30

Drury Lane, 1760-1761

Mother Cole, etc. (*Minor*): Nov. 22, 24, 25, 26, 28; Dec. 1, 3, 9, 22; Jan. 9, 19, 24; Apr. 22.
Buck (*Englishman in Paris*): Dec. 9. Foote Played this role at Covent Garden for Costollo's benefit on Apr. 21.
Lady Pentweazle, etc. (*Modern Tragedy*): Apr. 6; May 15.
Myrtle (*Conscious Lovers*-Steele): Apr. 25.
Scotchman (*Register Office*-Reed): Apr. 25, 27; May 1, 7.

Drury Lane, Summer 1761

Prologue (*All in the Wrong*-Murphy): June 15, 16, 18, 19, 22, 26, 29; July 23.

Mother Cole, etc. (*Minor*): June 26, 29; July 21; Aug. 7.

Young Philpot (*The Citizen*-Murphy): July 2, 4, 7, 9, 13, 16, 21; Aug. 5.

Distress (*The Wishes*-Richard Bentley): July 27, 28, 30; Aug. 3, 6.

Covent Garden, 1761-1762

Mother Cole, etc. (*Minor*): Nov. 10; Jan. 22; Apr. 30.

Young Wilding (*Liar*): Jan. 12, 13, 15, 22.

The Haymarket, Summer 1762

Orators: Apr. 28; May 1, 4, 6, 8, 11, 18, 20, 22, 25, 26, 29; June 1, 3, 5, 8, 10, 12, 16, 21, 23, 25, 29; July 1, 3, 6, 8, 10, 13, 15, 20, 22; Aug. 30; Sept. 6, 9, 10, 14, 16.

Young Wilding (*Liar*): June 21, 23, 25, 29; July 1, 3, 6, 22; Aug. 23, 25, 28; Sept. 9.

Mother Cole, ect. (*Minor*): July 8, 10, 13, 20; Sept. 2, 8, 11.

Young Philpot (*Citizen*-Murphy): Aug. 10, 13, 19, 23, 25, 27, 28; Sept. 3, 7.

Lady Pentweazle, etc. (*Modern Tragedy*): Sept. 10.

Lady Pentweazle (Act 1 of *Taste*): Sept. 11, 14, 16.

The Haymarket, Summer 1763

Orators: May 11, 18, 21, 28; June 3; July 4, 13; Aug. 8, 19, 29; Sept. 3.

Mother Cole, Smirk (*Minor*): June 20, 22, 24, 29; July 1, 8, 15, 25; Aug. 3, 12, 15, 26.

Major Sturgeon, M. Mug (*Mayor of Garratt*): June 20, 22, 24, 27, 29, 30; July 1, 4, 6, 7, 8, 11, 13, 15, 18, 20, 22, 25, 27, 29; Aug. 1, 3, 5, 8, 12, 15, 17, 19, 22, 24, 26, 29, 30, 31; Sept. 2, 3.

Young Wilding (*Liar*): June 30; July 11, 20, 27; Aug. 10, 17, 30.

Samuel Foote as the Devil in *The Devil Upon Two Sticks*. Courtesy of the Victoria Art Gallery and Municipal Libraries, Bath.

Lady Pentweazle (*Diversions of the Morning*): July 6, 7.
Young Philpot (*Citizen*-Murphy): July 18, 22, 29; Aug. 10, 11,
    24, 31; Sept. 7.
Buck (*Englishman Returned from Paris*): Aug. 5, 22.

Drury Lane, 1763-64

Major Sturgeon, M. Mug (*Mayor of Garratt*): Nov. 30; Dec. 2, 3,
    5, 7, 8, 9.
Gomez (*Spanish Friar*-Dryden): Dec. 5.

The Haymarket, Summer 1764

Sir Thomas Lofty, P. Pepperpot (*Patron*): June 13, 15, 18, 26, 28,
    29; July 3, 5, 10, 13, 20, 25; Aug. 6, 15, 31; Sept. 10.
Major Sturgeon, M. Mug (*Mayor of Garratt*): June 26, 28, 29;
    July 3, 5, 6, 10, 16, 25, 30; Aug. 1, 6, 10, 17, 20, 27; Sept. 5,
    11, 14.
Orators: July 6, 12, 23; Aug. 10, 22, 29; Sept. 7, 13.
Young Philpot (*Citizen*-Murphy): July 12, 13, 18, 27; Aug. 3, 13,
    24; Sept. 3.
Mother Cole, Smirk (*Minor*): July 16, 27; Aug. 13, 14; Sept. 3, 12.
Young Wilding (*Liar*): July 30; Aug. 1, 3, 8, 17, 27; Sept. 5, 11, 14.
Lady Pentweazle, etc. (*Tragedy à la Mode*): Aug. 29, 31; Sept. 1,
    7, 10, 13.

The Haymarket, Summer 1765

Zachary Fungus (*Commissary*): June 10, 11, 14, 17, 19, 21, 24, 26,
    28; July 1, 3, 5, 8, 10, 12, 17, 22, 26; Aug. 5, 12, 15, 19, 23, 26;
    Sept. 2, 4, 10, 12, 13.
Hartop (*Knights*): June 10, 11, 14, 17, 19, 21; Aug. 14.
Young Philpot (*Citizen*-Murphy): July 8, 10, 12; Aug. 8, 21;
    Sept. 11.
Young Wilding (*Liar*): July 15, 19, 24, 29; Sept. 11.
Major Sturgeon, M. Mug (*Mayor of Garratt*): July 15, 19, 24;
    Aug. 7, 12, 15, 19, 23, 26, 28; Sept. 2, 10, 13.

Orators: July 31; Aug. 7, 14; Sept. 3, 9.
Mother Cole, etc. (*Minor*): Aug. 9, 16, 28; Sept. 6.
Sir T. Lofty, P. Pepperpot (*Patron*): Aug. 21.

The Haymarket, Summer 1766

Mother Cole (*Minor*): June 18, 20, 24, 26; July 23, 25, 28; Aug.
  6; Sept. 2.
Orators: July 1, 3, 8, 10; Aug. 4.
Zachary Fungus (*Commissary*): July 15, 18, 21, 30.
Mayor Sturgeon, M. Mug (*Mayor of Garratt*): July 23, 25, 28, 30;
  Aug. 4, 6.
Fondlewife (*Credulous Husband*-Congreve): Aug. 21.

The Haymarket, Summer 1767

Mother Cole, etc. (*Minor*): May 29; June 2, 15; Aug. 19; Sept. 4.
Zachary Fungus (*Commissary*): June 4, 10, 19, 25; July 20; Aug.
  3; Sept. 1, 11.
Orators: June 5, 12; Aug. 25; Sept. 9.
Major Sturgeon, M. Mug (*Mayor of Garratt*): June 17, 19, 25;
  July 20; Aug. 3, 27; Sept. 7, 12.
Francisco (*Tailors*): July 2, 3, 7, 9, 13, 17, 29; Aug. 12, 19, 25;
  Sept. 1.
Sir Thomas Lofty, P. Pepperpot (*Patron*): Aug. 12, 27.
Fondlewife (*Credulous Husband*- Congreve): Aug. 14.
Young Philpot (*Citizen*-Murphy): Sept. 4, 9.

The Haymarket, Summer 1768

Devil, Hellebore, Squib (*Devil upon Two Sticks*): May 30; June
  1, 3, 6, 8, 10, 13, 15, 17, 20, 22, 24, 27; 29; July 1, 4, 6, 11, 15,
  20, 25, 29; Aug. 3, 8, 12, 17, 22, 29; Sept. 2, 5, 9, 12, 13, 15.
Major Sturgeon, M. Mug (*Mayor of Garratt*): May 23; Aug. 10;
  Sept. 7, 14.
Zachary Fungus (*Commissary*): July 13; Aug. 5, 26; Sept. 14.
Mother Cole, etc. (*Minor*): July 18; Aug. 15, 31.
Gomez (*Spanish Friar*-Dryden): Aug. 19.

The Haymarket, Summer 1769

Devil, Hellebore, Squib (*Devil upon Two Sticks*): May 15, 17, 19, 22, 26, 31; June 7, 12, 19; July 5, 24; Aug. 4; Sept. 4, 13, 15.

Zachary Fungus (*Commissary*): May 24; June 14; July 10; Aug. 2, 21; Sept. 8, 14

Mother Cole, etc. (*Minor*): May 29; June 9, 16; July 7, 21; Aug. 11; Sept. 12.

Major Sturgeon, M. Mug (*Mayor of Garratt*): May 29; June 9, 16; July 7, 21; Sept. 1.

Orators: June 2; July 28.

Ailwoud (*Dr. Last in his Chariot*-Bickerstaffe): May 21, 23, 26, 28, 30; July 3, 31; Aug. 18, 31.

Cadwallader (*Author*): Aug. 11, 16, 18, 21, 23; Sept. 8, 12, 14.

Fondlewife (*Old Bachelor*-Congreve): Aug. 25, 28.

Lady Pentweazle (*Taste*): Aug. 25.

The Haymarket, Summer 1770

Devil, etc. (*Devil upon Two Sticks*): May 16, 21; June 5, 13, 20; July 20; Aug. 6, 17, 29; Sept. 10, 15.

Zachary Fungus (*Commissary*): May 18, 25; June 1, 11; Aug. 3, 16; Sept. 13.

Cadwallader (*Author*): May 18, 30; June 8; July 11, 23; Aug. 10; Sept. 3, 12.

Thomas Lofty (*Patron*): May 28; June 8.

Major Sturgeon, M. Mug (*Mayor of Garratt*): May 28; June 1, 11; Aug. 20; Sept. 3, 13.

Mother Cole, etc. (*Minor*): June 15; July 27.

Luke Limp (*Lame Lover*): June 22, 25, 27, 29; July 2, 4, 6, 11, 16, 23; Aug. 1, 10, 20; Sept. 5, 12.

Fondlewife (*Old Bachelor*-Congreve): Aug. 24; Sept. 7, 14.

Lady Pentweazle (*Taste*): Aug. 24; Sept. 7, 14.

Young Philpot (*Citizen*-Murphy): Aug. 31.

The Haymarket, Summer 1771

Devil, etc. (*Devil upon Two Sticks*): May 15; June 3, 21; Aug. 5, 30; Sept. 11.

Major Sturgeon, etc. (*Mayor of Garratt*): May 20; June 12; Aug. 26; Sept. 2, 13.

Mother Cole, etc. (*Minor*): May 20; June 19; Aug. 12, 26; Sept. 13.

Luke Limp (*Lame Lover*): May 23.

Cadwallader (*Author*): May 23; June 19; Aug 14, 21; Sept. 6, 14.

Zachary Fungus (*Commissary*): May 29; June 17; Aug. 16.

Thomas Lofty (*Patron*): June 7.

Lady Pentweazle (*Taste*): June 7, 17; Aug. 16, 23; Sept. 12.

Young Wilding (*Liar*): June 12; Aug. 7.

Orators: June 14.

Solomon Flint (*Maid of Bath*): June 26, 28; July 1, 3, 5, 8, 10, 12, 15, 17, 19, 22, 26, 29, 31; Aug. 2, 9, 14, 21, 23, 28; Sept. 4, 10, 12, 14.

Don Lewis (*Love Makes a Man*-C. Cibber): Aug. 19; Sept. 6.

Fondlewife (*Old Bachelor*-Congreve): Sept. 2.

The Haymarket, Summer 1772

Solomon Flint (*Maid of Bath*): May 18, 20, 25, 29; June 5, 12, 22; July 22; Aug. 21; Sept. 4, 10.

Cadwallader (*Author*): May 20, 25; June 5; Aug. 5; Sept. 4, 8, 14.

Mother Cole, etc. (*Minor*): May 22; June 19; Aug. 17.

Major Sturgeon, etc. (*Mayor of Garratt*): May 22, 29; Aug. 21; Sept. 10.

Devil, etc. (*Devil upon Two Sticks*): May 27; June 1, 10, 24; July 27; Sept. 9.

Zachary Fungus (*Commissary*): June 8, 17; Aug. 5; Sept. 14.

Lady Pentweazle (*Taste*): June 8.

Thomas Lofty (*Patron*): June 15.

Matthew Mite (*Nabob*): June 29; July 1, 3, 6, 8, 10, 13, 15, 17, 20, 24, 29, 31; Aug. 3, 7, 12, 14, 19, 26, 28; Sept. 2, 7, 11, 15.

Bayes (*Rehearsal*-Villiers): Aug. 10, 24, 31.

Fondlewife (*Old Bachelor*-Congreve): Sept. 8.

The Haymarket, Summer 1773

Matthew Mite (*Nabob*): May 17, 22; June 4, 9; July 5, 16; Aug.
  30; Sept. 9.
Mother Cole, etc. (*Minor*): May 26; June 2, 11, 30; Aug. 11, 31.
Major Sturgeon (*Mayor of Garratt*): May 26; June 2, 9, 30; Sept. 8.
Solomon Flint (*Maid of Bath*): May 28; June 7, July 7; Sept. 8.
Devil, etc. (*Devil upon Two Sticks*): May 31; June 25; July 12;
  Aug. 23.
Cadwallader (*Author*): June 7, 9; July 16; Aug. 30; Sept. 14.
Bayes (*Rehearsal*-Villiers): June 18, 23; July 19.
Zachary Fungus (*Commissary*): July 2.
Robert Riscounter (*Bankrupt*): July 21, 23, 26, 28, 30; Aug. 2,
  4, 6, 9, 13, 16, 18, 25, 27; Sept. 1, 6, 10, 13, 14, 15.
Orators: Sept. 3.

The Haymarket, Summer 1774

Robert Riscounter (*Bankrupt*): May 16; June 1, 15; July 1, 8;
  Aug. 4; Sept. 2, 14.
Matthew Mite (*Nabob*): May 30; June 3, 13, 22; July 4, 13; Aug.
  8, 19.
Cadwallader (*Author*): June 3, 10, 17; July 1, 13; Aug. 24; Sept.
  14.
Luke Limp (*Maid of Bath*): June 6.
Major Sturgeon (*Mayor of Garratt*): June 6, 24; Sept. 2.
Devil, etc. (*Devil upon Two Sticks*): June 8, 20, 29; July 6; Aug.
  29; Sept. 12.
Mother Cole, etc. (*Minor*): June 10, 24.
Zachary Fungus (*Commissary*): June 17.
Bayes (*Rehearsal*-Villiers): June 27; July 11.
Aircastle (*Cozeners*): July 15, 18, 20, 22, 25, 27, 29; Aug. 1, 3, 5,
  10, 12, 15, 17, 22, 26, 31; Sept. 7, 9, 13, 15.
Thomas Lofty (*Patron*): Sept. 5.

The Haymarket, Summer 1775

Devil (*Devil upon Two Sticks*): May 15, 17, 29; July 5, 24; Aug. 18; Sept. 8.

Cadwallader (*Author*): May 16, 29; June 14, 28; July 12, 21; Aug. 14; Sept. 1.

Aircastle (*Cozeners*): May 19, 24; June 2, 16, 26; July 3, 21; Aug. 23; Sept. 14.

Matthew Mite (*Nabob*): May 22, 31; June 14; July 17; Aug. 4, 25, Sept. 11.

Mother Cole (*Minor*): May 26; June 9, 28; July 12, 26; Aug. 14; Sept. 1, 15.

Major Sturgeon (*Mayor of Garratt*): May 26; June 9, 21; July 19, 26; Aug. 16; Sept. 14.

Robert Riscounter (*Bankrupt*): June 5; July 19; Aug. 11.

Zachary Fungus (*Commissary*): June 7, 30; Aug. 9; Sept. 13.

Solomon Flint (*Maid of Bath*): June 12, 21; July 28; Aug. 21, 30.

Bayes (*Rehearsal*-Villiers): July 31; Aug. 7.

Thomas Lofty (*Patron*): Aug. 2.

Orators: Aug. 16.

Luke Limp (*Lame Lover*): Aug. 28; Sept. 6.

Gomez (*Spanish Friar*-Dryden): Sept. 4, 12.

The Haymarket, Summer 1776

Robert Riscounter (*Bankrupt*): May 20, 28; July 12.

Matthew Mite (*Nabob*): May 22; June 28; July 17; Aug. 12; Sept. 11.

Mother Cole (*Minor*): May 27; June 17; July 31; Aug. 14.

Cadwallader (*Author*): May 27; June 17, 24; July 31; Sept. 11.

Zachary Fungus (*Commissary*): May 30; June 12; Aug. 9.

Major Sturgeon (*Mayor of Garratt*): May 30; June 21; July 29; Aug. 9; Sept. 13.

Devil (*Devil upon Two Sticks*): June 14; July 3, 24; Aug. 16; Sept. 10.

Aircastle (*Cozeners*): June 19, 21, 24, 26; July 1, 8, 15, 19, 26; Aug. 5; Sept. 6, 14.

Hartop (*Knights*): June 26, 28; July 5, 17, 22; Aug. 7; Sept. 9.

Solomon Flint (*Maid of Bath*): July 5, 22; Aug. 7.

Orators: July 10.

Lady Pentweazle (*Taste*): July 10, 12, 15, 19, 26; Aug. 5, 12;
  Sept. 6, 14.

Thomas Lofty (*Patron*): July 29.

Father O'Donnavan (*Capuchin*): Aug. 19, 21, 23, 26, 28, 30; Sept.
  4, 9, 13.

Paul Plyant (*Double Dealer*-Congreve): Sept. 2, 12.

BIBLIOGRAPHY

Appleton, William W. *Charles Macklin: An Actor's Life.* Cambridge, Mass., 1960.

Askham, Francis. *The Gay Delavals.* New York, 1955.

Asmodeus. London, 1776.

Avery, Emmet L. *Congreve's Plays on the Eighteenth-Century Stage.* New York, 1951.

Baine, James. *The Theatre Licentious and Perverted . . . Partly Occasioned by the acting of a comedy entitled, The Minor.* Edinburgh, 1770.

Baker, D. E., I. Reed, and S. Jones, edd. *Biographical Dramatica; or a Companion to the Playhouse.* 3 vols. London, 1812.

Baker, H. B. *English Actors from Shakespeare to Macready.* 2 vols. New York, 1879.

Battestin, Martin C. "Fielding and 'Master Punch' in Panton Street," *PQ,* XLV (January, 1966), 191-208.

Belden, Mary M. *The Dramatic Work of Samuel Foote.* New Haven, 1929.

Bellamy, George Anne. *Apology for the Life of George Anne Bellamy.* 6 vols. London, 1785.

Bernard, John. *Retrospections of the Stage.* 2 vols. London, 1830.

Boaden, James. *Memoirs of Mrs. Siddons.* 2 vols. London, 1827.

———, ed. *Private Correspondence of David Garrick.* 2 vols. London, 1831-32.

Boswell, James. *Boswell for the Defense, 1769-1774,* edd. W. K. Wimsatt and F. A. Pottle. New York, 1959.

————. *The Life of Samuel Johnson, L.L.D.*, ed. G. B. Hill, rev. L. F. Powell. 6 vols. Oxford, 1934-50, 64.

————. *Observations, Good or Bad, Stupid or Clever, Serious or Jocular, on Esquire Foote's Dramatic Entertainment, intitled, The Minor*. By a Genius. Edinburgh, 1760.

————. *The Ominous Years, 1774-1776*, edd. C. Ryskamp and F. A. Pottle. New York, 1963.

————. *Private Papers of James Boswell from Malahide Castle in the Collection of Lt. Col. R. H. Isham*, edd. G. Scott and F. A. Pottle. 18 Vols. New York, 1928-34 (Privately printed).

Burney, Francis. *The Early Diary of Francis Burney*, ed. A. R. Ellis. 2 vols. London, 1913.

Burnim, Kalman A. *David Garrick Director*. Pittsburgh, 1961.

Byrnes, Joseph A. "Four Plays of Samuel Foote," unpublished Ph.D. dissertation, New York University, 1963.

Campbell, James. *The Memoirs of Sir James Campbell of Ardkinglass. Written by Himself*. London, 1832.

————. *The Case of the Duchess of Kingston*. London, 1775.

Chambers, Robert, ed. *The Book of Days*. 2 vols. Edinburgh, 1863.

Chesterfield, Philip Dormer Stanhope, Fourth Earl of. *The Letters of Philip Dormer Stanhope*, ed. Bonamy Dobree. 6 vols. London, 1932.

Churchill, Charles. *Poetical Works of Charles Churchill*, ed. Douglas Grant. Oxford, 1956.

Cibber, Theophilus. *Dissertations of Theatrical Subjects. As they have several Times been delivered to the Public (With General Approbation) By Mr. Cibber*. London, 1756.

————. *Theophilus Cibber to David Garrick Esq. with Dissertations on Theatrical Subjects*. London, 1759.

Colman, George. *Man and Wife, or The Stratford Jubilee*. London, 1770.

Colman, George the Younger. *Random Records*. 2 vols. London, 1830.

Cooke, William. *Memoirs of Charles Macklin*. London, 1804.

————. *Memoirs of Samuel Foote Esq.* 3 vols. London, 1805.

————. *The Table-Talk and Bon-Mots of Samuel Foote*. New Southgate, 1889.

Corner, Betty C. "Dr. Melchisedeck Broadbrim and the Playwright," *Journal of the History of Medicine,* VII (Spring, 1952), 122-135.

Cradock, Joseph. *Literary and Miscellaneous Memoirs.* 4 vols. London, 1828.

Cross, Wilbur L. *The History of Henry Fielding.* 3 vols. New Haven, 1918.

Cumberland, Richard. *Memoirs of Richard Cumberland. Written by Himself.* 2 vols. London, 1807.

Davies, Thomas. *Dramatic Miscellanies.* 3 vols. London, 1783-84.

———. *A Genuine Narrative of the Life and Theatrical Transactions of Mr. John Henderson.* London, 1777.

———. *Memoirs of the Life of David Garrick Esq.* 2 vols. London, 1780.

Decastro, J. *The Memoirs of J. Decastro,* ed. R. Humphreys. London, 1824.

Deelman, Christian. *The Great Shakespeare Jubilee.* London, 1964.

de la Torre, Lillian. *Villainy Detected.* New York, 1947.

Dibdin, James C. *The Annals of the Edinburgh Stage.* Edinburgh, 1888.

Dunbar, Howard H. *The Dramatic Career of Arthur Murhpy.* New York, 1946.

Edgeworth, Richard Lovell. *Memoirs of Richard Lovell Edgeworth,* ed. Maria Edgeworth. London, 1844.

England, Martha W. *Garrick's Jubilee.* Ohio State University Press, 1964.

An Epistle from Tully in the Shades to Orator M[acklin] in Covent Garden. London, 1955.

Everard, Edward C. *Memoirs of an Unfortunate Son of Thespis.* Edinburgh, 1818.

Fielding, Henry. *Joseph Andrews,* ed. Martin C. Battestin. Boston, 1961.

Fitzgerald, Percy. *Samuel Foote, a Biography.* London, 1910.

Foot, Jesse. *The Life of Arthur Murphy Esq.* London, 1811.

Foote, Samuel. *Apology for the Minor. In a Letter to the Rev. Mr. Baine.* Edinburgh, 1771.

————. *The Comic Theatre, Being a Free Translation of all the Best French Comedies. By Samuel Foote and Others.* 5 vols. London, 1762.

————. *The Dramatic Works of Samuel Foote.* 4 vols. London, n.d. [ca. 1778].

————. *A Letter from Mr. Foote, To The Reverend Author Of The Remarks, Critical and Christian, On the Minor.* London, 1760.

————. *The Roman and English Comedy Consider'd and Compar'd.* London, 1747.

————. *A Treatise on the Passions, so far as they Regard the Stage.* London, [1747].

————. *The Dramatic Works of Samuel Foote, With Remarks on each Play and an Essay on the Life, Genius, and Writings of the Author,* ed. Jon Bee [pseud. for John Badcock.] 3 vols. London, 1830.

Forster, John. *Biographical Essays.* London, 1860.

Fox, R. Hingston. *William Hunter: Anatomist, Physician, Obstetrician, 1718-1783.* London, 1901.

Garrick, David. *The Letters of David Garrick,* edd. David Little and George Kahrl. 3 vols. Cambridge, Mass., 1963.

————. *The Letters of David Garrick and Georgiana Countess Spencer, 1759-1779,* edd. Karl Spencer and Christopher Dobson. Cambridge for Roxburgh Club, 1960.

————. *Some Unpublished Correspondence of David Garrick,* ed. George P. Baker. Boston, 1907.

————. *Three Plays by David Garrick,* ed. Elizabath Stein. New York, 1926.

Genest, John. *Some Account of the English Stage from the Restoration in 1660 to 1830.* 10 vols. Bath, 1832.

George The Third, King. *The Correspondence of King George The Third from 1760 to December 1783,* ed. Sir John Fortescue. 6 vols. London, 1927.

Gibbon, Edward. *The Letters of Edward Gibbon,* ed. J. E. Norton. 3 vols. London, 1956.

Grant, Douglas. *The Cock Lane Ghost.* London, 1966.

Guest, Alan D., "Charles Adams and John Gilbert-Cooper," *TN,* XI (July-September, 1957), 138-145.

Henderson, John. *Letters and Poems by the Late Mr. John Henderson.* London, 1786.

Historical Manuscripts Commission, Eleventh Report, Pt. VIII. The Manuscripts of the Duke of Leeds. London, 1888.

————, *Thirteenth Report, Pt. VI. The Delaval Manuscripts.* London, 1893.

Hitchcock, Robert. *An Historical View of the Irish Stage.* 2 vols. Dublin, 1788.

Holcroft, Thomas. *Memoirs,* ed. W. Hazlitt. 3 vols. London, 1816.

Hotten, John Camden, *A Handbook to the Topography and Family History of England and Wales.* London, 1863.

Jackson, John. *The History of the Scottish Stage, from its First Establishment to the Present Times.* Edinburgh, 1793.

Johnson, Samuel. *Diaries, Prayers, and Annals,* ed. E. L. McAdam with Donald and Mary Hyde. New Haven, 1958.

————. *The Letters of Samuel Johnson,* ed. R. W. Chapman. 3 vols. Oxford, 1952.

Johnstone, Charles. *Chrysal, or the Adventures of a Guinea. By an Adept.* 4 vols. London, 1760-65.

Junius. *The Letters of Junius,* ed. C. W. Everett. London, 1927.

Kenrick, William. *Love in the Suds; a Town Eclogue, Being the Lamentation of Roscius for the loss of his Nyky.* London, 1772.

Kinne, W. A. *Revivals and Importations of French Comedies in England, 1749-1800.* New York, 1939.

Kirkman, J. T. *Memoirs of the Life of Charles Macklin Esq.* 2 vols. London, 1799.

Knight, Joseph. *David Garrick.* London, 1894.

Lee, Umphrey. *The Historical Backgrounds of Early Methodist Enthusiasm.* New York, 1931.

Lewes, Charles Lee. *Comic Sketches; or the Comedian his own Manager.* London, 1804.

Lichtenberg's Visits to England as Described in his Letters and Diaries. Transl. and edd. Margaret L. Mare and W. H. Quarrell. Oxford, 1938.

The London Stage 1660-1800, Pts. 3, 4, and 5, ed. Arthur H. Scouten and George Winchester Stone, Jr., Charles B. Hagan 2 3 and 2 vols. respectively. Carbondale, Ill., 1961, 1962, 1969. Carbondale, Ill., 1961, 1962.

Lynch, James J. *Pit, Box and Gallery: Stage and Society in Johnson's London.* Berkeley and Los Angeles, 1953.

Mackenzie, Henry. *The Anecdotes and Egotisms of Henry Mackenzie,* ed. Harold W. Thompson. Oxford, 1927.

Macklin's Answer to Tully. London, 1755.

MacMillan, Dougald. *Drury Lane Calendar 1747-1776.* Oxford, 1938.

Madan, Martin. *Christian and Critical Remarks on . . . The Minor.* London, 1760.

Mavor, Elizabeth. *The Virgin Mistress. A Study in Survival: The Life of the Duchess of Kingston.* London, 1964.

M'Culloch, David. *Gallovidian.* XVII (1919), 159-161.

Memoirs of the Life and Writings of Samuel Foote Esq., the English Aristophanes: To Which are added the Bon-mots, Repartees, and Good Things Said by that Great Wit and Excentrical Genius. . . . London, 1777.

Moore, Thomas. *Memoirs of the Rt. Honourable Richard Brinsley Sheridan.* 2 vols. London, 1827.

More, Hannah. *Memoirs of the Life and Correspondence of Mrs. Hannah More,* ed. William Roberts. 2 vols. New York, 1835.

Murphy, Arthur. *The Englishman From Paris.* 1756. Introduced and edited by Simon Trefman (Augustan Reprint Society, 137). Los Angeles: Clark Memorial Library, University of California, 1969.

———. *The Life of David Garrick, Esqu.* 2 vols. London, 1801.

———. *An Ode to the Naiads of Fleet Ditch.* London, 1761.

———. *The Spouter, or the Triple Revenge.* London, 1756.

———. *The Way to Keep Him and Five Other Plays by Arthur Murphy,* ed. John Pike Emery. New York, 1956.

Nettle, Humphrey [probable pseud. for William Jackson]. *Sodom and Onan. A Satire inscribed to* [portrait of Foote and a picture of a human foot] *esq., alias the devil upon two sticks. By Humphrey Nettle.* London, 1776.

Neville, Sylas. *The Diary of Sylas Neville,* ed. Basil Cozens-Hardy. London, 1950.

The Newgate Calendar, ed. Henry Savage. Hartford, Conn., 1926.

Nichols, John. *Literary Anecdotes of the Eighteenth Century.* 9 vols. London, 1812-15.

Nicholson, Watson. *The Struggle for a Free Stage*. London, 1906.

Nipclose, Nicholas [pseud.]. *The Theatres or a Poetical Dissection by Sir Nicholas Nipclose, Baronet*. London, 1771.

O'Keefe, John. *Recollections of the Life of John O'Keefe*. 2 vols. London, 1826.

Orrery Papers, ed. Countess of Cork and Orrery. 2 vols. London, 1903.

Oulton, Walley C. *The History of the Theatres of London*. 2 vols. London, 1796.

Peake, Richard B. *Memoirs of the Colman Family*. 2 vols. London, 1841.

Pearce, C. E. *The Amazing Duchess. Being the Romantic History of Elizabeth Chudleigh, Maid of Honour, The Honourable Mrs. Harvey, Duchess of Kingston and Countess of Bristol.* 2 vols. London, 1911.

Pilkington, Letitia. *Memoirs of Letitia Pilkington, 1712-1755.* 4 vols. New York, n.d.

Pope, Alexander. *The Poems of Alexander Pope,* ed. John Butt. New Haven, 1963.

Polwhele, Richard. *Biographical Sketches in Cornwall*. 3 vols. London, 1831.

———. *The History of Cornwall.* 7 vols. London, 1816.

———. *Traditions and Recollections.* London, 1826.

Pounce, Peter [pseud. of Richard Lewis.] *The Robin Hood Society: A Satire with Notes Variourum*. London, 1756.

The Register of Marriages, Baptisms and Burials of the Parish of St. Mary, Truro Co. Cornwall. Exeter: The Devon and Cornwall Record Society, 1940.

Samuels, Arthur P. I. *The Early Life Correspondence and Writings of the Rt. Hon. Edmund Burke, LL.D.* Cambridge, 1923.

Scouten, Arthur. "On the Origin of Foote's Matinees," *TN*, VII (January-March, 1953), 28-31.

Shepherd, T. B. *Methodism and the Literature of the Eighteenth Century*. London, 1940.

Sherbo, Arthur. *New Essays by Arthur Murphy*. East Lansing, Mich., 1963.

Sherrard, O. A. *A Life of John Wilkes*. New York, 1930.

Sichel, Walter. *Sheridan*. 2 vols. New York, 1909.

Snagg, Thomas. *Recollections of Occurrences, The Memoirs of Thomas Snagg,* ed. Harold Halison. London, 1951.

Steele, Elizabeth. *The Memoirs of Mrs. Sophia Baddley.* 6 vols. London, 1787.

Sterne, Laurence. *The Letters of Laurence Sterne,* ed. Lewis P. Curtis. Oxford, 1935.

Stockwell, La Tour. *Dublin Theatres and Theatre Customs,* 1637-1820. Kingston, Tenn., 1938.

Stone, George W. Jr. "The Authorship of Tit for Tat, A Manuscript Source for 18th-Century Theatrical History." *TN,* X (October-December, 1955), 22-28.

Taylor, John. *Records of My Life.* 2 vols. London, 1832.

Thaler, Alwin. *Shakespeare to Sheridan.* Cambridge, Mass., 1922.

Theatrical Biography: or Memoirs of the Principal Performers of the Theatres Royal, Drury Lane, Covent Garden, Haymarket, together with Critical and Impartial Remarks on their Respective Merits. 2 vols. London, 1772.

Theatrical Review. London, 1758.

Tyerman, Luke. *The Life and Times of the Reverend George Whitefield, B.A. of Pembroke College, Oxford.* 2 vols. New York, 1877.

Victor, Benjamin. *The History of the Theatres of London and Dublin.* 3 vols. London, 1761-71.

Walpole, Horace. *The Letters of Horace Walpole,* ed. P. Cunningham. 9 vols. London, 1891.

——. *The Letters of Horace Walpole,* ed. P. Toynbee. 16 vols. London, 1903.

——. *The Yale Edition of Horace Walpole's Correspondence,* ed. W. S. Lewis. Vols. 1-22, 28-29. New Haven, 1937.

Weatherly, E. H. "Foote's Revenge on Churchill and Lloyd." *HLQ,* LX (1945), 49-60.

Werkmeister, Lucyle. "Notes for a Revised Life of William Jackson." *N&Q,* CCVI (1960), 62-82; XXVII (1961), 16-54, 128-162.

Weston, Thomas. *Memoirs of that Celebrated Comedian and Very Singular Genius, Thomas Weston.* London, 1776.

The Whitefoord Papers, ed. W. A. S. Hewins. Oxford, 1898.

Wilkes: An Oratorio. As Performed at The Great Room in Bishopsgate-Street. Written by Mr. Foote. The Music by Signor Carlos Francesco Baritini. London, 1769.

Wilkinson, Tate. *Memoirs of His Own Life.* 4 vols. York, 1790.
————. *The Wandering Patentee.* 4 vols. York, 1795.
Willcocks, M. P. *A True-Born Englishman, Being the Life of Henry Fielding.* London, 1947.
Wimsatt, W. K. "Foote and a Friend of Boswell's: A Note on *The Nabob.*" *MLN*, LVII (May, 1942), 325-335.
The Works of the English Poets, ed. A. Chalmers. Vol. XV. London, 1810.

Newspapers and Magazines

Critical Review
Daily Advertiser
Evening Post
Examiner
Exshaw's Magazine
Gazeteer and Daily Advertiser
General Advertiser
Gentleman's Magazine
Gray's Inn Journal
Literary Magazine
Lloyd's Evening Post
London Chronicle
London Monthly
Monthly Chronicle
Monthly Mirror
Monthly Review
Morning Chronicle
Public Advertiser
St. James's Chronicle
Town and Country Magazine
Universal Museum and Complete Magazine
Westminster Magazine

INDEX